PENGUIN BOOKS

THE CRYSTAL SPIRIT

George Woodcock was born in Winnipeg in 1912 and came as a small child to England, where he remained until 1949. He has taught English at the University of Washington, and English and Asian Studies at the University of British Columbia, but resigned from teaching in 1963 with the rank of Associate Professor to devote himself to writing. He was editor of *Now* from 1940–47, was one of the editors of the anarchist papers *War Commentary* and *Freedom* during the same period, and is now editor of *Canadian Literature*, which he founded in 1959. He has held a Guggenheim Fellowship, a Canadian Overseas Fellowship, and various Canada Council awards; his study of George Orwell, *The Crystal Spirit*, won the Governor-General's Literary Award for 1966; he has recently been elected a Fellow of the Royal Society of Canada. He has published more than twenty books, ranging from volumes of verse to biographies (of Godwin, Aphra Behn, Kropotkin and Proudhon).

Apart from his book on Orwell, he has written three other volumes of criticism, *The Writer and Politics*, *Odysseus Ever Returning* and *The Paradox of Oscar Wilde*. He has also written *Anarchism* (published in Pelicans) and several historical works, including *The Greeks in India* and *The British in the Far East*. He has travelled widely in Europe, Asia and the Americas, and out of his travels have come books like *Ravens and Prophets*, *To the City of the Dead*, *Incas and Other Men*, *Faces of India*, and *Asia: Gods and Cities*. His most recent book is *Canada and the Canadians*.

GEORGE WOODCOCK

The Crystal Spirit

A STUDY OF
George Orwell

PENGUIN BOOKS

Penguin Books Ltd, Harmondsworth, Middlesex, England
Penguin Books Australia Ltd, Ringwood, Victoria, Australia

—

First published by Jonathan Cape 1967
Published in Penguin Books 1970

—

Copyright © George Woodcock, 1966

—

Made and printed in Great Britain
by C. Nicholls & Company Ltd
Set in Linotype Pilgrim

CONTENTS

Preface 7

PART ONE
The Man Remembered 9

PART TWO
Life Against Odds: *The Themes of Orwell's Fiction* 47

PART THREE
The Revolutionary Patriot: *Conservatism and Rebellion in Orwell's World-View* 177

PART FOUR
Prose Like a Window-pane: *Orwell as Critic and Stylist* 227

A Selective Bibliography 279

Index 281

PREFACE

MANY people have argued that the man they knew as George Orwell was more important as a personality than as a writer, for what he was than for what he said. I suspect that time will reveal this opinion to be a fallacy. Even in his least perfect writings Orwell still stands out as different from his contemporaries, yet no one reflects more clearly or more poignantly the peculiar anxieties of the age in which he lived. To speak for a generation without being typical of it is one of the marks by which we can tell the exceptional writers of any time – the writers who survive in the affections and memories of readers; if that is not enough, Orwell shows also that peculiar concern with the purity and intelligibility of the written language which in England has been the mark of the great literary reformer from John Dryden down to the present.

Yet, fallacious though it may be to assume that Orwell or any other writer is greater than his works – for how else can the greatness of a writer better emerge than through his writing? – the fact remains that those who knew Orwell have never been able to perform that act of faith demanded by so many modern critics, to see the writings isolated from the man. Always that gaunt, gentle, angry and endlessly controversial image intervenes, if only to remind one of how often his works were good talk turned into better prose.

This fact explains the form of the present book. I had intended to write a merely critical study of Orwell's books, but I found that until I had – as it were – exorcized the memory of the man by committing my recollections to paper, I could not approach his writings with any degree of objectivity. But once those recollections had been put on paper, they seemed to take their place naturally with the other aspects of Orwell which go to make up the four-sided figure that emerges in this book – the figure of the man as I (but not necessarily others) knew him, of the writer who built his major works around a single and enduring myth appropriate to the twentieth-century world, of the man of contradictory yet strangely consistent ideas, of the penetrating critic who turned his examination upon himself as well as on others and who in the process transformed himself by an almost conscious act of the will into one of the purest and finest prose writers of any English age.

I have made no attempt to produce a biography, partly because Orwell specifically wished that no such book should be written, and partly because I may well stand too near the subject to attain the objectivity such a work would demand. This book remains, as it was intended to be, a critical study, if one interprets that term in the free way Orwell himself would have sanctioned. Except for my own recollections and the letters which Orwell wrote to me, I have been content to examine the writings of my subject and the published recollections of those many other people who knew him and were unable – even when they were eager – to escape from the influence of his personality. Like these others I have written my introductory section on Orwell as I knew him out of a sense of inner necessity, but in doing so I think I have presented a sketch of the man a little different from any other that has yet appeared, and – more important – have exposed the attitude, affectionate but at the same time critical, which I developed towards Orwell a quarter of a century ago, and from which the rest of this book naturally develops.

I would end by expressing my gratitude to Sonia Brownell Orwell for permission to quote from George Orwell's letters and works.

PART ONE

THE MAN REMEMBERED

I

WHEN I remember George Orwell, I see again the long, lined face that so often reminded one not of a living person, but of a character out of fiction. It was the nearest I had seen in real life to the imagined features of Don Quixote, and the rest of the figure went with the face. For Orwell was a tall, thin, angular man, with worn Gothic features accentuated by the deep vertical furrows that ran down the cheeks and across the corners of the mouth. The thinness of his lips was emphasized by a very narrow line of dark moustache; it seemed a hard, almost cruel mouth until he smiled, and then an expression of unexpected kindliness would irradiate his whole face. The general gauntness of his looks was accentuated by the deep sockets from which his eyes looked out, always rather sadly. In contrast to the fragile, worn-down look of the rest of him, his hair grew upward into a kind of brown crest, vigorous and until the end untouched by grey.

The resemblance to Don Quixote was appropriate, for in many ways Orwell can only be understood as an essentially quixotic man. He regretted the fading of a past society which, for all its faults, seemed to him more generous and colourful than the present. He defended, passionately and as a matter of principle, unpopular causes. Often without regard for reason, he would strike out against anything that offended his conceptions of right, justice or decency, yet, as many who crossed lances with him had reason to know, he could be a very chivalrous opponent, impelled by a sense of fair play that would lead him to the public recantation of accusations he had eventually decided were unfair. In his own way he was a man of the Left, but he attacked its holy images as fervently as he did those of the Right. And however much he might on occasion find himself in uneasy and temporary alliance with others, he was – in the end – as much a man in isolation as Don Quixote. His was the isolation of every man who seeks the truth diligently, no matter how unpleasant its implications may be to others or even to himself.

But Don Quixote and Sancho Panza are, as Orwell himself pointed out, inseparable companions. In his essay on comic postcards, 'The Art of Donald McGill', he put to his readers the question: 'If you look into your own mind, which are you, Don Quixote or Sancho Panza?' He did not wait for an answer; he continued:

Almost certainly you are both. There is one part of you that wishes to be a hero or a saint, but another part of you is a little fat man who sees very clearly the advantages of staying alive with a whole skin. He is your unofficial self, the voice of the belly protesting against the soul. His tastes lie towards safety, soft beds, no work, pots of beer and women with 'voluptuous' figures. He it is who punctures your fine attitudes and urges you to look after Number One, to be unfaithful to your wife, to bilk your debts, and so on and so forth. Whether you allow yourself to be influenced by him is a different question.

By and large, Orwell did not let himself be greatly influenced by the little fat man within, at least in the grosser ways which he outlined in his essay, but there was in his work, and in his conversation, a concern for the substance and texture and above all the smell of physical life which certainly belonged far more in the province of Sancho Panza than in that of Don Quixote. This is one way of saying that Orwell, like Walt Whitman and William Blake, tended to be somewhat proudly a man of contradictions, and the simultaneous presence in his nature of the Don and Sancho gave his personality a fascinating and slightly enigmatic originality that has led since his death to something approaching an Orwell cult. Orwell has been hailed – as Wilde hailed himself – as a man in life and work symbolic of his age and its preoccupations; he has also been represented as a kind of secular saint of the Cold War age. But he was much too interested in himself as a person to welcome his posthumous elevation to the impersonal status of a symbol, and in his 'Reflections on Gandhi' he made his views on sainthood clear

enough to deter any but the most insensitive from the ungrate-
ful task of officiating at his canonization.

Orwell was too solitary to be a symbol and too angry to be
a saint. But he succeeded in becoming a writer who set down,
in the purest English of his time, the thoughts and fantasies of
an individual mind playing over the common problems of our
age. What made him exceptional – and more than a little eccentric in the eyes of his contemporaries – was the fact that he also
tried to work out his theories in action and then to give his
actions shape in literature. The triad of thought, act and artifact
runs through the whole of Orwell's writing life; the pattern is
not always so neatly arranged as I may appear to be suggesting,
but it is never entirely absent, and one has difficulty in envisag-
ing a future in which critics will ever be able to think of Orwell's writings separately from his life.

I met Orwell first towards the end of 1942, when he was
working in the Indian Section of the B.B.C. in London; through
our common friend Mulk Raj Anand, he sent me an invitation
to take part in a discussion on poetry which he was organizing.
Earlier in the same year we had engaged in a rather heated
polemic in the *Partisan Review* over one of Orwell's London
Letters in which he had attacked the English pacifists with the
curious and – it seemed to me – unsound argument that they
were really unadmitted power worshippers. In my reply I had
made very personal remarks about Orwell's inconsistencies; as
on paper he had seemed greatly enraged, I was surprised at his
invitation to the B.B.C. But I accepted it, mostly, I think, to
show that I bore as few ill feelings as Orwell himself appeared
to do.

A few days later I went to the wartime studios which the
B.B.C. had improvised in the basement of a requisitioned de-
partment store in Oxford Street. The panel which Orwell had
gathered together was an impressive one for a single broadcast
on a foreign network. Mulk Raj Anand, Herbert Read, and
William Empson I already knew; Edmund Blunden and Orwell
I had not met before. Orwell was wearing his rarely changing
uniform of an old tweed sports coat, leather-patched at the

elbows, and baggy corduroys. I was impressed by the size of his hands and feet; the latter were enormous – size twelve – which made it difficult for him to get shoes during the austerity war years. He greeted me in his flat-toned voice, with a reserved but not unfriendly smile. At that time I was running a market garden in Middlesex, and Orwell questioned me about it; he seemed to approve of the fact that I was engaged in manual work and that my hands were chapped and ingrained with soil.

The radio programme turned out to be a made-up discussion which Orwell had prepared quite skilfully beforehand, and which the rest of the participants were given a chance to amend before it went on the air. All of us objected to small points as a matter of principle, but the only real change came when Orwell himself produced a volume of Byron and, smiling round at the rest of us, suggested that we should read 'The Isles of Greece' to show that English poets had a tradition of friendship for the aspirations of subject peoples. At that time the British government was opposed to the Indian independence movement (Gandhi and Nehru were still in prison), but all of the participants in the broadcast supported it in sentiment at least, and as Herbert Read spoke the ringing verses of revolt, the programme assumed a mild flavour of defiance which we all enjoyed. Orwell, I noticed, had a very rudimentary idea of radio production, and his own voice was too thin to make him an effective broadcaster.

After the broadcast was completed, we went to a public house in Great Portland Street frequented by B.B.C. men, and here Orwell discoursed rather cynically on the futility of our having taken so much trouble over a programme to which he doubted if more than two hundred Anglophile Indians would bother to listen. He was already experiencing the frustration of a job that concentrated mostly on the dissemination of official propaganda.

I learned about his feelings on this point shortly afterwards when we began to write to each other over our various points of disagreement. The first of Orwell's letters began on a characteristic note. 'I am afraid I answered rather roughly in the

Partisan Review controversy. I always do when I am attacked – however, no malice either side, I hope.' Orwell liked to start friendships by clearing up any resentments his sometimes intemperate way of expressing himself may have caused. Julian Symons, whom he had accused of Fascist thinking, received an apology on their first meeting, and to Stephen Spender, whom he had attacked before they actually became acquainted, Orwell remarked that he found it very difficult to continue a literary feud with any writer after actually encountering him, 'because when you meet anyone in the flesh you realize immediately that he is a human being and not a sort of caricature embodying certain ideas.'

Later in his early correspondence with me, Orwell discussed his connexion with the B.B.C. 'I doubt whether I shall stay in this job much longer,' he said, 'but while here I consider I have kept our propaganda slightly less disgusting than it might otherwise have been. . . . To appreciate this you have to be as I am in constant touch with propaganda Axis and Allied. Till then you don't realize what muck and filth is normally flowing through the air. I consider that I have left our little corner of it fairly clean.'

In fact he was involved in a typically Orwellian dilemma. His revolutionary Socialist ideas did not make him any less of a thorough English patriot, dedicated to defending the people and the countryside of England even if he had little use for most of its existing institutions, and when he was rejected medically for Army, Navy and Air Force alike, he decided to do what he could as a reputedly very inefficient Home Guard sergeant and as a B.B.C. official. Patriotism aside, he believed that the left-wing libertarian socialism which he had adopted in 1936 could only survive if the Nazis were defeated, though he felt that the immediate establishment of some kind of socialized economy in England might be an incentive to fight more effectively. On the other hand his broadcasting experience taught him how language may be perverted and its real meaning eventually destroyed when it is put to the use of even the most benevolent propaganda; there is no doubt that his experience at the B.B.C.

provided him with the basic raw material that went into the portrayal of the Ministry of Truth and the devising of the propaganda language of Newspeak in *Nineteen Eighty-Four*.

He was so obviously unhappy in broadcasting that I was not surprised when I heard towards the end of 1943 that he had managed to get himself released from the B.B.C. and had joined *Tribune* as literary editor. *Tribune*, which still flourishes, was then the organ of the dissident wing of the Labour Party led by Aneurin Bevan; it was sharply critical of the Churchill government. Apart from the Communists, who fell into a special category because their actions were governed entirely by the exigencies of Russian policy, the *Tribune* group was the farthest left among the factions supporting the war, and in their paper pro-war and anti-war positions found a meeting-ground; for, apart from its critical attitude towards the coalition government, *Tribune* gave space, particularly in its literary pages, to many writers far nearer in their views to the independent attitudes of the Anarchists, Trotskyists and Independent Labour Party than they were to the policy of the official Labour Party. It was the kind of paper in which there was room for a writer like Orwell, and I think on the whole he enjoyed the two or three years he spent there.

It was at this time that I saw Orwell again. I was living at Hampstead, in Parliament Hill Fields, and I would often take the bus from South End Green into the centre of London. One morning, when I climbed on to the upper deck, I caught sight of Orwell's crest of hair and his familiar grimy trench coat towards the front of the bus. He had evidently seen me crossing the road, for as I came up the stairs he turned round and waved to me. I sat beside him. He immediately began to talk, with the urgency of a man who has to get something off his mind, about our disagreements in the *Partisan Review* and in our later correspondence. I was somewhat surprised, since I felt this had been cleared up in our letters, but Orwell obviously felt some direct and personal reference was necessary. 'There's no reason to let that kind of argument on paper breed personal ill-feeling,' he remarked. Obviously I had passed whatever test Orwell regarded as necessary before he could accord his esteem, and he wanted to be friendly. From that time we never again mentioned our original disagreement, and whenever our opinions differed I found Orwell blunt but genial in argument. But, as I learned later, he was not always willing to make peace so easily. On one occasion a Communist poet who had published a bitter personal attack on him offered to shake hands when they met in a Fleet Street public house. Orwell turned away in angry silence. Afterwards he told me of the incident. 'What a smelly little hypocrite S. is!' he concluded. 'Just like the rest of them! If he could do it without risking his cowardly little hide, he'd take the greatest delight in pushing me under a bus!' After his experiences in Spain, Orwell never ceased to detest the Stalinists, both collectively and personally, and he knew very well that, with good reason, they reciprocated his feelings.

As the bus began to drive off, Orwell pointed out the large rambling bookshop which then stood at the corner of South End Green and Pond Street. 'I worked there about ten years ago,' he said noncommittally, but seemed disinclined to enlarge on the statement; the shop was the model for the bookshop where Gordon Comstock worked in the early chapters of *Keep the Aspidistra Flying.* While the bus drove on through the bombed wastes of Kentish Town, he began to tell me of his experiences with the police at the time when he was writing his essay on Henry Miller, 'Inside the Whale'. Somehow – through Communists, he suspected – the vice squad of Scotland Yard had discovered that he was getting copies of Miller's banned novels through the post from Paris, and he endured several visits and a good deal of interference with his correspondence before they would finally accept his argument that he was a serious student of literature and not a pornographer intent on corrupting the young. In the end they allowed him to keep the books, but this concession did not in any way predispose him towards them. In taking over many of the attitudes of British working men, he had adopted their traditional distrust of the police. 'I have no particular love for the idealized "worker" as he appears in the bourgeois Communist's mind,' he had said a few years earlier in *Homage to Catalonia*, 'but when I see an actual flesh-and-blood worker in conflict with his natural enemy, the policeman, I do not have to ask myself which side I am on.'

I saw Orwell fairly often while he was working at *Tribune*, where even more than his predecessors he opened the review pages to writers of almost every shade of political opinion. He was not a good editor; his generosity too often clouded his discernment about writers and their work. He persuaded many good writers to work for him; I remember articles by E. M. Forster, Herbert Read, Cyril Connolly, Stephen Spender. But he also published a great deal of shoddy trash by young writers who had no promise to fulfil, and he did this mainly, I think, from kindness rather than from lack of judgment. He found it extremely difficult to return an article with a coldly-worded rejection slip, and he said to me more than once that no writer who had earned a hard living by reviewing should ever be trusted with the task of editing.

Orwell made up for his shortcomings as an editor by becoming a first-rate occasional essayist, and in the years between 1943 and 1947 the page one turned to first in a new issue of *Tribune* was always that on which Orwell, under the general title of 'As I Please', discoursed on any facet of life or letters that struck his fancy at the time. It was the best short essay writing of the forties, and most of it still reads amazingly well today. Orwell's versatility was astounding; he rarely failed to find a subject – a popular song, an aspect of propaganda, the first toad of spring – on which there was something fresh to say in a prose that, for all its ease and apparent casualness, was penetrating and direct. The years of book-reviewing, an occupation which has taken the edge off many a promising talent, seemed not merely to have developed Orwell's facility, but also to have sharpened his power to catch and develop those aspects of books or situations which the unobservant eye misses but which often contain the essential clues to understanding.

Sometimes I would call on Orwell in his small, crowded office in the Strand, and talk to him over a desk piled with books and manuscripts, behind which he looked pent in with no room for his long legs. The typewriters would clatter in our ears from the neighbouring desks and the V 2s would go off in the distance like the rockets falling in *Nineteen Eighty-Four*. We would go out to lunch in the upstairs dining-room of a rather decayed wine tavern in the Strand, sometimes with Herbert Read or Julian Symons. On one of these occasions – it was towards the end of the war, when London restaurant food was at its worst – the only dish offered was boiled cod with bitter turnip-tops. I found the combination of flavours appalling, but Orwell, who extracted a boyish enjoyment out of the hardships of the time, ate his fish and greens with relish. 'I'd never have thought they'd have gone so well together!' he remarked reproachfully to me when I sent my plate back almost untasted.

2

MY ACQUAINTANCE with Orwell broadened into friendship in the latter part of 1944. Though affinities of personality and attitude obviously played an important part in the process, the immediate cause was a common concern for the defence of civil liberties. As always happens at such times, the more intransigent minorities of opinion during the Second World War were sometimes rather harshly treated, and many pacifists, Anarchists and left-wing Socialists were imprisoned or otherwise harried by the authorities. The situation aroused a great deal of discussion among British intellectuals. A few – mainly Communists and Tories – argued that freedom of criticism and protest should be temporarily relinquished in safeguarding the greater freedoms for which Britain was struggling. Others, including Orwell and most of his friends and close associates, held that the liberties of speech and writing were the most important of the freedoms over which the war was being fought, and that, once abandoned, they might never be regained. Even at that time Orwell already saw very clearly the results that might follow from imposing ways of writing and thinking convenient to the government, and his attitude then anticipated the warnings he expressed some years later in *Nineteen Eighty-Four*.

The issue was brought to a head late in 1944, on an evening of dense London fog, when the Special Branch of Scotland Yard raided the offices of the Anarchist paper *War Commentary* and took away files, lists of subscribers and other material. The raid provoked immediate protests from London writers. One group-letter, which Herbert Read and I circulated, was signed by – among others – E. M. Forster, Stephen Spender and T. S. Eliot. Orwell, who had been attacking the Anarchists in his *Partisan Review* articles, declared a truce on them as soon as they became the victims of an immoderate exercise of authority, and signed another group-letter, which was circulated by Paul Potts. These protests went unregarded, and in May 1945, just before the end of the war in Europe, four of the editors of *War Commentary* were tried at the Old Bailey, under special wartime statutes against anti-militarist propaganda. A defence committee was organized, under the chairmanship of Herbert Read, with Aneurin Bevan as vice-chairman, but this did not prevent three of the accused from being sentenced to terms of imprisonment. Orwell, who had given publicity to the case in *Tribune*, now published, with Dylan Thomas, George Barker and several other writers, a protest not merely against the sentence but also against the decision of the government to bring proceedings when the war was drawing to an end. He thought it augured badly for peacetime freedom of expression.

During the trial of the editors of *War Commentary*, the National Council for Civil Liberties took little active interest in the case. This indifference on the part of an organization set up to protect basic freedoms of speech and writing was attributed, rightly or wrongly, to the infiltration of the council by Communists and their sympathizers, and the various people who had played a part in organizing defence during the *War Commentary* case decided that at least a temporary organization of a more militant character should be set up to aid the victims of prosecutions under the restrictive wartime regulations which still remained in force some time after the end of hostilities. The Freedom Defence Committee was therefore organized in the summer of 1945, and led a precarious but active life until 1949. Its leading supporters, though they included a few political leaders, like H. J. Laski, then chairman of the Labour Party, and a handful of M.P.s, were mainly drawn from the literary and artistic worlds, where the feelings about getting rid of all restrictions on freedom of expression were strongest. Among the more active were E. M. Forster, Bertrand Russell, Cyril Connolly, Benjamin Britten, Michael Tippett, Henry Moore, Osbert Sitwell and Augustus John. Herbert Read was chairman and Orwell became vice-chairman. As a member of the working committee, I was delegated to transmit to Orwell the invitation to accept this position, and I recollect that he was at first hesitant. 'I don't want to get back on the administrative treadmill,' he said. He was just beginning to extricate himself from editorial duties at *Tribune*, and wanted to devote more of his time to writing books. But, on the condition that no great demands would be made on his time, he agreed; he became much more helpful, both materially and morally, than his initial caution had led me to expect. When we moved into a basement office near Euston Road, he made a gift of his late wife's typewriter, and now and then, particularly after the royalties on *Animal Farm* began to flow in, he made quite substantial donations to the funds. The cheques were always signed Eric Blair, but this was the only connexion in which, at this time, he appeared to use his real name; the assumed *persona* of 'George Orwell' had taken almost complete control, and he always identified himself, in conversation and in signing letters, as George and never as Eric.

Orwell did not merely give money. He took a close interest in the committee's activities which, as I realize when I look through his letters to me, continued until his last illness. Occasionally he would buttonhole some influential person on the fringes of the Labour government whom we wished to interest in a case of manifest injustice, and he wrote his *Tribune* essay

'Freedom of the Park' in support of a campaign we had launched against police interference with the traditional right of political minorities to sell their publications at the Marble Arch entrance to Hyde Park. Once at least he even spoke at a public meeting we organized in Conway Hall in support of a general amnesty for people still in prison, many months after hostilities had ended, under various wartime laws and regulations. Orwell appeared on the platform with Herbert Read, Fenner Brockway and a few other leaders of the libertarian Left. I think he was rather unhappy in his unaccustomed role as public speaker, and his voice, weakened by the throat wound he had received during the Spanish Civil War, did not carry very well. Yet I do not agree with Julian Symons, who has also written about this occasion, that he was a bad speaker; there was so much unpretentious conviction in his manner, and so much plain common sense in what he had to say, that his audience listened with complete attention and applauded him, I remember, more warmly than the professional orators of the evening.

As far as I know, Orwell's vice-chairmanship of the Freedom Defence Committee was the only office he ever held in any organization of this type; I think he stayed with us to the end because we worked very amateurishly and never developed a bureaucratic hierarchy or, indeed, a permanent organization. The committee was set up as an *ad hoc* body to work in the special situation that existed just after the war, and, having got a few people out of prison and eliminated a few small tyrannies by policemen and civil servants, it faded away, without any formal dissolution, towards the end of 1949. Orwell liked its informality, though he himself at times was liable to get somewhat pedantic over procedure; I remember his arguing long and obstinately about the respective appropriateness of the phrases 'on principle' and 'in principle' in a resolution we were drafting. He also liked the people with whom it brought him into contact. Orwell's natural place was among the English radical dissenters, the fighters for rights, the defenders of minorities, the people whose anger over injustices went beyond partisan boundaries; he had disagreed with many such people on the issue of the war, but once it was over he tended to pick up his connexions with them once again, and the Freedom Defence Committee was one of the means by which he did so.

3

I HAVE devoted some space to this aspect of Orwell's last decade because, apart from Julian Symons, in a reminiscent essay in the *London Magazine*, no one else who has written about him has mentioned this interlude of libertarian public activity. To me it is memorable chiefly because it led to steadily closer contacts with Orwell. We began to meet informally, outside the ambience of civil liberties and editorial offices, and by the spring of 1945 we were visiting each other in our respective homes, which in Orwell's case was a clear sign of approval. He tended, as Symons remarked, to compartmentalize his personal relationships almost obsessively, and relatively few of the many people he knew were invited to his North London flat. He even managed to segment this inner Orwell circle, as one might call it, so carefully as to keep its various strangely assorted members separated from each other. One of his regular visitors at this time was an irascible verse-writer who had vowed deadly hatred to me for a review I had written of his poems; Orwell managed things so adroitly that we never met in his flat. Even so, one did occasionally say or hear others saying, 'I don't know what Orwell sees in X'. What Orwell did see, almost certainly, was an interestingly individual personality; censorious though he might be in print, he was, as his burning desire to make up paper quarrels on first acquaintance suggests, very tolerant towards the people he knew well.

What made Orwell such an excellent journalist and often gave his novels a touch of that reality which goes beyond mere verisimilitude was his intense interest in the concrete aspects of living, in 'the surface of life', as he would say. As one got to know him, one realized how his writing seemed to extend and

amplify his daily life and conversation. Now, when I reread his
books, and skim again through his journalistic pieces in *Tribune*, the *Observer*, and, earlier on, the *New English Weekly*,
finding them still fresh and original after twenty years, I am
perpetually reminded of the conversation on evenings we spent
together in one or the other of our flats, or walking over Hampstead Heath on a summer afternoon, or, occasionally, dining in
Soho and going on to the Café Royal or to one of the public
houses where writers gathered, the Wheatsheaf in Rathbone
Place, or Victor Berlemont's York Minster ('the French house')
near the bombed ruin of St Anne's, Soho, or the Swiss tavern in
Old Compton Street.

  Orwell's flat, where he lived with his sister Avril, then un-
married, and with his small adopted son Richard, to whom he
was extravagantly devoted, was in Islington, perched under the
roofs of a tall Georgian house in Canonbury Square, then a
lower-middle-class outpost on the edge of a great workers' district. Orwell was highly conscious of the geography of classes,
and the whole area, with its bombed houses and flooded base-
ments and ruins red in the summer with willow-herb, had the
kind of seediness which he liked to portray in his novels and
which creates so much of the atmosphere of books like *Keep
the Aspidistra Flying* and *Nineteen Eighty-Four*. His attitude to
London was ambivalent; he claimed to hate it, and he was
certainly much happier when he lived in the country, but the
city still fascinated him, particularly marginal districts like Islington and the less respectable fringes of Hampstead. To live in
such districts probably gave him a comforting illusion of nearness to the British working man – that nearness which he had
sought so often and so vainly. A street or so from Canonbury
Square stood a large working-class tavern, a kind of gin palace,
with cut-glass screens and a big garden filled with tables, where
the proletarians would sit on a summer's evening in whole
families, with the fathers and mothers downing pints of old-
and-mild while the children shouted on the swings which the
publican had cannily provided. Orwell liked to go there occasionally, always keeping a weather eye open so that he might

avoid the embarrassment of running into one of the little group of Stalinist writers who lived in the district. But he did not appear to know any of the working men who frequented the pub, and he certainly seemed out of place among them, a rather frayed sahib wearing shabby clothes with all the insouciance an old Etonian displays on such occasions. I always found it difficult to think how he could have passed himself off so convincingly as a tramp in the adventures he describes in *Down and Out in Paris and London* and in *The Road to Wigan Pier*. But the little world of the tramps and the slightly larger world of writers and painters were probably, a generation ago, the only classless areas of English life, and for that reason they were quite exceptional. Between the worker and the most radically minded of middle-class men there was – as Orwell observed sharply when he wrote *The Road to Wigan Pier* – a great gulf fixed, and this gulf he never really crossed.

Orwell's own apartment reflected his attempt to reconcile his intellectualism with his interest in a working-class culture that was already moribund among the people. It was a dark and almost dingy place, with a curiously Dickensian atmosphere. In the living-room stood a great screen plastered over with shellacked pictures cut from magazines and a collection of china mugs, celebrating various popular nineteenth-century festivals, crowded on top of the crammed bookshelves. He gathered objects around him for their curiosity rather than their aesthetic charm, though at the same time he was intensely sensitive to natural beauty, the beauty of landscapes, birds and even humble creatures like toads. By the fireplace stood a high-backed wicker armchair, of an austerly angular shape which I have seen nowhere else, and here Orwell himself would always sit, like a Gothic saint in his niche. The small room which he called his study looked like a workshop, with its carpenter's bench, its rack of chisels and its smell of newly cut wood; Orwell was very fond of manual work, and when he was in London he would sometimes do a little joinery as a relaxation from writing, though the simple bookshelves and brackets which he showed me displayed no evidence of special dexterity. Most of his writing he actually did by typewriter, sitting at the large round table in his living-room.

Orwell was not entirely indifferent to comfort, but he certainly set no great store by appearances and his periods of hardship had given him an easy contempt for the trappings of the bourgeois life. His way of dressing, even when he was relatively prosperous, remained the shabby corduroys and the worn tweed jacket, with a thick, dark-coloured Viyella shirt, a shaggy tie and shoes that were never well polished. He liked trench coats, bulky knitted scarves, and leather gauntlets. I never saw him wearing a suit or, in any weather, a hat.

John Morris, who disliked Orwell as a result of their association at the B.B.C., suggested in *Penguin New Writing* that this sartorial eccentricity manifested a childishly self-conscious rebellion against the proper standards of polite behaviour. But it seemed to me that, having once escaped from middle-class conventions, Orwell just did not find them worth the trouble of resuming. At the same time he did take a boyish pleasure in imitating a few working-class habits. For example, he would often pour his tea into his saucer and blow on it vigorously before he drank it, and if anyone appeared to be shocked, he would be delighted and regard it all as a great joke. A similar boyishness of nature led him to practise feats of endurance and austerity which taxed his weak health, but which provided him with the subject-matter for two of his best books, *Homage to Catalonia* and *Down and Out in Paris and London*, and which might have produced, if only he had lived long enough, an excellent account of the hardships of farming in the Hebrides. He seemed to have naturally modest needs, and long periods of semi-voluntary poverty had reduced his demands on life, but when anything good came his way he rarely rejected it, as one realized after the publication of *Animal Farm* when he at last enjoyed something approaching prosperity. But to that aspect of his later years I shall be returning.

Whenever one arrived at Orwell's flat, or when he walked into our attic apartment in Highgate, his ailing bronchi wheezing from the long climb up several flights of stairs, there was first a period of silence, for Orwell, though gregarious, was also a shy man. Then after a while, the conversation would warm up, over a meal (usually high tea at Orwell's) or sitting before a coal or peat fire, with Orwell butter-fingeredly rolling cigarettes of the strongest black shag he could find and drinking tea as dark and almost as thick as treacle. Sometimes, when he was in a reminiscent mood, the talk would develop into a monologue on his part. His voice, which retained a slight but recognizable vestige of the Eton accent, was rather low and level in tone, and it had a fascinating kind of monotony which seemed to throw into relief the vividness of his descriptions. His monologues mainly concerned those parts of his life which were dealt with in his autobiographical works and in the semi-autobiographical parts of his novels, the writings on Burma, on Paris and Spain, on the lower depths of English life which in those days still seemed to anyone brought up in the middle classes more distant and hardly less exotic than a foreign country. It seemed as though one were listening to a leisurely, rather didactic but nonetheless very entertaining gloss on his various books. At other times we would be guided by Orwell's passion for odd facts, and would converse on the strangest variety of subjects, hopping erratically from point to point. However banal our subject might appear when we first lit upon it, Orwell would usually discuss it with such thoroughness and humour that it would be lifted completely out of its pristine dullness. He might talk about tea, for example, and ways of making it, or about various kinds of fuel and their respective merits, and would bring in such a wealth of illustration and reminiscence and so many odd tags of information that one was stimulated to enter into the subject with as much zest as he. And then a week or two later, one would find that this conversation had become part of his writing and formed the basis of one of his highly readable essays in *Tribune*. I think it was this close relationship between his talk and his writing that enabled Orwell to be at once such a prolific and such a generally successful journalist. Once an idea had taken shape and even a degree of polish in conversation, it was a fairly simple matter to write it down. Some of Orwell's articles, as he admitted rather shame-facedly, were actually typed out immediately and published in their first draft, without any substantial revision. On anything that was to appear in book form, or on one of those rather monumental pieces which he contributed to *Horizon* or *Partisan Review* or *Now*, he took much greater pains.

There were other times when the conversation ranged over the more portentous fields of politics, and Orwell would ex-pound his fears on the future of society, and dilate on the way in which the concern for freedom and truth had grown weak in the popular consciousness, as well as among writers and poli-ticians. In this way he told us all the basic ideas of *Nineteen Eighty-Four*, though, with characteristic modesty, he talked little about the details of the novel, and until I saw it finally in print I had only the sketchiest idea of the plot, though I knew all the themes by heart. One day, in the spring of 1946, Orwell took out of one of his bookshelves a paperbacked book. 'I've been looking for this for a long time,' he said, 'but I still can't find a copy of the English version.' It was *Nous Autres*, the French translation of Zamyatin's *We*, and a few weeks later Orwell wrote for *Tribune* a descriptive essay on this fascinating anti-Utopia. But he gave no indication of the extent to which the chance acquisition of this volume would help to determine the shape of *Nineteen Eighty-Four*, which bears the ineradicable marks of Zamyatin's influence. When Orwell talked in this apocalyptic vein he would paint a horrifying Gothic picture of the fate that might befall us, and here, as some of the more pessimistic parts of *Coming Up for Air* suggest, he was moti-vated by long-held fears which the reading of *We* merely helped to crystallize in a fictionally viable form.

Politically, Orwell was at his best as the critic, the iconoclast, in some ways – possibly owing to the Gallic strain in his family – remarkably similar to French writers like Péguy and Proud-hon. After he returned to England in 1927 and resigned from the Imperial police in Burma, he described himself rather vaguely as an Anarchist, and continued to do so for several years; even after he began to call himself a Socialist in 1936, he significantly fought beside the Anarchists in the internecine struggle between the Communists and their libertarian opponents during the Barcelona May Days of 1937. From that time until his death his relation with the Anarchists was noticeably ambivalent.

When I first knew him, Orwell was a supporter of the Labour Party, though I doubt if he was a card-carrying member. It was the left wing of the party with which he associated, the wing led by Aneurin Bevan, Jennie Lee and Michael Foot, and after Labour came into power in 1945, and began to impose its programme of Crippsian austerity, a rather squalid foretaste of *Nineteen Eighty-Four*, his enthusiasm cooled perceptibly and rapidly. From my own contact with him at this time, I believe Julian Symons was substantially correct when he said, in his *London Magazine* article, that Orwell retained his faith in libertarian socialism until his death, but that in the end this belief 'was expressed for him more sympathetically in the personalities of unpractical Anarchists than in the slide-rule Socialists who made up the bulk of the British Parliamentary Labour Party'.

This does not mean that Orwell ever again became an avowed Anarchist. But he passed from a sharp and immoderate wartime criticism of the Anarchists because of their anti-militarism to a position of interested tolerance, so that between 1945 and his death, Anarchist intellectuals, including Herbert Read, Marie Louise Berneri and me, were among his closest friends. He contributed at least one and possibly more review articles to *Freedom*, the weekly which replaced *War Commentary* in 1945 as the political organ of the Anarchists, and he became a loyal and interested supporter of *Now*, the literary magazine which I was running at the time. He was the first person to send a substantial cheque to the fund which I established in a vain attempt to stem the magazine's losses, and to one of the issues, in 1946, he contributed his magnificent and terrible essay, 'How the Poor Die'. This was after the publication of *Animal Farm*; American magazines were bidding for his work, and he could certainly have demanded a handsome fee for such a piece of writing instead of the minute token payment I was able to offer.

But Orwell never cut away the literary ladders by which he himself had climbed, and he was always willing, when he had the time, to write for impecunious little magazines.

I think his wavering attitude towards anarchism, shifting from a general commitment in the early thirties to critical hostility during the war years and back to friendly interest in the last five years of his life, was connected with the peculiar nature of his own socialism, which, with all its contradictions and its tendency to take pendulum swings from extreme idealism to extreme common sense, had far more affinity with Proudhon's variety than with Marx's. When Orwell talked most eloquently about socialism, it was always when he was engaged in showing the faults and dangers of existing Socialist movements. Whenever I discussed with him his views of what socialism should actually be, the creed that emerged was a very simple one. He was mainly concerned with the implementation of those fairly general ideas which he brought together under the heading of 'decency', ideas like brotherhood, fair play and honest dealing which he had absorbed from writers like Dickens, but he was not very adept at close political discussion, and he had a temperamental reluctance to think in terms of elaborate social plans or clearly defined party platforms.

What concerned him much more deeply than political programmes were the general principles of conduct, particularly conduct affecting other men, which had been developed in the long tradition of English radical dissent, and which were quickly losing ground in modern political life, in the world of the concentration camps and the partisan rewriting of history. It was important to tell the truth. It was important to preserve the objectivity of history. It was important above all to create a world in which every man's right to self-respect would be jealously preserved. This was why Orwell hated political doctrinaires, professional do-gooders, and faddists of all kinds.

It was when he talked to me about the State, that apple of discord which split the Socialist movement in the nineteenth century, that Orwell seemed particularly confused. On one side he was still influenced by the traditions of the sahib class into which he had been born, traditions of dedicated public service coupled with the wielding of unchallenged authority. But he also cultivated an anti-authoritarian strain of thought that was never far from the surface in his reactions to established government. So there were occasions when he would speak, in tones that might have seemed appropriate to a converted Blimp, of extensive and disciplined nationalization of industries, of state control over wide sectors of social life. But at other times – and here I felt his real inclinations were emerging – he seemed to envisage a decentralized society and workers' control of industry – something rather like the Guild Socialist vision, with a great deal of room for individual initiative. Similarly he would argue that authors should be state-supported, and at other times appear to contradict himself by maintaining that the less a writer had to do with any organized body, the better for him and his work. 'There are always strings attached,' he sometimes said, and then I would know he was thinking of his years at the B.B.C.

Although conversations with Orwell ranged widely, there were certain strictly avoided areas. He had developed an extraordinary reticence about intimate matters, which Richard Rees rather aptly described as *pudor*. Even his anger was demonstrative only on paper, and when he was in the company of someone he disliked he was most likely to express his disapproval by an agonizing and gloomy silence. While his consideration for other people, which he sometimes displayed practically in the way of great helpfulness and generosity, indicated the presence of deep feelings, he showed them rarely, except towards his son Richard, to whom his devotion was touchingly obvious. He was not uninterested in women – after all, he married twice – but he never made a display of the fact, and one extraordinarily beautiful girl who was on very friendly terms with both of us remarked to me with some pique that Orwell was the only one among her male acquaintances who never made her feel that he was aware of her as a woman.

Orwell's *pudor* prevented him from discussing a whole range of intimate aspects of his own life. For example, he only once mentioned to me his first wife Eileen, who died suddenly in 1944 and whom I never met. Neither he nor his sister Avril ever talked very much about their family or their childhood, and as far as my conversations with him went, he might have been born somewhere towards the end of his time at Eton. One soon learned to respect his reticences; anything less would have meant the loss of a friend.

Undoubtedly this almost fanatical reserve had a great deal to do with the request in Orwell's will that no biography of him should be written, a request which to many people seemed inconsistent with his choice of the autobiographical form for so many of his books and with the strong autobiographical elements that appear in all his novels. In the long run a biography can hardly be avoided; already, with the publication of many of Orwell's letters, and of the reminiscences of his relatives and friends, a kind of phantom biography does exist, and undoubtedly, when all those who knew him are dead, someone – probably the wrong person – will at last write the definitive life of George Orwell.

However irrational the request, Orwell's friends have respected it, though they have also speculated on the connexion between this wish to keep certain personal matters from the light of day and the relationship between George Orwell and his *alter ego* Eric Blair. George Orwell, first merely a *nom de plume*, began to emerge in the early thirties, but almost to the end of the decade Orwell still signed his letters Eric and accepted the use of this name by his friends. By the early forties he had become George Orwell to almost everybody but his bank manager. And it was George Orwell who turned Eric Blair, under various guises, into a character in literature and decided, with an artist's arbitrariness, which aspects and which adventures of his other self should be recorded. The 'I' in *Down and Out in Paris and London* and *The Road to Wigan Pier* is no more and no less George Orwell than the Marcel of *À la recherche du temps perdu* is Marcel Proust, and the autobiographical form of his works can be deceptive, if it is taken too literally, for Orwell rarely tells of his own experience except to make a point illustrating some general argument, usually of a political or social nature. At least overtly, he does not confess for the sake of confessing, though in works like *Such, Such Were the Joys* one feels a personal need impelling him in addition to the avowed intent to tell his experiences for the sake of exposing the tyrannies practised on children in the name of education. Generally he was highly selective in the autobiographical material he used in his books or essays; there was rarely anything that could be interpreted as a romantic uncovering of the depths of the self, and it was obviously to prevent any such uncovering by others that he forbade the writing of a biography. His published statements and the *persona* he revealed so guardedly to his friends comprised all that he wished to be known about himself. Yet, as we shall see later on examining his books, that hidden self is rarely absent, and emerges most strongly in the various forms of personal alienation which he portrays and discusses.

4

ORWELL was one of those rare men whom success did not harm. On the contrary, one noticed a definite mellowing of his character during the lamentably brief period between the successful publication of *Animal Farm* and the onset, at the end of 1947, of the illness that continued until his death at the beginning of 1950. He became noticeably less inclined to imagine himself the victim of literary conspiracies, and he found much pleasure in sharing his good fortune with others, particularly after the American Book-of-the-Month Club accepted *Animal Farm* in 1946. In that year Orwell had modestly estimated, in reply to a questionnaire circulated by *Horizon*, that a sufficient weekly income for an author would be six pounds if he were single and ten pounds if he were married. In these terms, he found himself, with the royalties from *Animal Farm* and the fees for magazine-article commissions which began to flow from the United States, not merely comfortably off, but positively well-to-do.

When he received the news of the Book-of-the-Month Club's decision, Orwell rang me up and invited me to lunch with him in celebration. By now he had abandoned the dreary public houses of the Strand which one associated with his *Tribune* days, and was patronizing the Greek and Italian restaurants of Percy Street. We met in a Tottenham Court Road public house, and as we walked to Percy Street Orwell explained to me at length that we were going to a restaurant he had begun to visit only the previous week, because the head waiter in the restaurant where he formerly lunched had objected to his taking off his jacket to eat. I have forgotten the name of the restaurant to which we did go, but I do remember Orwell standing up, conspicuous because of his height, and hanging his jacket over the back of his chair. With a look he challenged me to follow his example; I did. At that time wartime restrictions of restaurant meals were beginning to relax, and the lunch was an excellent and lavish one, with aperitifs, wine and brandy; it was a far cry from the boiled cod and turnip-tops in the Strand a few years before, and Orwell seemed to enjoy the change.

Over lunch, Orwell discussed the effect which the success of *Animal Farm* would have on his future. I thought at the time that his ideas were very realistic. He intended to put most of the money he got from the Book-of-the-Month Club into a trust fund for his son Richard. There was nothing in the way he spoke to suggest that he had any premonition that he would be dead within four years; he was merely acting from a sense of caution bred of many illnesses. He also wanted to buy a house in the Hebrides, and told me that he had been thinking about this all through the war; rather sardonically, he said that now his intention was reinforced by a desire to get as far away as possible from the threat of destruction by the atom bomb. From what I know of Orwell's almost perversely obstinate courage, I doubt if this was ever a really important reason for his wishing to leave London; the nostalgia for a simpler and cleaner way of life which emerges so poignantly in *Coming Up for Air* and even gives pathos to parts of *Nineteen Eighty-Four* was, I am sure, a much more pressing motive. Apart from his own feelings, he wanted to bring up his son in the country rather than the city, and later on he was delighted when Richard, still only four years old, seemed to be taking enthusiastically to life on the farm. For the rest, he hoped to abandon the journalistic work he had been carrying on since 1940, and to spend his time – at least in the foreseeable future – on writing novels and major critical essays.

By the austere standards of England in 1946, the bill which Orwell paid for lunch that day was a stiff one – round about six guineas – and I felt obliged to contribute in some way to the celebration of his good fortune. I decided that it had to be something in the way of an unusual treat, and I remembered that one of the Soho pubs, the Dog and Duck, had mysteriously acquired a small cache of real absinthe. So we crossed Oxford Street and stood in the tiny bar, crowded with beer-boozers drinking against closing time, while the barmaid slowly dripped water through a cube of sugar into the milky liquid. Some of our fellow customers were curious, and the barmaid explained at embarrassing length, with dark references to people who wasted good money on frivolities; there was still a lot of puritanical feeling about extravagant spending in London at that time, and we began to realize that the regulars of the Dog and Duck regarded us with suspicious disfavour, so that as soon as the absinthe was ready we drank it quickly and hurried out. Unwittingly, I had made Orwell rather unhappy, since the incident underlined the gap between the modest bourgeois luxuries he could now afford to give himself and his friends, and the standards of the working class for which he still felt an obscure though slowly receding admiration. However, that was not what he talked about as we walked away down Frith Street, both feeling a little sheepish. 'Didn't it cost rather a lot, George?' he asked solicitously. It had in fact cost only a fraction of the bill he had settled half an hour before, but he knew enough about the life of young professional writers – this was the year of my first book – to realize that the pound I had paid out was one of the very few in my possession. Naturally, like Gordon Comstock in *Keep the Aspidistra Flying*, I dissembled.

It must have been almost immediately after this meeting that Orwell went up to the Hebrides and found the deserted farmhouse, Barnhill, which he bought on the island of Jura. From that time we naturally saw much less of him, but letters arrived quite frequently in which he gave vivid little pictures of his life there, and kept us posted on his activities. Returning from Switzerland in August 1946, for example, I found a letter waiting for me in which he said that he had just started a novel which he hoped to finish in 1947. This became *Nineteen Eighty-Four*, and was destined, though none of us then imagined it, to be his last book.

Knowing Orwell's passion for tea, my wife and I, coffee drinkers, would save up our rations and every now and again send him a packet of Typhoo Tips, which produced the dark, strong brew he liked. One of these packets, in September 1946, evoked a letter in which Orwell described existence on Jura; it reflected the intense interest he always took in the concrete aspects of life – particularly rural life – and also in its social overtones.

Thanks ever so for the tea – it came just at the right moment because this week the whole of the nearest village is being brought here in lorries to get in the field of corn in front of our house, and of course tea will have to flow like water while the job is on. We have been helping the crofter who is our only neighbour with his hay and corn, at least when rain hasn't made it impossible to work. Everything is done here in an incredibly primitive way. Even when the field is ploughed with a tractor the corn is still sown broadcast, then scythed and bound up into sheaves by hand. They seem to broadcast corn, i.e. oats, all over Scotland, and I must say they seem to get it almost as even as can be done by a machine. Owing to the wet they don't get the hay in till about the end of September or even later, sometimes as late as November, and they can't leave it in the open but have to store it all in lofts. A lot of the corn doesn't quite ripen and is fed to the cattle in sheaves like hay. The crofters have to work very hard, but in many ways they are better off and more independent than a town labourer, and they would be quite comfortable if they could get a bit of help in the way of machinery, electrical power and roads, and could get the landlords off their backs and get rid of the deer. These animals are ʼo common on this particular island that they are an absolute curse. They eat up the pastures where there ought to be sheep, and they make fencing immensely more expensive than it need be. The crofters aren't allowed to shoot them, and are constantly having to waste their time dragging carcasses of deer down from the hills during the stalking season. Everything is sacrificed to the brutes because they are an easy source of meat and therefore profitable to the people who own them. I suppose sooner or later these islands will be taken in hand, and then they could either be turned into a first-rate area for dairy produce and meat, or else they would support a large population of small peasants living off cattle and fishing. In the eighteenth century the population here was 10,000 – now less than 300.

In letters like this one felt that Orwell was not merely displaying his recently acquired knowledge of the remote Scottish countryside and its ways of life, but was also expressing a conviction that the so-called progress which had been going on for the past three or four generations, and which had accelerated since his childhood, was disrupting a naturally balanced society in which a frugal but satisfying agrarian existence had been viable. But he allowed for the possibility of that trend being eventually diverted, and I found it an interesting indication of the open and undoctrinaire kind of socialism which he professed that he should consider the re-creation of a peasant class a possible solution to the social ills of rural Scotland. Or was perhaps his longing to re-establish the past getting the better of his desire to achieve a Socialist future which he must have known would become, if it were built by the Labour Party of the 1940s, the very kind of mechanized and centralized society that he foresaw with the greatest apprehension?

About this time I was commissioned by Dwight Macdonald, then editing *Politics* in New York, to write a long critical essay on Orwell. I found that several of Orwell's books which are now freely available in paperbacks had gone out of print and were virtually unobtainable. Even the London Library had no copy of *Keep the Aspidistra Flying*, and, having tried all my friends in vain, I wrote to Orwell asking if he could possibly lend me one. I did not get the novel, but I did receive a reply that showed the sharply critical standards Orwell applied to books of his own which, for all their evident imperfections, have stood the test of time reasonably well. After remarking that it was 'very flattering' to be the subject of an article in *Politics*, he continued:

I haven't a copy of *Keep the Aspidistra Flying*. I picked up a copy in a secondhand shop some months back, but I gave it away. There are two or three books which I am ashamed of, and have not allowed to be reprinted or translated, and that is one of them. There is an even worse one called *A Clergyman's Daughter*. This was written simply as an exercise, and I oughtn't to have published it, but I was desperate for money, ditto when I wrote *Keep the A*. At that time I simply hadn't a book in me, but I was half-starved and had to turn out something to bring in £100 or so.

Both books would have satisfied any ordinary journeyman writer, but Orwell took his literary craftsmanship very seriously. His writing seemed effortless, but this was only because of the exacting discipline he imposed on structure and verbal texture alike.

My article appeared in *Politics* during the following winter, after Orwell had returned to London. It was the first serious essay on Orwell's work that had yet appeared, and on some points it was very critical, particularly of those inconsistencies of thought which it is easy to uncover in almost anything Orwell wrote about politics. The day after the issue arrived in England, I went into the Freedom Bookshop, and there I found Orwell. He had just bought *Politics*, and was obviously intent on reading the article as soon as he could. I felt rather apprehensive; I had got into trouble with London literary friends over much less critical comments on their work. That evening Orwell rang me up; he liked the essay and thought it was as good a first study as any writer could expect. He objected only to one paragraph, in which I had accused him of political opportunism for arguing that conscription could not be avoided in time of war but that as soon as hostilities were ended it must be resisted as an infringement on the liberties of the individual. But even here his protest took a surprisingly mild form. 'I have my reasons for arguing like that,' he said, but he never explained them.

Orwell stayed in London from October 1946 to April 1947. It was the hardest winter we had endured for many years, and Orwell suffered from severe attacks of bronchitis which kept him in bed for weeks on end. I remember more than once going round to his flat in the middle of the day and finding him in pyjamas and a shaggy dressing-gown, looking exceptionally gaunt and pale, but working at his typewriter on a review or article for some editor to whom he had made a promise he did not wish to break.

After Orwell left for Jura in April 1947 we did not see him again; for him it was the last of the good summers. He invited us to join him in the Hebrides whenever we felt inclined, and sent an elaborate timetable of trains, boats, buses and hired cars. But that year we could not afford the fares for the two-day journey from London, and we had to be content with the letters that arrived fairly frequently until the autumn. Looking through them, I find Orwell telling me details of the island life – he had just started cutting peat, 'which I think is really less work than cutting wood' – and approving of my intention at that time to write a book on Oscar Wilde. 'I've always been very pro-Wilde,' he commented. 'I particularly like *Dorian Gray*, absurd as it is in a way.' I suspect that Orwell's liking for Wilde was based mainly on his natural sympathy for the defeated, since there is little in common between the austerity of his own work and the lushness of Wilde's, except perhaps a shared liking for surface colour, which in Orwell's case comes out most strongly in *Burmese Days*. However, he did realize, more than most people, that there was a very serious side to Wilde's character, and when I edited a new edition of *The Soul of Man Under Socialism*, which appeared at the end of 1947, he wrote an article on the leader page of the *Observer*, in which he talked of Wilde's ideas as a contribution to socialist thought that merited discussion. Wilde's libertarian attitude was really not far removed from his own. Nevertheless, when one remembered his attacks on intellectual Socialists and on 'pansy poets' during the 1930s, his liking for Wilde did seem a typical Orwellian inconsistency.

It was at this time, in August, that Orwell took a decision which many of his friends regarded with foreboding. He announced that, apart from a trip to London in November, he intended to winter on Jura. With his precarious health, and after the bad attacks of bronchitis during the preceding winter, it seemed the height of quixotic folly for him to remain in the damp, raw autumn and winter climate of the Hebrides, but he was the kind of man with whom, one knew beforehand, it was useless to argue once he had made up his mind. Moreover, he had thought up plenty of reasons for staying, and he detailed them to me in a letter which made me feel that he had really found in the remote and fairly primitive communities of Jura something approaching that semi-idyllic 'golden country' so nostalgically evoked in his novels.

I can work here with fewer interruptions, and I think we shall be less cold here. The climate, although wet, is not quite so cold as England, and it is much easier to get fuel.... Part of the winter may be pretty bleak and one is sometimes cut off from the mainland for a week or two, but it doesn't matter so long as you have flour in hand to make scones. Latterly the weather has been quite incredible, and I am afraid we shall be paying for it soon. Last week we went round in the boat and spent a couple of days on the completely uninhabited Atlantic side of the island in an empty shepherd's hut – no beds, but otherwise quite comfortable. There are beautiful white beaches round that side, and if you do about an hour's climb into the hills you come to lochs which are full of trout but never fished because too unget-atable. This week of course we've all been breaking our backs helping to get the hay in.... After September the weather gets pretty wild, though I know there are very warm days even in mid-winter.

It has often been suggested since Orwell's death that a suicidal impulse drove him to the Hebrides. I think the evidence of all the letters he wrote to his friends from those almost deserted islands shows that he went there seeking not self-destruction but life and renewal, and that, as John Wain has said, it was a tragic irony that the climate of Jura should have helped to speed his death.

In the event, Orwell did not make his November trip to London. He had felt unwell intermittently during the summer, he had overtaxed his strength helping with farm work, and in October he and Richard were wrecked on a fishing trip. He told me:

Yes, we did nearly get drowned, and ended up by managing to scramble ashore on a tiny islet after losing both the engine and the oars from the boat, so that we couldn't get off again. Very luckily some lobster fishermen happened to pass and saw the fire we had lit, so we got away after a few hours. Richard enjoyed every minute of it except when he was in the water.

All these circumstances helped to undermine his precarious health, but in the last week of October he was still planning to leave for London, and told me to expect him about the seventh of November. Almost immediately after writing he took to his bed; he was seriously ill with tuberculosis of the left lung. He stayed bedridden, at home, for two months, and when he next wrote me, in January 1948, it was from a hospital on the mainland in Lanarkshire to which he had been removed a fortnight before. His ailing lung was being put out of action, but he remarked stoically, 'I have been a bit less like death since being here,' and he was hopeful of being about again by the summer and of getting a correspondent's job in a warm climate to see him through the following winter.

Sickness did not diminish Orwell's interest in what went on around him. He commented on books which I sent him, talked about nineteenth-century travel writing about South America and its 'wonderful Arcadian atmosphere', and became much concerned over the public attitude towards civil liberties and the record of the Labour government in this field. An agitation for discriminatory legislation against former Fascists had been going on in *Tribune*, and the Labour Party had embarked on a purge of Communists in the Civil Service, using methods of investigation which did not allow suspects to confront their accusers. Orwell's comments to me on these two issues seem particularly revealing of his state of mind at this time. On the question of the ex-Fascists he wrote in January:

I hope the F.D.C. is doing something about these constant demands to outlaw Mosley and Co. *Tribune*'s attitude I think has been shameful, and when the other week Zilliacus wrote in demanding what amounts to fascist legislation and creation of second-class citizens, nobody seems to have replied. The whole thing is simply a thinly disguised desire to persecute people who can't fight back, as obviously the Mosley lot don't matter a damn and can't get a real mass following. I think it's a case for a pamphlet, and I only wish I felt well enough to write one. The central thing one must come to terms with is the argument, always advanced by those advocating repressive legislation, that 'you cannot allow democracy to be used to overthrow democracy – you cannot allow freedom to those who merely use it in order to destroy freedom'. This of course is true, and both Fascists and Communists do aim at making use of democracy in order to destroy it. But if you carry this to its conclusions, there can be no case for allowing any political or intellectual freedom whatever. Evidently therefore it is a matter of distinguishing between a real and a merely theoretical threat to democracy, and no one should be persecuted for expressing his opinions, however antisocial, and no political organization suppressed, unless it can be shown that there is *a substantial threat to the stability of the state*.

Two months later, in March, Orwell wrote to me of the case of the Communist civil servants, and asked me to make sure that the Freedom Defence Committee took some kind of stand.

It's not easy to have a clear position [he allowed], because, if one admits the rights of governments to govern, one must admit their right to choose suitable agents, and I think any organization, e.g. a political party, has a right to protect itself against infiltration. But at the same time, the *way* in which the government seems to be going to work is vaguely disquieting, and the whole phenomenon seems to me part of the general breakdown of the democratic outlook. Only a week or two ago the Communists themselves were shouting for unconstitutional methods to be used against the Fascists, now the same methods are to be used against themselves, and in another year or two a pro-Communist government might be using them against us. Meanwhile the general apathy about freedom of speech, etc., constantly grows, and that matters much more than what may be on the statute books.

By showing Orwell defending two groups he detested, these letters demonstrate the genuineness of his libertarian convictions, and also, since they were written during the long interludes of illness that broke the actual writing of *Nineteen Eighty-Four* into two parts, they indicate the kind of anxieties which were present in his mind at this time. In public apathy, and in the disregard of basic freedoms by a Labour government and by the intellectuals of the *Tribune* group with whom he had formerly been associated, he saw the kind of dangers that might conceivably end in some society similar to that of his fictional Oceania.

During the spring and early summer of 1948 Orwell seemed to be recovering steadily. In April he told me that, in spite of some bad side effects, the streptomycin treatment appeared to have done so well that there was no longer any trace of infection in his lungs. In July his recovery seemed so advanced that the doctors gave in to his burning desire to return to Jura, on condition that he lived very quietly and took a great deal of rest. 'It will be rather a bore not being able to go fishing, etc., but it's worth it. I don't mind being in bed as I have got used to writing there.' On the twenty-third of July he wrote me a brief, hasty note on a scrap from an exercise book to say that he was leaving the hospital and going back to the island. 'They seem to think I'm pretty well cured and will end up perfectly O.K. so long as I don't relapse during the next few months.'

But the return to Jura meant a return from the peculiar mental isolation that seems to enfold all tuberculosis hospitals to the preoccupations of Orwell's ordinary life. He began to pick up the threads of writing, and with that to feel again the sense of urgency that in recent years had inspired so much of his work. For well over half a year he had done nothing on *Nineteen*

Eighty-Four, and now he decided that he must finish the book. He wrote a few brief articles and reviews for the *Observer* and other papers to earn some ready money, but otherwise he concentrated on finishing the novel, writing few letters in comparison with the considerable correspondence he had kept going from hospital. Many miles away from the nearest doctor, he steadily overtaxed his strength during the summer months. By September he began to relapse, but, though he was in 'a ghastly state', he did not leave the island for treatment until December; he insisted on finishing his novel beforehand. 'The effort of doing so didn't make me any better,' he said. He talked about pressing letters from publishers and about the fact that he had earned very little money since 1947, but there was such an urgency about his desire to finish the book that I suspect these were only rationalizations. *Nineteen Eighty-Four* was unashamedly a book with a message, and even during his illness, as the letters I have quoted suggest, he was anxious for that message to get on its way to the public as quickly as possible, though he did not foresee how widely it would spread or how strangely it would be misinterpreted. It is also likely that when his health did begin to grow worse again in September, Orwell realized more strongly than before the possibility of not recovering and worked on because he wished to present in complete form the book which was to become his testament.

When I heard from Orwell for the last time, early in 1949, he had left Scotland and was being treated at a sanatorium in the Cotswolds. He seemed relatively content there, and some of the grim old Orwellian humour came back when he discussed his treatment. 'They are giving me something called PAS which I suspect of being a high-sounding name for aspirins, but they say it is the latest thing and gives good results. If necessary I can have another go at streptomycin, which certainly seemed to improve me last time, but the secondary effects are so unpleasant that it's a bit like sinking the ship to drown the rats.' He was still interested in the affairs of the Freedom Defence Committee, which was now waning fast. Characteristically he expressed regret at not being able to contribute to the funds as generously as in the past. He had found sickness expensive, and until *Nineteen Eighty-Four* came off the press he felt that he must continue to be economical. With the caution of a professional writer with a long experience of low incomes, he thought that he would be lucky if he made five hundred pounds out of the novel. In spite of the success of *Animal Farm*, he did not realize, or was unwilling to acknowledge, that at forty-five he had become a successful and even a fashionable writer.

In the spring of 1949 my wife and I left England for Canada. ('The sort of country that could be fun for a bit, especially if you like fishing,' Orwell had commented when he heard of our plans.) Our last weeks in London were busy with the multitudinous arrangements that were necessary in the Age of Austerity before one could transfer one's home from England to any other country. We thought of paying Orwell a farewell visit, but never found the time for it. It was one of the omissions one regrets after it cannot be rectified. When we reached Canada I wrote two or three letters to Orwell; he was too sick to answer. Later I heard from Julian Symons that his condition had taken a serious turn for the worse, and that he was now in the University College Hospital in London. Then, at a party in Vancouver on a snowy evening in the first days of 1950, one of the guests came in and told me that the news of Orwell's death had just come over the radio. A silence fell over the room, and I realized that this gentle, modest and angry man had already become a figure of world myth.

PART TWO

LIFE AGAINST ODDS

*The Themes of
Orwell's Fiction*

THE myth of Orwell is that of the tortured, tragic writer, who died in his prime after a life of heroic hardships, and left as his testament the haunting and admonitory nightmare of a future dominated by communism. He appears in the myth as a figure hardly recognizable by those who knew him, a being of apocalyptic vision, touched by genius, gifted with tongues, but at heart the epitome of the plain man in our democratic age, inventing words like *doublethink* that have passed into the colloquial language and proclaiming his horrifying revelation to the faithful in terms which they are convinced they understand.

The faithful in this case are the most heterogeneous following a writer can ever have accumulated. They include, on the Right, Conservatives and free-enterprisers of every colour, from Christopher Hollis and the more educated followers of Barry Goldwater to the editors of *Time* and that blind and miserable news-vendor who thrust a copy of *Nineteen Eighty-Four* into the hands of Isaac Deutscher in New York, saying, 'You must read it, sir. Then you will know why we must drop the atom bomb on the Bolshies!' Far to the Left, the neo-Orwellians also include the Anarchists, who have hailed *Nineteen Eighty-Four* as the exposition in brilliant fiction of all that Bakunin ever said against the Marxist view of the State. Between the extremes come the middle-of-the-way Socialists, who remember Orwell's links with the British Labour Party, and are just as willing as the Conservatives to accept the picture of him as the singleminded foe of communism, precisely because this allows them to forget that Orwell saw the seeds of *Nineteen Eighty-Four* waiting for germination in every Socialist system, and that more than a decade before, in *The Road to Wigan Pier*, he had made the most savage attack on doctrinaire socialism ever launched from the Left.

Finally, there are the intellectuals of camps and campuses who have united in claiming Orwell as their own, from the

American ex-Trotskyists, who were his fellow contributors to the *Partisan Review*, to those drab young English writers, singularly misnamed by journalists 'the angry young men', who found in Orwell's view of working-class life a false affinity with their own predilection for the greyer aspects of existence in contemporary Britain. In comparison with such dubious disciples, Orwell still shines out, half a generation later, as a noble and colourful figure, large in act and vision, the almost complete opposite of the narrow-visioned academics who have closed in during the present generation on the literary worlds of both Britain and North America. He was himself an intellectual of the autodidactic kind, yet the persistent attacks on the intellectual caste which recur in his books, from *Keep the Aspidistra Flying* in the mid thirties until his death, and which reach a rather shrill intensity in the London Letters he sent to *Partisan Review* during the war years, are completely sincere. He knew that intellectuals are in constant danger of being trapped in their own mental constructions, of becoming cultists or coterie men, and he would have regarded the superficial 'Orwellism' that has flourished among them in recent years as a malady no less dangerous than the Stalinist and pacifist cults which he denounced during the 1940s.

When people of widely differing viewpoints – Conservatives and Anarchists, Socialists and Liberals, ageing academics and young writers born old – find encouragement for their attitudes in a single author's work, we can reasonably assume that each of them is missing something, and that the work, considered as a whole, must be a good deal more complex than it appears at first sight. Orwell did not seek to be all things to all men; far from it. And if today he arouses echoes in such various minds, it is due more than anything else to the paradoxical fact that in aspiring to make his prose pure and transparent, he wrote with an appearance of simplicity which concealed the protean complexity that often characterized his thoughts and arguments.

A great deal of this complexity came from the fact that Orwell was a man who tended to glory in his contradictions and in the unsystematic nature of his thought. He was the last of a nineteenth-century tradition of individualist radicals which bred such men as Hazlitt, Cobbett and Dickens. He tended to move rather eccentrically and elusively between the poles of opinion to which most men remain tethered once they have taken up an attitude at the end of youth; in his most radical moods he was never afraid to sound what seemed to his critics the jarring note of conservatism. His outlook, in fact, was the reverse of sectarian, and he detested 'the smelly little orthodoxies' as he called them, by which he meant all the closed systems of thought from Catholicism to communism. His own limitations of thought and feeling, his obsessions and his enthusiasms, were always personal and temperamental rather than partisan and theoretical.

The appearance of inconsistency which one so often detects in following the opinions Orwell expressed on a given subject over a relatively brief period arose from the shift in his attitude which took place whenever the subject moved from the abstract and general to the concrete and personal. One finds him, for example, denouncing with great feeling the principles and institutions of imperialism, yet when he comes down to particulars he is willing to grant that British imperialism is better than the newer imperialisms that will follow it, and when he reaches the personal level he points out the virtues of good imperial administrators and suggests that even the worst of them deserve our sympathy. 'The life of the Anglo-Indian officials,' he said in *Burmese Days*, 'is not all jam. In comfortless camps, in sweltering offices, in gloomy dank bungalows smelling of dust and earth-oil, they earn, perhaps, the right to be a little disagreeable.' He was even willing to say more than a good word for Kipling.

Perhaps the most striking example of Orwell's desire to be fair to his opponents as persons even when he detested everything they stood for is shown in his attitude towards Hitler. Orwell loathed every tenet and every act of Nazism, and if he devoted more time to the exposure of the rival creed of communism, it was only because he felt that there was more danger of the Communists being able to deceive and dominate the Left in democratic countries. Yet he was unable to close his heart even to Hitler as a human being, and in the beginning of the war he had the moral courage to write in the *New English Weekly* an article which is a model of the imaginative understanding of an enemy's character. He said:

I have never been able to dislike Hitler. Ever since he came to power – till then, like nearly everyone, I had been deceived into thinking that he did not matter – I have reflected that I would certainly kill him if I could get within reach of him, but that I could feel no personal animosity. The fact is that there is something deeply appealing about him. One feels it again when one sees his photographs. . . . It is a pathetic, doglike face, the face of a man suffering under intolerable wrongs. In a rather more manly way it reproduces the expression of innumerable pictures of Christ crucified, and there is no doubt that this is how Hitler sees himself. The initial, personal cause of his grievance against the universe can only be guessed at; but at any rate the grievance is there. He is the martyr, the victim, Prometheus chained to the rock, the self-sacrificing hero who fights single-handed against impossible odds. If he were fighting a mouse he would know how to make it seem like a dragon. One feels, as with Napoleon, that he is fighting against destiny, that he *can't* win, and yet that somehow he deserves to. The attraction of such a pose is of course enormous: half of the films one sees turn upon such a theme.

This passage does not merely show that Orwell could understand the charismatic appeal Hitler made to vast numbers of Germans, so that they identified their own personal and collective grievances with his. It also demonstrates a number of the component aspects of Orwell's *persona* as a writer: scrupulous honesty, shown particularly in his admission of his own earlier underestimation of Hitler's importance; curiosity about the unusual in human mentality; willingness to go against accepted attitudes; even a slightly perverse streak of defiance which makes him state a little too forcibly a case which he knows will be unpopular. Most significant of all is the fact that Orwell presents Hitler not as the creator of a mass party or as the ruler of a nation, ensconced on the pyramid of power, but as a solitary figure, alone with his grievance and doomed, in the end, to failure.

In other words, Hitler as Orwell sees him resembles the typical Orwellian anti-hero. From Flory in *Burmese Days* to Winston Smith in *Nineteen Eighty-Four*, the central figure of every Orwell novel is a solitary, detached by some scar in his past from the world in which he finds himself, compelled to live the double existence of the misfit and, after inevitable and ineffectual rebellion, doomed to fail and be destroyed or finally and hopelessly to be enslaved. Here we reach the point where polemical contradictions merge in the artist's consistent vision.

2

IN *Nineteen Eighty-Four*, Orwell's final, most ambitious novel, the struggle of the solitary anti-hero forms the fictional pattern underlying the grim polemical picture of Utopia achieved. In didactic terms Orwell is trying to convey the view he held during the years between 1946 and 1948, that in every modern society without exception there were tendencies which, allowed to develop unchecked, might bring us within a generation into a world where all the values of truth and justice, mercy and freedom, decency and equality, which we have cherished since Brutus laid his hand on Caesar, would be sacrificed to make way for a new world in which Utopia would emerge in its own gross and terrifying caricature under the sign of 'a boot stamping on a human face – for ever'.

At this point the general and the individual tragedies are joined. For the boot stamping on the face was not merely a political image. It was the symbol of a personal nightmare that had been haunting Orwell at least since 1937, when he was given a foretaste of the totalitarian Utopia through his participation in the Spanish Civil War as a member of the militia attached to a left-wing dissident party, the POUM, which was eventually hunted down and almost exterminated by the Communists in Catalonia. Images of stamping boots and crushed faces, of human compassion destroyed by political brutality, began to appear in his writings and his conversation long before he had even conceived *Nineteen Eighty-Four*. George Bowling, the hero of *Coming Up for Air* (written in 1938), attends a Left Book Club meeting in a respectable London suburb, and all at once imagines himself within the mind of the professional anti-Fascist who is speaking.

> I saw the vision that he was seeing. And it wasn't at all the kind of vision that can be talked about. What he's *saying* is merely that Hitler's after us and we must all get together and have a good hate. Doesn't go into details. Leaves it all respectable. But what he's *seeing* is something quite different. It's the picture of himself smashing people's faces in with a spanner. Fascist faces, of course, I *know* that's what he's seeing. It was what I saw myself for the second or two that I was inside him. Smash! Right in the middle! The bones cave in like an eggshell and what was a face a minute ago is just a great big blob of strawberry jam. Smash! There goes another! That's what's in his mind, waking and sleeping, and the more he thinks of it, the more he likes it. And it's all O.K. because the smashed faces belong to Fascists. You could hear all that in the tone of his voice.

What Bowling sees going on secretly in the mind of the anti-Fascist speaker becomes explicit and open in the statements of the Inner Party official O'Brien in *Nineteen Eighty-Four* when he uses the image of the boot on the face to represent the ever-lasting reign of terror for its own sake which the Inner Party imposes on the people of Oceania. For Winston Smith at the very same moment it represents the extremity of his personal defeat. And in this connexion it is interesting, and a little startling, to find Orwell in 1943 applying a similar image to himself when he writes to a friend complaining about the propaganda work he has to do at the B.B.C. and ending with the bitter sentence: 'At present I'm just an orange that's been trodden on by a very dirty boot.'

The fact that such images, applied both in fiction and towards his own personal life, begin to appear as early as 1938 and are repeated over the decade until the completion of *Nineteen Eighty-Four* weakens the arguments of those who contend that the darkness of Orwell's vision in his final novel was due to his sickness or to his sense of impending death. There is a great deal of reason to conclude that, so far as Orwell was concerned, the writing of *Nineteen Eighty-Four* was a kind of cathartic process, a purging of all the apprehensions that had been haunting him unendurably for many years. It is true that after the novel was completed he himself blamed some of its crudities of expression and form, such as the neo-Gothic torture scenes in Room 101, on his illness, but the framing nightmare had been present in his mind for a whole decade, and I believe that the urgency with which he completed the novel, at great peril to his health, was due largely to an inner need to end a task that would finally expel the darkness from his system.

One must also remember that the grim political forebodings and personal nightmares to which Orwell gave expression in *Nineteen Eighty-Four* did not dominate him even then to the exclusion of very different thoughts. At this point we have to consider the significance of the novel's second face. Orwell was in many ways a man of extraordinary mental and emotional resilience, and the source of his self-regenerative power lay in his joy in the ordinary, common experiences of day-to-day existence and particularly of contact with nature. He fed from the earth, like Antaeus, and his happiest recollections of youth, like his happiest letters, were concerned in some way or another with rural experiences.

The pleasures he most enjoyed, even as an adult, were those of an Arcadian simplicity, as one can see from looking through the occasional essays he wrote for *Tribune*. He enjoyed planting fruit trees and seeing them grow, he liked watching birds and toads, collecting moths and catching fish. Though when I knew him he never had the voice to sing them, he got a great deal of pleasure out of popular songs, in which he found the Socialist movement sadly lacking, and when he said in one of his essays that he would sooner have written 'Come Where the Booze is Cheaper' than 'The Blessed Damozel' he was not being merely perverse; the music-hall song was associated in his mind with the tangible pleasure of ordinary, uncomplicated people, while Rossetti's poem could only have been written by an aesthete who had achieved an almost complete divorce between art and life, even his own life. Apart from popular songs, I never heard Orwell express any opinions about music, and Rayner Heppenstall maintains that he had no ear at all for classical compositions. This would fit in with his essentially naturalistic attitude, for classical music has always been the most unnatural and abstract of the arts. In painting his taste was definitely for the styles that seemed best to reflect the colour and movement of natural life, and his interest ended with the post-impressionists. I still have a postcard reproduction of a Degas painting which he sent me, and I remember a Gauguin print pasted on the great screen in his living-room, but after Cézanne the only painter who attracted his attention was Dali, whom he regarded as a psychological monstrosity rather than a significant painter. Even in literature Orwell distrusted any aesthetic other than a naturalistic and popular one. Once only, in the Trafalgar Square scene in *A Clergyman's Daughter*, did he write anything that could be regarded as experimental in the Joycean sense, and while *Coming Up for Air* derives a great deal from Proustian time-juggling and Proust's theories of memory, there is little sign of influence of the French writer on the actual style of this or any other Orwell book.

Later I shall discuss in much greater detail Orwell's views on the aesthetics of writing. The point I wish to make at present is that his naturalism permeated every aspect of his outlook. The craftsmanlike clarity to which he aspired in his prose was intended not only to present his arguments clearly but also to portray with impressionistic vividness the character of the visible world as he saw it, that almost Keatsian world where beauty and truth become each other's manifestations in the same way as, in Orwell's view, the quality of prose is inextricably linked with the intention of veracity.

I mention Keats, and I am reminded that while every writer on Orwell has noticed the extent to which he was influenced by Victorian writers, few have paid much attention to the parallels between his attitudes and those of the Romantics. Yet when he turned to verse he wrote like a bad Shelley; his solitary heroes had all a touch of diminished Byronism; and his attitude towards the people resembled Wordsworth's. Like Wordsworth, he sought, in his deliberate colloquialism, to use what the Romantic poet described as 'a selection of the language really used by men'. Like him again, he turned for a vision of the desirable way of life to a past in which he thought men lived according to more natural rhythms than the suburbanites who even in his day were quickly becoming the typical modern men of the Western world. The passage from the preface to *Lyrical Ballads* in which Wordsworth justifies his choice of rural characters, settings and themes parallels closely Orwell's arguments in favour of the country life. Wordsworth said:

Humble and rustic life was generally chosen because, in that condition, the essential passions of the heart find a better soil in which they can attain their maturity, are less under restraint, and speak a plainer and more emphatic language; because in that condition of life our elementary feelings coexist in a state of greater simplicity, and, consequently, may be more accurately contemplated, and more forcibly communicated; because the manners of rural life germinate from those elementary feelings, and, from the necessary character of rural occupations, are more easily comprehended, and more durable; and, lastly, because in that condition the passions of men are incorporated with the beautiful and permanent forms of nature.

In such terms Orwell might have justified the idyllic description of nature was unavoidable – in fact, tragically so.

Orwell did not merely idealize this kind of life in fiction. He sought to attain it personally in the 1930s, when he retreated from a hack's attic in Kentish Town to the Hertfordshire village of Wallington, and tried to live by running a small shop, keeping chickens and cultivating a large garden. Towards the end of his life he followed the same urge by departing even farther from the malign centres of civilization in his flight to the Hebrides, where rural life was at that time still unmechanized and simple, and where contact with 'the beautiful and permanent' forms of nature was unavoidable – in fact, tragically so.

While Orwell considered that a rustic life, far from the cities he hated, was the best of all, he also believed that the life of working men, at least outside the suburban industrial estates that were growing up around London, had retained some of the natural vigour of rural existence; in *The Road to Wigan Pier* he presents the working class as possessing a distinctive way of life and even a distinctive culture which make them almost a different species from the middle class, more robust, more human, above all more natural.

In a working-class home – I am not thinking at the moment of the unemployed, but of comparatively prosperous homes – you breathe a warm, decent, deeply human atmosphere which it is not easy to find elsewhere. I should say that a manual worker, if he is in steady work and drawing good wages – an 'if' which gets bigger and bigger – has a better chance of being happy than an 'educated' man. His home life seems to fall more naturally into a sane and comely shape. I have often been struck by the peculiar easy completeness, the perfect symmetry as it were, of a working-class interior at its best. Especially in winter evenings after tea, when the fire glows in the open range and dances mirrored in the steel fender, when Father in shirtsleeves sits in the rocking chair at one side of the fire reading the racing finals, and Mother sits on the other with her sewing, and the children are happy with a pennorth of mint humbugs, and the dog lolls roasting himself on the rag mat – it is a good place to be in, provided you can be not only in it but sufficiently *of* it to be taken for granted.

An idyllic – impossibly idyllic – picture no doubt, but real enough to Orwell when he envisaged it as a contrast to the shabby-genteel villas inhabited by the poor but pretentious members of the lower upper middle class from which he came. The adjectives he uses are particularly significant: *decent, human, sane, comely*, the typical adjectives of Orwellian approval, defining the virtues of solid, ordinary men, and combined appropriately with an emphasis on *completeness* and *symmetry*. What Orwell is trying to show us is a life which, because of the simplicity and naturalness of the demands of those who live it, has achieved an equilibrium which no middle-class life can rival.

But when Orwell went and actually lived for several months of 1936 among the miners and unemployed workers of the north of England, and tried to establish with them the kind of relationship he had built up in the 'squalid little democracy' of tramps when he mingled with them in 1929 (the experience described in the latter part of *Down and Out in Paris and London*), he found that the barriers of class were almost as impenetrable as those that divide one Hindu caste from another.

For some months I lived entirely in coal miners' houses. I ate my meals with the family, I washed at the kitchen sink, I shared bedrooms with miners, drank beer with them, played darts with them, talked to them by the hour together. But though I was among them, and I hope and trust they did not find me a nuisance, I was not one of them, and they knew it even better than I did. . . . Whichever way you turn this curse of class difference confronts you like a wall of stone. Or rather it is not so much like a stone wall as the plate-glass pane of an aquarium; it is so easy to pretend that it isn't there, and so impossible to get through it.

We might vary the image by seeing the glass as that of the window through which Orwell looks at his ideal working-class interior, a passionately interested spectator, but outside the window and painfully conscious of it.

One may argue that Orwell's experience was exceptional because he went among miners, a working-class group which in England has always tended to take on, even in its relations with other working-class groups, the exclusive and self-perpetuating character of a caste rather than a class. But with any other group he would hardly have found contact much easier, since a generation ago the English class structure was still so elaborately stratified that it was difficult for middle-class people much less shy and reserved than Orwell to form intimate relationships with English working people. In any case, whether or not Orwell's sense of the failure of communication with the miners corresponds to objective truth, for him it was subjectively real; he stood on the other side of the barrier from those decent, human, sane and comely people, who were exploited by his own class, yet who by their natural energy had managed to survive and retain their virtues almost as a different people; Orwell does not use Disraeli's image of the Two Nations, but he does talk of the 'alien cultures' of bourgeois and proletarian.

This aspect of Orwell's view of society appears again in *Nineteen Eighty-Four* when he describes the 'proles' – the working caste of Oceania who, whatever the Party may decide, manage to continue obstinately their earthy lives and to follow their stupid pleasures, living like happy moles under the surface of the totalitarian nightmare which encloses and suffocates the members of the Party. Thus, Orwell suggests, life will always go on, finding its own underground ways, never wholly suppressed or defeated, no matter what social or political lava flow may harden above it. The proles of Oceania will never try to overthrow the state that has risen above them; at most they will make little futile protests like the woman who shouts out in the cinema against the showing of war-horror films to children. Their revolution consists merely in existing, as they are, naturally, and we may assume that they will continue to survive, as less ambitious species survived the dinosaur, long after the political terror has passed into the history it sought to destroy.

But there is a tragic corollary to this proposition. Winston Smith, Party member, is seeking always to get back to an ancient and more natural way of life where such things as historical truth, golden landscapes, sexual love and human idiosyncrasies are once again allowed. Realizing that the proles live a more natural and in some ways even a freer life than the members of the Party, he tries to make contact with them, sexually on at least one occasion when he patronizes a tart in a slum street, and at another time with intellectual curiosity, when he corners an aged prole in a tavern and tries to learn from him what life was really like before the Party came into power. In both cases he fails; the prostitute, enticing in the half-light, turns out to be a disgusting toothless hag, whom he nevertheless joylessly enters in a vain search of some indefinable release, while the old man has so little of the historical sense Winston expected of him that he can remember only a few personal trivialities from the distant past.

Winston's failure to establish a relationship with the proles is, of course, far more complete than the failure Orwell experienced when he took the road to Wigan Pier. For Orwell could talk to the miners, gain enjoyment and information from what they said, while the only prole to whom Winston managed to talk in this way, Mr Charrington the antique dealer, turned out to be a high officer in the Thought Police, whose aim had been all along to tempt Winston into self-betrayal. The division here is not merely between classes or castes. It is a complete splitting apart of the Don Quixote-Sancho Panza duality which Orwell regarded as characteristic of every normal human being. Deprived of all intellectual and spiritual life, the proles had become complete Sancho Panzas, following the natural life at an almost animal and instinctual level. The Party members, taught to eschew all physical pleasure, to avoid all emotions except hatred, represent the Quixote principle gone to seed in arid intellectuality.

This means that Party members are deliberately alienated from any natural way of life. Winston and Julia embark on their insurrection through passion, through that undisciplined sexual activity which the ruling party regards as dangerously subversive activity. When Winston discovers that the rural hideout to which Julia leads him is the golden country of his recurrent dreams, and when they lie awake in the bedroom above the antique shop, they experience a brief illusion of liberation, of having won their way through to a full and happy life such as they had never experienced before. But the woodlands of spring where they make love are bugged with microphones, and the bedroom is fitted out with two-way television screens in which their every act is observed and their every word is recorded by the Thought Police. They are doomed to defeat, to surrender, to mutual betrayal, and to the total destruction of every natural impulse as they are tortured back into a conformity that is a living death. The moral of their experience is that those who in Orwell's Utopia belong to the elite are doomed; if they accept their situation, they are committing an act of moral and intellectual suicide as human individuals, and if they attempt to change it they are destroyed in the process. They can never escape from their pasts; unlike the Party, they cannot rewrite the histories which have made them what they are.

Here we have a representation of total alienation; not merely the individual but the whole class to which he belongs has pursued the logic of caste division to the ultimate conclusion, and has detached itself not merely from the rest of humanity but also from the past and from anything else that might divert its members from the single objective of maintaining power – the rule of the Party – for its own sake.

There are many aspects of the theme of alienation in *Nineteen Eighty-Four* which I have not mentioned and which I shall discuss later, but I have sketched the main outline of the human as distinct from the polemical aspect of the book in order to bring forward in its final and most ruthlessly developed form a situation which recurs throughout Orwell's fiction, and which one can regard as providing the leitmotif for his career as a novelist. A man, or in the case of *A Clergyman's Daughter* a woman, conscious that first youth and all its illusions are past, finds himself rebelling against the life he is now living, and particularly against his role as a member of the lower ranks of the ruling elite (for, just as Winston Smith belonged only to the Outer Party, so all of Orwell's other leading characters belong to the class of English people whom he called 'the shock-absorbers of the bourgeoisie'). In one way or another the vision of a golden country and an escape to a more natural – or at least less hypocritical and less complicated – way of life appears, and in his own manner each hero goes in search of it. For a time he lives a double life, concealing his real inclinations from others and perhaps even from himself. But in the end the guise of the double is ineffective; it is penetrated, and, even if he has escaped, he is hauled back to his place in society. In the process he loses his vision of the golden country, and now, unsupported even by his illusions, he has to face the reality of his world and, even more appallingly, the reality of himself. Every novel ends on the note of sad resignation, or tragic despair.

None of Orwell's characters is a self-portrait, but each shares some experiences with his creator, embodies some of his characteristics, and gives expression to some of his current preoccupations. Even the least Orwellian of them in outward appearance, the bluff and vulgar insurance salesman George Bowling, manages to give voice to an extraordinary number of Orwellian thoughts about the state of the world in 1938 by the time *Coming Up for Air* has reached its end. The pattern of alienation dominant in the fate of every one of them takes its form from the complex of personal myths within which Orwell saw his own life enclosed.

3

THE search for these myths takes us back first of all to the point at which Orwell decided to rebel against his own class and its view of the world and man's duties within it. The crucial date was 1927, when, on leave from police service in Burma at the age of twenty-four, he resigned from his post and became a full-time writer, though not for several years a professional in the sense of earning his living at his new occupation.

This decision was reached after a period of growing disillusionment on Orwell's part with the tasks he found himself performing as a servant of British imperialism, and it is in his literary references to Burma that we first encounter alienation in its peculiarly Orwellian form. Of the period when Orwell's attitude was undergoing its vital transition we know little beyond what he himself has chosen to tell us. He had temporarily lost touch with the future men of letters who were his fellows at Eton, and the people among whom he moved in Burma were not of the kind who kept letters or wrote down their recollections of the gauche young official who departed so quickly from among them. The only revealing outside glimpse we get of him during his Burmese service is provided by an Old Etonian, Christopher Hollis, who passed through Rangoon in 1925, a year after Orwell had joined the service, and three decades later wrote down what he remembered of an evening they spent together: 'On the side of him which he revealed to me at that time there was no trace of liberal opinions. He was at pains to be the imperial policeman, explaining that these theories of no punishment and no beating were all very well at public schools but that they did not work with the Burmese. . . .' Hollis goes on to say that Orwell was, 'as those who were out in Burma bear witness, a good police officer' (though he calls none of these nameless witnesses forward to testify), and he nds his passage on Orwell in Burma by remarking: 'It is also typical of him that at the same time, as I afterwards learned, he insisted on befriending an Englishman who was greatly cold-shouldered by Rangoon society for having married an Indian lady, even though the marriage seemed to Orwell a folly.'

On the reasons for Orwell's departure from Burma, the secondary sources are equally laconic. Even his sister Avril, in the reminiscences she broadcast in 1959, merely recorded that during a holiday in Cornwall after his return from Burma in 1927 her brother told his mother that he had resigned his commission and would not be going back to the East. 'Of course she was rather horrified, but he was quite determined that what he wanted to do was to write.' But no reasons are given for the determination, and we must be content with the explanations which Orwell himself provides.

The evidence is contained mainly in three autobiographical pieces and, in a less direct form, in Orwell's first novel *Burmese Days*. The autobiographical pieces are the two narrative essays 'A Hanging' and 'Shooting an Elephant', and a few pages of *The Road to Wigan Pier*. Like most writers of autobiography, Orwell tampered with facts in the interests of artistic proportion and didactic emphasis. He warns us of this in *The Road to Wigan Pier* when he remarks of *Down and Out in Paris and London* that 'nearly all the incidents described there actually happened, though they have been rearranged'. The phrase 'nearly all' is delightfully Orwellian in its almost naïve frankness, but its punctilious honesty is a guarantee that what its writer tells us is substantially and subjectively true. And since it is the subjective rather than the objective aspects of his experiences that find their way into his books and shape them, this is the kind of truth we are seeking.

'A Hanging' is the only work of his earliest phase as a writer – the only work signed by Eric Blair – which Orwell considered worth preserving. It first appeared in 1931 in the *Adelphi*, then edited by Richard Rees, who became Orwell's close friend after their meeting in 1930. Eric Blair contributed his apprentice work to this magazine in the form of mediocre verse and rather self-consciously literary book reviews. George Orwell – the surname that of a river which meanders through the East Anglian countryside – first appeared in 1933 as the writer of *Down and Out in Paris and London*.

It is obvious as soon as one reads 'A Hanging' why this alone of the earlier writings should have been picked for preservation. In the Blair reviews, Orwell is still very self-consciously trying out the English language and testing his own notions about the aims of literature, which at this moment do not include political argument; his style is at times as Wildean as some of his pronouncements, such as his chiding remark to J. B. Priestley that 'a novelist is not required to have good intentions but to convey beauty'.

When we turn from such characterless aestheticism to 'A Hanging', the change is in every way extraordinary. It is as if a different person were speaking. A man is describing something he has experienced directly and deeply, something that has gnawed at his mind so long that memory has given it a life and shape of its own. In writing it down he discovers, almost automatically, a style appropriate to the incident and to his own reactions.

It was in Burma, a sodden morning of the rains. A sickly light, like yellow tinfoil, was slanting over the high walls into the jail yard. We were waiting outside the condemned cells, a row of sheds fronted with double bars, like small animal cages.

It is not yet the colloquial manner of the mature Orwell, but it is direct, economical, with a touch of vivid imagism, and little left of other people's phrases. The writer has found his manner, and needs only to develop it.

The incident in 'A Hanging', the execution of a nameless Indian coolie for an offence that is never revealed to us, was one of the crucial events in Orwell's Burmese days. 'I watched a man hanged once,' he said elsewhere. 'It seemed to me worse than a thousand murders.' And he added: 'I never went into a jail without feeling (most visitors to jails feel the same) that my place was on the other side of the bars.'

The desire to identify with those on the other side of the bars is not stated explicitly in 'A Hanging', but it is there, clearly enough, in the key paragraph of revelation, where the author tells us what the experience means to him. Suddenly, on his way to the gallows, the man about to be hanged steps aside to avoid a puddle.

It is curious, but till that moment I had never realized what it means to destroy a healthy, conscious man. When I saw the prisoner step aside to avoid the puddle I saw the mystery, the unspeakable wrongness, of cutting a life short when it is in full tide. This man was not dying, he was alive just as we are alive. All the organs of his body were working – bowels digesting food, skin renewing itself, nails growing, tissues forming – all toiling away in solemn foolery. His nails would still be growing when he stood on the drop, when he was falling through the air with a tenth of a second to live. His eyes saw the yellow gravel and the grey walls, and his brain still remembered, foresaw, reasoned – even about puddles. He and we were a party of men walking together, seeing, hearing, feeling, understanding the same world; and in two minutes, with a sudden snap, one of us would be gone – one mind less, one world less.

Observe the shift in the last sentence, from 'he and we' to 'one of us'. The prisoner is no longer a strange alien figure with vague liquid eyes, the moustache of a film comic, the 'bobbing gait of the Indian who never straightens his knees'. He has become a human being, a unique personality about whom, had he lived, one could have been curious.

The incident goes on to its planned conclusion, the hooded

man standing on the scaffold, his voice calling on Rama like a tolling bell, and the officials of several races who take part in the grim fulfilment of the law shudder in apprehension until the signal is given and the man dies. Then they walk away, relieving their tension by joking like people after a funeral. 'We all had a drink together, native and European alike, quite amicably. The dead man was a hundred yards away.' This is the final irony – that Europeans, Burmese and Indians can only come together and drink amicably after an incident which had shocked them out of the customary ways of imperial life, with its rigid patterns symbolized by the exclusive English Club which forms the pivotal centre of action in *Burmese Days*.

A last aspect of 'A Hanging' remains to be considered, since it anticipates a recurrent feature of Orwell's later books, and that is the use of animal imagery. The condemned men are kept in animal cages, the warders handle the prisoner as if he were a fish, and finally a dog appears, 'from goodness knows whence', in the prison compound, and bounds up to the prisoner, trying to lick his face. When the prisoner calls on his god, it is the dog who answers with a whine, and when the prisoner has been hanged, it is the dog who races first behind the gallows. 'But when it got there it stopped short, barked, and then retreated into a corner of the yard, where it stood among the weeds, looking timorously out at us.' It is almost as if the world of nature had broken in and condemned the unnatural proceedings of men. The animal kingdom is identified with that oppressed other world of humanity towards which the narrator, in that moment preceding the hanging, has felt a sudden opening of sympathy. Many years later the identification becomes complete in the fable of *Animal Farm*.

'Shooting an Elephant' was actually written in 1936, almost ten years after Orwell's departure from Burma, when John Lehmann asked him for a piece which he could publish in *New Writing*. He appears to have recollected the incident very vividly just before he wrote the story, but he had obviously been thinking of it intermittently ever since it happened. In *Burmese Days*, written several years before, the hero Flory, on his first meeting with Elizabeth Lackersteen, describes to her 'the murder of an elephant which he had perpetrated some years earlier'.

At the time to which 'Shooting an Elephant' relates, Orwell was subdivisional police officer in the town of Moulmein; the narrative begins with a description of the hatred he felt surrounding him in this town where anti-British feeling was particularly strong. The sense of alienation from his environment which the situation produced in him was intensified by the fact that by now, towards the end of his tour of duty, he was no longer the young Conservative whom Hollis had met in 1925, but had made up his mind that 'imperialism was a bad thing and the sooner I chucked up my job and got out of it the better'. In secret he was 'all for the Burmese and all against their oppressors, the British', but by their very insolence the subject people made any human contact with them impossible, and even aroused Orwell's unwilling hostility; as he said elsewhere, 'Orientals can be very provoking.'

The central incident is a simple one. An elephant in 'must' has gone on the rampage; Orwell is called to deal with the situation and finds that the animal has trampled a coolie to death. He decides that he should kill the elephant, and though when he finds it calmly browsing the attack of 'must' seems to have passed and it is perfectly well-behaved again, the watching crowd of Burmese leaves him no alternative – if he is to maintain his prestige as a sahib – but to go through with the murder, which he does, botching the job but finally killing the beast.

Writing with the hindsight of a man who has had time – by 1936 – to work out his ideas and who now calls himself a Socialist, Orwell turns his tale into a little essay on the predicament of the man of feeling who serves an imperial government.

And it was at this moment, as I stood there with the rifle in my hands, that I first grasped the hollowness, the futility of the white man's dominion in the East. Here was I, the white man with his gun, standing in front of the unarmed native crowd – seemingly the leading actor of the piece; but in reality I was only an absurd puppet pushed to and fro by the will of those yellow faces behind.

I perceived at this moment that when the white man turns tyrant it is his own freedom that he destroys.

Orwell is making two points. First, a ruling class sacrifices its own freedom in more or less exact proportion to the degree of tyranny with which it exercises its power; in later books he carries this idea to its logical conclusion until in *Nineteen Eighty-Four* absolute power equals absolute loss of freedom to members of the Party. The second point, that the ruled dominate the rulers, will be abandoned by Orwell once he begins to understand the nature of totalitarian power.

Already, by the time he wrote 'Shooting an Elephant', Orwell was aware of the fundamental incompatibility between the means necessary for holding power and the ideal of a natural way of living that was lurking in his mind, and so the killing of the elephant, which for Eric Blair the police officer was an unpleasant necessity, becomes in the hands of Orwell the artist a symbolic event, much more self-consciously rendered than the death of the hanged man which he had described five years before. The rifle Orwell uses, 'a beautiful German thing with cross-hair sights', is the instrument of an irresistible mechanical power which wreaks on the great animal 'a mysterious, terrible change. He looked suddenly stricken, shrunken, immensely old.' Orwell fires a second and then a third shot.

That was the shot that did for him. . . . But in falling he seemed for a moment to rise, for as his hind legs collapsed beneath him he seemed to tower upwards like a huge rock toppling, his trunk reaching skywards like a tree. He trumpeted, for the first and only time. And then down he came, his belly towards me, with a crash that seemed to shake the ground even where I lay.

The elephant, like a rock, like a tree, becomes identified in that splendid, trumpeting moment of downfall with the whole world of nature, and its crash shivers the solidity of the very earth on which its killer lies. The animal, Orwell remembers, seemed to be dying 'in some world remote from me where not even a bullet could damage him further'. So the agent of domination becomes also the enemy of nature ; just as his occupation of policeman makes human contact with the oppressed people impossible, so his act of killing the elephant makes the world of natural life seem infinitely detached from him.

In both 'A Hanging' and 'Shooting an Elephant', Orwell was deliberately shaping and rearranging his material. Each narrative is told, not as a fragment of autobiography, but rather in the form of a short story condensing months of actual thought into a moment of revelation, and ending in an ironic anticlimax, which in 'Shooting an Elephant', as we turn away from the animal's Himalayan agony, is devastating. 'I often wondered whether any of the others grasped that I had done it solely to avoid looking a fool.'

There is less artistic shaping, though perhaps more intellectual rationalization, in the account of his general reactions to Burma which, in the same year as he published 'Shooting an Elephant', Orwell embedded in the more frankly polemical pages of *The Road to Wigan Pier*, where he compares and relates his attitudes to Burmese 'natives' and English workers. He remarks that before he went to Burma at the end of his teens he had grown up 'a snob and a revolutionary', reading 'advanced' writers at Eton, yet at the same time firmly convinced that working people were vulgar and repulsive. Above all, he was convinced that they smelled, and 'the thought of it made me sick'.

When he reached Burma the particular agonies of the British class situation no longer bothered him, since the people of the inferior race were not physically repulsive to him. 'One looked down on them as "natives", but one was quite ready to be physically intimate with them; and this, I noticed, was the case even with white men who had the most vicious colour prejudice.' Yet these alien, attractive and exasperating Burmese were the very people over whom Orwell had to act as the agent of an unwanted government. 'Not only were we hanging people and putting them in jail and so forth; we were doing it in the capacity of unwanted foreign invaders.'

Orwell could not help identifying himself with these people whom his duty as a policeman forced him to suppress. The result was a secret evolution of thought in 'the almost utter silence that is imposed on every Englishman in the East', an evolution that led him into the phase of anarchistic rebellion in which he believed that 'all government is evil, that the punishment always does more harm than the crime and that people can be trusted to behave decently if only you will let them alone'. The oppressors, he felt, were always wrong, and the oppressed were always right. By the 'oppressed' he first of all meant the Burmese, whose faces still haunted him when he left their country. But after 1927 he transferred his feelings to the working class in England. He admits that his interest in them stemmed at first merely from the fact that he perceived an analogy between them and the Burmese. 'Here in England, down under one's feet, were the submerged working class, suffering miseries which in their different way were as bad as many an Oriental ever knows.'

But, though the identity of the victims changed, the essential relationship remained the same. Orwell continued to view society according to the imperialist model he had observed in Burma. Instead of seeing an England populated by people of the same race, divided as it always has been into a number of merging classes and subclasses between which individuals could pass with considerable mobility, he tended always to see it in the simpler terms of a colonial world, a world of master race and subject race. At the top were the few exploiting capitalists and landlords, and immediately below them the less prosperous men of their own breed who did the dirty work as administrators, professional men and officers in the services; then came the great gulf that divided the upper and middle from the lower classes with such emphasis that they formed two nations, just as the British and the Burmese were two nations. Consequently, even in Britain, the relation of the establishment to the rest of the country was essentially imperial, that of an alien elite governing the great mass of white 'natives'.

The Burmese and later the British workers in fact played a dual role in Orwell's imagination. They were the oppressed, for whom one must fight because conscience dictated it. But there was also the feeling that they had retained some of the secrets of life – the desirable secrets which the sophisticated and the powerful had lost. Both groups lived in unscientific mental landscapes, haunted by strange and childish superstitions, bound by extraordinary taboos, but at the same time they seemed to have kept a surer and more natural grasp on life, which comes out in the lusty and uninhibited vulgarity of their pleasures, of the Burmese *pwe* dances and the English music halls. There was a strange obstinate vitality about them which, in Orwell's view, intellectuals never possessed. Theirs was the Sancho Panza world without which the Don Quixotes could not live.

I am not suggesting that Orwell preached or even held unconsciously to a Lawrencean cult of blood and the dark gods, or that he shared with Yeats a longing for a more primitive but more hierarchical life. Obviously he did not. Everything in him, down to the very clarity of his prose, reacted against cults of unreason, and if at times he let himself think of a less complicated society, it was in terms of anarchical rather than hierarchical primitiveness. Orwell's affinities were in fact less with Lawrence and Yeats than with William Morris, another libertarian Socialist who distrusted doctrinaires, and *News from Nowhere*, with its golden world in which past and future have come together and submerged the evil present, might have served as an image for his ideal world. Like Morris, he felt that in their decent, balanced and essentially conservative lives, the oppressed – the miners of Lancashire and the peasants of Burma or, later on, of Jura – had retained more faithfully than their rulers the essence of the good past, and that for this reason it was they who held – if anyone held it – the chance of making a better world in the future.

The ambiguous relationship between the members of a ruling elite and the members of the racial or social underworld is first shown clearly in all its psychological involutions in Orwell's one novel of the East, *Burmese Days*.

4

Burmese Days was the second of Orwell's books to be published, appearing under his adopted name in 1934, but it had been conceived and may well have been substantially completed before he wrote *Down and Out in Paris and London*, which is based on later experiences. It is probable that Orwell was already shaping *Burmese Days* in his mind when he came back from the East in 1927 and announced his intention of taking up the career of writing.

Burmese Days therefore represents his first attempt to transmute into a more completely fictional form than in 'A Hanging' his insights into the relationship between society and the self-conscious rebel, particularly the rebel from a ruling elite. I found myself tempted a moment ago to use the expression 'more purely artistic form', but nothing Orwell wrote was merely or, with the sole exception of *Animal Farm*, flawlessly a work of art. 'It is as if I have been forced into becoming a pamphleteer,' he once remarked ruefully, and though he dated his definitely 'political' phase from the Spanish Civil War ('By the end of 1935 I had still failed to reach a firm decision'), even *Burmese Days* is largely a didactic novel, interspersed with informative or homiletic passages about imperialism and its effects, and aimed much more deliberately than *A Passage to India*, with which it is often compared, at inducing a political reaction in its readers.

In *Burmese Days* the central character, the timber merchant Flory, resembles Orwell in many ways, but he is certainly no portrait, differing from him in many characteristics and in some important aspects of his experience. Yet the temptations of biographical interpretation are so great that critics have been reluctant to abandon entirely the search for some clue which will suggest that Flory is in some way Orwell's double. Christopher Hollis, for example, acknowledges that it would be false and uncharitable to assume that Flory, weak and degenerate as he is, can be an actual self-portrait; nevertheless, he advances the curious proposition that 'Flory is clearly to some extent Orwell as he imagined that he might have been if he had stayed in Burma'.

It seems to me quite unnecessary to suppose that Orwell was so concerned with might-have-beens that he constructed a character to fit his speculations on this subject. The idea that Flory can be seen in any real way as a self-portrait is further discredited by the fact that, like other writers, Orwell tended to distribute his own experiences, reactions and even personal characteristics among several characters in a single book. It is Westfield who follows his occupation in Burma, that of police superintendent, and Orwell confessed later that the incident of the brutal interrogation of a suspected thief in Westfield's presence was based on an experience of his own. We can also assume that Westfield's reaction closely resembled the reaction which Orwell himself experienced, particularly if the incident took place in his early 'loyal' years.

'All right, put him in the clink,' said Westfield moodily, as he lounged away from the table with his hands in his pockets. At the bottom of his heart he loathed running in these poor devils of common thieves. Dacoits, rebels – yes; but not these poor cringing rats !

Similarly, one can detect an echo of Orwell's own austerity and fastidiousness in Verrall, the arrogant young officer, and an exaggeration of his sensitivity to Burmese insolence in Ellis's enraged and violent reaction to schoolboy insults which sets off the riot that is one of the novel's main set pieces.

Flory's tragedy, indeed, is his own and that of his class, but it is not Orwell's in any direct and personal sense. For Orwell escaped from the East, whereas Flory was drawn back. But the impossibility of actual identification does not prevent us from finding at least significant parallels between crucial experiences in Flory's life and incidents in Orwell's earlier years which he considered important enough to fuse into his personal myth. For example, Flory is made conspicuous in childhood – and afterwards – by the birthmark which earns him the nickname of 'monkey-bum', just as Orwell (if we are to allow even the most minimal literalness to the experiences in an English private school which he describes in *Such, Such Were the Joys*) felt himself made conspicuous and contemptible by the mark of poverty. Here we touch the primary alienation, the unearned outcast's mark, which all Orwellian heroes share with their creator. It is an alienation whose roots lie deep in childhood, but which does not reveal itself completely until much later in life; Burma gave it shape for Orwell as it did for Flory.

In *Burmese Days* – and this may illustrate the difficulty which Orwell felt in dealing with his own early years – Flory's marked youth is sketched lightly in two paragraphs of a brief recapitulation of his life which appears early in the novel. His birthmark, with all its associations of mockery, stays with him until, in the moment of death, it at last fades away. But it is Burma, to which, like Orwell, he comes when he is 'not quite twenty', that shapes him into the mature, unhappy man, in the end so unlike his creator.

The action of *Burmese Days* is framed within the malign aspect of Asian life as personified by U Po Kyin, the villainous Burmese magistrate who acts as a grotesque *deus ex machina* throughout the novel, pulling the strings of intrigue and, in the ruthless pursuit of his own ambitions, bringing about unexpected perturbations in the lives of the tiny group of white sahibs. This aspect of the novel, of course, gives expression to the idea Orwell harboured at the time that in an imperial situation the rulers become, against their wills, the puppets of the ruled. It also illustrates his excellent grasp of that curious duality of the Asian mind which allows the most ruthless of Machiavellian behaviour towards one's enemies to be reconciled with its opposite, the Buddhist doctrines of non-attachment and of salvation by means of good works which adjust the balance of Karma.

At the centre of the frame is the English club at Kyauktada, goal of U Po Kyin's ambitions and citadel of the resident English, where their internal struggles are fought out and where many of the crucial incidents in the novel take place. But the club is not merely a centre of action. It is also, in the minds of English, Burmese and Indians alike, the symbol of the imperial caste system, the manifestation of the separateness of the ruling elite from the subject race; while it remains all-white, the English officials and traders of Kyauktada can still feel that their domination is secure, that the barrier which exists between them and the 'natives' will, despite all casual and even physical contact, be maintained. On the other hand, U Po Kyin sees membership in the club as the means by which he can work his way forward in the government service until he becomes the equal, perhaps even the superior, of his English colleagues, while for the Indian Dr Veraswami, pathetic, idealistic and incorruptible, it represents the haven where, shining in reflected glory, he will be immune from all attacks. Flory's one overt rebellion, which is enough to damn him in the eyes of his fellow whites, is that he at last summons the courage to propose Veraswami, who is his friend, for membership. In doing so he not only offends the fanatical and completely sincere prejudices of the rival timber merchant, Ellis; he also, as the policeman Westfield points out, goes against the 'five chief beatitudes of the pukka sahib', which Orwell lists thus:

> Keeping up our prestige;
> The firm hand (without the velvet glove);
> We white men must hang together;
> Give them an inch and they'll take an ell; and
> Esprit de corps.

These injunctions sound very much like the code of a secret order, and the white society of Upper Burma, as Orwell portrays it, is the earliest prototype of the ruling elite of Oceania which he described fourteen years later in *Nineteen Eighty-Four*. It differs from the Party in one important respect, that it maintains its solidarity not by physical power, but solely by the strength of an amazingly inflexible public opinion.

It is a world in which every word and every thought is censored. ... Free speech is unthinkable.... Your opinion on every subject of any conceivable importance is dictated for you by the pukka sahibs' code. . . . You are a creature of the despotism, a pukka sahib, tied tighter than a monk or a savage by an unbreakable system of taboos.

The system requires that the line of division between the rulers and the ruled always be rigidly maintained, and demands not merely a passive acceptance but emphatic agreement; the scenes in which Ellis furiously worms out Flory's reservations on the question of inequality between whites and Asians anticipate the much more elaborate and grotesque scenes in *Nineteen Eighty-Four* in which O'Brien lays bare all the petty disloyalties that lurk in Winston Smith's mind.

While one is in the system, rebellion has to be maintained secretly, as Orwell tells us he himself maintained it while in Burma, and as Flory does up to the point where a rather complicated series of motives sets him on the path to open revolt. Only with the greatest caution do rebels in such a world communicate with each other, like members of an underground organization in a dictatorship. Flory speaks his most heterodox thoughts only to Dr Veraswami, and then in bantering tones, so that the doctor refuses to take them seriously. And in *The Road to Wigan Pier* Orwell introduces an extraordinary description of an encounter – perhaps his only encounter – with a fellow dissident.

I remember a night I spent on the train with a man in the Educational Service, a stranger to myself whose name I never discovered. It was too hot to sleep and we spent the night talking. Half an hour's cautious questioning decided each of us that the other was 'safe'; and then for hours, while the train jolted slowly through the pitch-black night, sitting up in our bunks with bottles of beer handy, we damned the British Empire – damned it from the inside, intelligently and intimately. It did us both good. But we had been speaking forbidden things, and in the haggard morning light when the train crawled into Mandalay, we parted as guiltily as any adulterous couple.

The incident, as Orwell narrates it, is hauntingly similar to the scenes in *Nineteen Eighty-Four* in which, in the imagined security of the various hiding-places where they meet, Winston

Smith and Julia talk treason against the Party. Critics who have some familiarity with India under the British Raj have disputed Orwell's picture of the invisible tyranny which ruled over the white community, and in literal terms they are probably right, for Orwell had always a predilection for exaggeration and wild statement. On the other hand, there is no doubt that emotionally he experienced in Burma the existence of a minor terror that was no less thorough because it was neither codified nor violently enforced, and that later his paranoic inclinations gave sanction to this image until it took on an artistic life and became incorporated in the pattern of tyranny and alienation that runs through all his work. Having been used in *Burmese Days*, the half-true and half-imaginary scheme of imperial despotism lay dormant in his mind until he had use for it again when he came to construct the much more thorough group tyranny of *Nineteen Eighty-Four*.

But Flory's allegiance, like that of every sahib, is owed not merely to the alien power which protects him as a merchant and for which, if necessary, he will fight physically. There is a more painful and more ambiguous allegiance, to the country and the people among whom the best years of his manhood have been spent. In his early twenties Flory becomes acclimatized to Burma, enjoying it with a certain youthful, lusty innocence which is reflected in the fine descriptive section, reminiscent of the early Turgenev, where Orwell rather lyrically narrates the passage of the Burmese seasons as Flory experienced them in those early years.

In his later twenties Flory begins to experience a sense of revolt, the revolt of an intelligent man increasingly given to solitary reading; at the same time he begins to feel lonely among his fellow countrymen. Since the war intervenes and creates exceptional circumstances, it is not until ten years after his first arrival in Burma that his first leave falls due. On the ship he longs for England, for release from the 'horrible country' of Burma. But at Colombo there is a wire calling him back; three representatives of his firm have died of blackwater fever. Ten days after leaving Rangoon he is in Burma again, with the servants crowding round him with presents and hanging garlands around his neck.

Something turned over in Flory's heart. It was one of those moments when one becomes conscious of a vast change and deterioration in one's life. For he had realized, suddenly, that in his heart he was glad to be coming back. This country which he hated was now his native country, his home. He had lived here ten years and every particle of his body was compounded of Burmese soil. Scenes like these – the sallow evening light, the old Indian cropping grass, the creak of the cartwheels, the streaming egrets – were more native to him than England.

There is an obvious ambiguity in this passage. Is Orwell really suggesting that pleasure at returning to a country one has both loved and hated for a decade is a sign of deterioration in one's life? Or is it a subjective reaction on Flory's part due to a sense of guilt about the kind of life he has lived in Burma? And, if so, what are the sources of that guilt? Is it merely the guilt of sharing in political repression? Or is it something at once more elusive and more profound?

As we read on through *Burmese Days*, we realize that the experiences that come to Flory as a result of his life in Burma are – leaving aside for the present his position in the white community – of two kinds. First there is an intense, almost empathetic reaction to the physical environment – landscape, trees, streams, villages and, above all, animals and birds; 'in all novels about the East,' Orwell once remarked, 'the scenery is the real subject-matter.' And then there is his more complex relationship with the Burmese and the other Asian people of Kyauktada.

The first type of experience is illustrated by an incident which takes place fairly early in the novel, before Flory becomes deeply involved in the web of circumstances that will finally entangle him in ruin and destruction. In one of the fits of irritable boredom that often descend on him after enjoying his Burmese mistress, Ma Hla May, he walks out one evening along the dusty road that leads from Kyauktada into the jungle. The forest is dusty, shrivelled in its hot-season dryness: the only birds visible are dull and ragged, and the heat draws a poisonous stench out of the leaves. The scene corresponds exactly to Flory's mood. But after a while he comes to a stream of clear water beside which the trees are taller, the bushes greener and covered with flowers. He follows the stream along a cattle path to a deserted pool, which is one of his habitual haunts.

Here a peepul tree grew, a great buttressed thing six feet thick, woven of innumerable strands of wood, like a wooden cable twisted by a giant. The roots of the tree made a natural cavern, under which the clear greenish water bubbled. Above and all round dense foliage shut out the light, turning the place into a green grotto walled with leaves.

Into the pool Flory steps, and sits almost submerged. Shoals of small silvery fish swim about him. A flock of green pigeons settles in the dome of the peepul tree, invisible because of their colour, but setting the whole tree 'shimmering, as though the ghosts of birds were shaking it'. Finally, one of them flutters down, unaware of Flory's presence, and settles on a lower branch.

A pang went through Flory. Alone, alone, the bitterness of being alone! So often like this, in lonely places in the forest, he would come upon something – bird, flower, tree – beautiful beyond all words, if there had been a soul with whom to share it. Beauty is meaningless until it is shared. If he had one person, just one, to halve his loneliness! Suddenly the pigeon saw the man and dog below, sprang into the air and dashed away swift as a bullet, with a rattle of wings. One does not often see green pigeons so closely when they are alive. They are high-flying birds, living in the treetops, and they do not come to the ground, or only to drink. When one shoots them, if they are not killed outright, they cling to the branch until they die, and drop long after one has given up waiting and gone away.

It is a decorative, rather keyed-up piece of writing of a type to which Orwell reverted in his later years only in very brief passages, except for the long and ecstatic narrative of a rural childhood in *Coming Up for Air*, a narrative which also revolves around pools where fish are swimming. In each case the pool lies partly in the naturalistic and partly in the symbolic realm.

Flory feels 'happy and at peace' after 'the clear water', which is rarely found in the miry Burmese landscape. Entirely enclosed within its green shade, the pool brings refreshment through immersion in the clear element, the descent into innocence. The vestiges of an Anglican childhood clung to Orwell more tenaciously than he ever cared to admit, as was shown by his later novel of loss of faith in a country rectory, *A Clergyman's Daughter*, and by his extraordinary knowledge of hymns, which he remembered more exactly than any other agnostic I have ever met. The baptismal implications of this scene are obvious: Flory is immersed in the renewing water, and the dove descends. There follows the ecstasy of beauty recognized, and the immediate pang as he is reminded of his loneliness. But it is not only loneliness that Orwell is concerned with. Also, in the rather gauche disquisition on the habits of the green pigeon that ends the incident, he suggests the presence of an unattainable desire, a desire for something which, in trying to capture it, one may only destroy. That desire, I suggest, is for a permanent access to a more natural life, a desire which runs all the way through *Burmese Days* and, needless to say, is never satisfied.

Long before *Animal Farm* was even conceived, Orwell's feeling for the world of non-human beings (which must have provided at least one link of sympathy with Buddhist Burma) was thoroughly exemplified in *Burmese Days*, where animals appear not only as images, but also as unconscious participants in the action of the novel. It is almost as if, even outside the framing intrigue of U Po Kyin, there is a conspiracy of the land whose agents, in animal forms, intervene at crucial moments to help determine the fates of the human characters. Flory's ill-starred relationship with Elizabeth Lackersteen begins when he rescues her from the attack of a fearsome-looking but harmless buffalo. It reaches its point of highest promise when they go out on a hunting expedition, Elizabeth kills her first bird, and Flory shoots a leopard, earning Elizabeth's intense admiration; the leopard's mouldering skin becomes a symbol of the deterioration of Flory's hopes. Later Flory is thrown by a horse in Elizabeth's presence, and this horse and another, coming saddled and riderless out of the jungle, provide the first sign to him that Elizabeth may have become Verrall's mistress; this sends him into agonies of jealousy from which even the pleasure he usually gains from watching birds – in this case the tiny nameless yellow finches which he sees feeding on grasses in the jungle – is no longer active. Finally, in the catastrophic scene where Ma Hla May comes into the church and abuses him before the whole white community for having cast her off, he is betrayed by his own dog Flo, who runs fawning up to her as a familiar person and so confirms their relationship; this ends all his hopes with Elizabeth and leads to his suicide. Through its animals, whom Flory in his own way loves, the land of Burma has played its part in destroying him, though not, as we shall see, without his cooperation.

On a lower metaphorical level, animal imagery is used throughout the book in describing Asians, though only rarely and in very special ways in describing Europeans. U Po Kyin is described as a crocodile, and his wife, Ma Kin, has a simian face. Male Indians remind Orwell of dogs; the Dravidian butler at the club has 'liquid, yellow-irised eyes like those of a dog', and Dr Veraswami's face 'recalled that of a black retriever dog'. The two pathetic Eurasians, Mr Francis and Mr Samuel, who live on Buddhist charity, behave like 'a pair of dogs asking for a game'. The Burmese, on the other hand, often call up feline associations. Ma Hla May is 'like a cat', has 'kitten's teeth', and when she is expelled from Flory's house goes off with a kitten which Flory had once given her. The younger wife of Flory's servant Ko S'la is a 'fat, lazy cat', and Elizabeth, who regards all Burmese as 'so coarse-looking, like some kind of animal', asserts that the men have 'heads like tomcats'. One could go on at much greater length, but the examples I have given are sufficient to show how Orwell frequently compares Asians with the animals which provided the 'good times' of his youth, whereas he resorts to such a comparison only once, and then negatively, in reference to one of the European characters, the venomous

Mrs Lackersteen, Elizabeth's aunt, who, when all her genteel defences are broken down during the siege of the club by the Burmese mob, lies 'looping about in one of the long chairs like a hysterical snake'.

Finally there is a very signficant animal identification in the case of Flory himself. On the night before he meets Elizabeth Lackersteen, Flory cannot sleep because of the noise which the pariah dogs are making as they bay the moon on the maidan. He takes his rifle, intending to shoot the dog which has caused him the most annoyance, but he has 'not the nerve to fire it in cold blood'. And then, as he watches the dogs running like their own ghosts across the maidan, he remembers how earlier in the evening he had weakly echoed Ellis's ranting against the idea of admitting an Asian to membership of the club, and becomes in his own mind the 'sneaking, idling, boozing, fornicating, soul-examining, self-pitying cur'. It is at this point that Orwell introduces the recapitulative flashback of Flory's past, and then brings us forward to that individual on his veranda, raising his rifle and at last letting drive at the pariah dog. But the dog is unhit; it is Flory, the self-styled cur, who is hurt by the bruise which the heavily kicking rifle immediately raises on his shoulder. The link between the man and the animal out on the maidan illuminates Flory's situation. The pariah dog, distrusted by its fellow animals, has no place in the other world of men. Flory, the solitary, distrusted by his fellow white men, has no place in the other world of animals and the Asians who resemble them.

Yet it is this world to which he is drawn constantly, the world of animals and birds, the world of Burmese villages at noon and evening, of the crowd, noise, and smells in the market of Kyauktada, of the coarse and colourful splendours of the *pwe* dances. But in the end he fails to make terms with it, and this is because, fundamentally, his attitude remains that of the alien. He rebels against the elite to which he belongs, and yet when he tries to escape from it into the different world that excites his sympathies and stirs his romantic nature, he is still chained by the conventions of the *sahiblog*. His past has made him what he is; it is too late to cross the barrier that divides him from another way of life, just as it had been too late ever since his childhood for Orwell to cross the invisible barrier that divided him from the miners of Lancashire.

The consequence is that Flory's relationship with anyone belonging to the subject races is incomplete and carries with it a touch of the brutality that always – in Orwell's view – enters into the intercourse of master race and subject people. Ko S'la, his servant, is the person he has known longest in Burma – since the first day of his arrival there, in fact – and in some ways they are very close to each other.

Like all bachelors' servants Ko S'la was lazy and dirty, and yet he was devoted to Flory. He would never let anyone else serve Flory at table, or carry his gun or hold his pony's head while he mounted. On the march, if he came to a stream, he would carry Flory across on his back. He was inclined to pity Flory, partly because he thought him childish and easily deceived, and partly because of the birthmark, which he considered a dreadful thing.

Yet the relationship between the two men remains always that of master and servant; they never enter into each other's minds. As for Ma Hla May, who shares Flory's bed and whom he bought from her peasant parents two years before for three hundred rupees, she is only one of the many Burmese girls he has lived with and used, regarding them as strange dolls rather than human beings, and never feeling for them any love, until in the end he expels them from his life. When he casts off Ma Hla May for the sake of Elizabeth, she reproaches him, and stirs a guilt-ridden conflict.

He could not look at her; he stood helpless, pale, hangdog. Every word she said was justified, and how tell her that he could do no other thing than he had done? How tell her that it would have been an outrage, a sin, to continue as her lover? He almost cringed from her, and the birthmark stood on his yellow face like a splash of ink.

There is poetic justice – too much of it for the plausibility of the novel – in the fact Ma Hla May should in the end be one of the principal instruments of Flory's destruction.

Elizabeth, her unwitting accomplice, is the first of the series of temptresses who in all but one of Orwell's novels lead the heroes, through the illusion that it is possible to escape from loneliness, towards their various defeats. In the reader's eye, Elizabeth is a shallow-minded philistine snob, who arrives in Burma with her prejudices ready made – designed by nature, as Orwell remarks in the last sentence of the novel, for the position of a *burra memsahib*. But such are the illusions created by the glimpse of a petal-like cheek and by the pain of one's own solitude, that Flory believes her to be the 'civilized girl' of whom he has always dreamed, the girl who would share his inner, secret life, would 'carry away from Burma the same memories as he carried . . . who would love Burma as he loved it and hate it as he hated it'.

But Elizabeth merely hates Burma, hates it as only *burra memsahibs* can hate an Eastern country. Furthermore, her up-bringing has made her neurotically afraid of anything intellectual, bohemian, or un-Britishly odd. The consequence is a series of almost grotesque misunderstandings, as Flory, still thinking that she is 'civilized', tries to carry on her education in the wonders of Oriental life by taking her to a *pwe* dance in the native quarter and explaining its artistic significance, by leading her into the stench and turmoil of the bazaar, and by introducing her to the Chinese merchant Li Yeik and his discon-certing household. Each occasion ends in the revelation to Elizabeth that Flory is something less than a pukka sahib. How-ever – leaving aside the interlude with Verrall – there are ups as well as downs in their relationship; the ups occur when Flory accidentally reveals conventionally heroic aspects of his character which appeal to Elizabeth's boarding-school romanti-cism. He rescues her from the buffalo, which she cannot believe is really harmless. He saves the situation by daring and presence of mind when the Burmese mob attacks the club. And, most im-portant of all, he introduces Elizabeth to the aristocratic pursuit of shooting.

This is the point, as Malcolm Muggeridge has remarked in his otherwise somewhat inaccurate study of *Burmese Days*, at which Flory's passion for Elizabeth at last seems credible, as their hands meet over the body of the jungle cock which Elizabeth has shot. It may tell us something about Orwell that this one convincing love scene in the novel is full of sadistic implications; certainly it tells us a great deal about Flory's predicament. For there is a direct correlation between Elizabeth's feelings for Flory and the slaughter of birds and animals. 'She was conscious of an extraordinary desire to fling her arms round Flory's neck and kiss him; and in some way it was the killing of the pigeon that made her feel this.' From this point there is no reason to be surprised at any of Elizabeth's demonstrations of heartlessness.

Another aspect of the shooting expedition is revealed with the reappearance of the green pigeons, the birds which had aroused Flory's ecstasy of appreciation and his pangs of loneliness on the evening before he first met Elizabeth. Then he had longed for someone to share in the appreciation of that beauty; now he finds only someone to share in its destruction, and nothing can demonstrate more clearly the difference in character and viewpoint between Flory and Elizabeth than the conversation which takes place after he has shot two of the green pigeons. Flory displays their corpses, pointing out their beauty, dwelling tenderly on the jewel-like colouring of the breast feathers, reciting a poetic Burmese tale about them. 'Are they good to eat?' is all Elizabeth has to ask. 'Very,' he says; 'even so, I always feel it's a shame to kill them.' 'I wish I could do it like you do!' says Elizabeth enviously. The whole conversation shows the frank brutality that underlies her soulless flower-like beauty. It also demonstrates the contradiction in Flory's attitude, for the beauty which he loves he is also willing to destroy so as to prove himself in the eyes of this empty and worthless girl.

What Flory seeks in Elizabeth is support and comradeship in the rebellion against the unwritten code of the sahibs, and, ironically, it is under the stimulus of his meeting with her that he at last shows his rebellion openly and insists, as he had not dared to do before, on the election of his friend Veraswami to the club. Once such a feeling of hope and revolt has been stirred, it is impossible for him to return to the old life of secretiveness and brutalized passions. But his views about the 'natives', and his bookishness, which is really another kind of rebellion, are what Elizabeth distrusts most of all in him, and when she finally rejects him it is because of that which has made him different from other sahibs, and has doomed him to be a rebel and a self-condemned outcast.

It was not what he had done that horrified her. He might have committed a thousand abominations and she could have forgiven him. But not after that shameful, squalid scene, and the devilish ugliness of his disfigured face in that moment. It was, finally, the birthmark that had damned him.

Flory has found that the only way he can really escape from the condition of being a sahib, the only rebellion he can finally make against the elite to which he belongs, is death. If Ma Hla May personifies the Burmese land which he has injured by killing its most beautiful beings and the Burmese people whom he has insulted by demanding intimacy without equality, Elizabeth in her turn personifies that unspoken corporate spirit of the ruling community which half-consciously detects the treasons of its members and punishes them by scorn and rejection. Cut off from his last hope of personal fulfilment within the ruling elite to which he belongs, faced by the impenetrability of that other world to which he has been attracted, Flory is doomed.

There has always, in fact, been only one way in which a white man could ever cast off his foreignness and immerse himself in Asia, and that is through religious renunciation, through the abandonment of all his past when he assumes the ochre vestment of the *sannyasin* or the orange robe of the Buddhist monk. But this never occurs to Flory, and there is no evidence that it occurred to Orwell, at least while he was still in Burma.

5

THE renunciation that Flory never achieved became the keynote for almost a decade of his creator's life and work after returning from the East in 1927. In his mind Orwell had already rebelled against the imperialist system, and now that he returned to England he rebelled in action against the replica of imperialism which he discovered when he looked with new eyes at English society. In order to write about this discovery, and to gain the experience he considered necessary for that purpose, he quite deliberately chose a life of poverty and evaded any kind of occupation that might lead him away from the path he had selected.

There have been suggestions that this may be a romanticized view of Orwell's motives at this period. T. R. Fyvel, a journalistic associate of Orwell during the 1940s, claims that Orwell blamed external circumstances for his poverty.

Many years later, when I tackled Orwell on the subject, he said that in actual fact he had found it difficult to find work on returning from Burma. He had little money, few social connexions, and no special trade; it was a time of unemployment; a respectable job would have been difficult enough.

It is quite possible that Orwell did give Mr Fyvel such an explanation; he did not like being 'tackled' on any detail of his personal life, and he was inclined to throw up evasive smokescreens whenever anyone tried to pry information out of him. The fact is that in 1927, when Orwell came back from Burma, jobs were still quite easy to get, and even in the 1930s it was not difficult for an Old Etonian, with the kind of friends Orwell had made at school, to find employment. There is no evidence that Orwell ever sought anything more than casual teaching or tutoring work, and he appears to have been too proud to ask more than one of his friends, the mysterious B. of *Down and Out in Paris and London*, for help.

We have also Orwell's very emphatic statement that even before he had left Burma he already felt repelled by the idea of a successful career in any conventional sense, since he believed it could not be achieved without some kind of exploitation. 'At that time failure seemed to me the only virtue. Every suspicion of self-advancement, even to "succeed" in life to the extent of making a few hundreds a year, seemed to me spiritually ugly, a species of bullying.' It is not likely that a man who thinks in this way will spend his time or effort looking for a good job. But if he feels as guilty as Orwell did, it is likely that he will sooner or later begin to think in terms of renunciation, even if it does not take on a religious colouring, and this is precisely the development which Orwell's thoughts followed:

What I profoundly wanted, at that time, was to find some way of getting out of the respectable world altogether. I meditated upon it a great deal, I even planned parts of it in detail; how one could sell everything, give everything away, change one's name and start out with no money and nothing but the clothes one stood up in. But in real life nobody ever does that kind of thing; apart from the relatives and friends who have to be considered, it is doubtful whether an educated man *could* do it if there were any other course open to him. But at least I could go among these people, see what their lives were like and feel myself temporarily part of their world. Once I had been among them and accepted by them, I should have touched bottom, and – this is what I felt: I was aware even then that it was irrational – part of my guilt would drop from me.

This avowal occurs in *The Road to Wigan Pier*, which Orwell wrote in 1936, and it is followed by an account of how he decided that he would disguise himself and go down to the East End of London to mingle with various types of social outcast. Having changed into appropriately dirty working-class clothes, he set off for Limehouse, and there, screwing up his courage, he entered the dark doorway of a building with a notice in the window: *Good Beds for Single Men*.

I was still half afraid of the working class. I ... wanted to become one of them, but I still thought of them as alien and dangerous; going into the dark doorway of that common lodging-house seemed to me like going down into some dreadful subterranean place – a sewer full of rats, for instance.

As the ultimate torture of Room 101 in *Nineteen Eighty-Four* later revealed, there was nothing Orwell feared more than rats. Inside the lodging-house, having paid his ninepence, he went into the frowsty underground kitchen. No one took any notice except a drunken young stevedore who lurched towards him. Orwell stiffened for a fight. 'The next moment the stevedore collapsed on my chest and flung his arms round my neck. " 'Ave a cup of tea, chum!" he cried tearfully; " 'ave a cup of tea!" I had a cup of tea. It was a kind of baptism.'

The idea of baptism, of sacramental initiation, even if only with a cup of tea, suggests the high seriousness with which Orwell at this time took the idea of renouncing his past and stepping down into the lower depths of society. And, though in hindsight at the beginning of his Socialist period he is willing to say – as we have seen – that 'in real life nobody does that sort of thing', in the course of his last twenty years he did manage to achieve a great deal of his programme. He changed his name so thoroughly that I have met people who knew him for years in the 1940s and did not realize that he had been born any other than George Orwell. He even made a good start on changing his personality. He abandoned the elaborately caste-ridden world of the upper middle class, first for the 'squalid little democracy' of the tramps, and then for the classless society of the literary intelligentsia. For years he lived on the remote frontiers of the world where money counted, enduring poverty in smelly Paris hotels and dank Essex cottages, in the middle 1930s keeping a shop that brought him an average income of a pound a week, and heading off to a life of Hebridean primitiveness as soon as the six-year interval of the war had ended. Even if he had survived his last illness and had continued to enjoy the unexpected financial success which attended his last two books I suspect he would have found a way of making himself poor again; he fled to Jura partly because he tired very quickly of the novelty of comparative wealth.

But this process lasted for twenty years, and it had not come to an end when he died, for just before his final collapse he was still planning changes in his life and new approaches to writing which would enable him to delve deeper into the problems of human relationships. At present we are concerned only with the books that belong to the first part of this period, the nine years between Orwell's return from Burma and his departure early in 1936 on his first Socialist expedition to that mythical destination well known to joking North-countrymen, Wigan Pier. Apart from the writings on Burma which I have already discussed, Orwell wrote three books during these nine years: the semi-autobiography, *Down and Out in Paris and London*, and two novels, *A Clergyman's Daughter* and *Keep the Aspidistra Flying*. In each of these works the hero – or heroine in the case of *A Clergyman's Daughter* – descends into the lower depths of society; in each a variant on the theme of renunciation is played out; in each the renunciant fails to maintain his separation from the elite to which he belongs, and returns to his middle-class place in society knowing more about himself and about the world; in each of the two novels a defeat is implied, though the defeats vary in nature. There is one other important piece of writing relating to this period, the essay 'How the Poor Die', which I published in *Now* in 1946; the manuscript Orwell handed to me was, I gathered, a revised version of an earlier piece written towards the end of the 1930s but not published at that time.

Down and Out in Paris and London shows how cautiously we must approach any of Orwell's works usually considered autobiographical; there is an obvious discrepancy between the account given in this book in 1933 of his reasons for going among the outcasts of England, and the account three years later in *The Road to Wigan Pier*. In *The Road to Wigan Pier*, as we have seen, he suggests that his first contact with the lower depths of society occurred when he went on a planned expedition to find out who inhabited these obscure regions and how they lived. In *Down and Out in Paris and London*, he asserts that his earliest experience of common lodging-houses and casual wards took place almost accidentally, when he returned penniless from Paris and found that an expected job had not materialized. Thereupon, apparently without contacting his relatives or any of his friends except the mysterious B., from whom he did not like to borrow any more money, he exchanged his second-best suit for a set of tramp's clothes and dropped into the depths, *down* from his station in society and *out* of his class. This part of his story certainly sounds implausible; it is hardly the way a middle-class person would decide to tide over a period of destitution, unless he had thought of it beforehand and had some particular reason already in mind for following such a desperate course.

Some circumstantial support is given to the account in *The Road to Wigan Pier* by the evidence of Orwell's friends that he was in the habit, at least by 1930, of going regularly on planned expeditions into the slums. He kept a suit of shabby clothes for this purpose at Ruth Pitter's Chelsea studio, and one evening at about the same period he arrived at Richard Rees's flat, changed into his tramp's garb, and set off with the hope of getting arrested for drunkenness and seeing the inside of a prison; the attempt was frustrated because the police sergeant recognized his Eton accent and released him next morning with a fatherly lecture.

It is the self-conscious deliberation of these adventures that is significant; the whole idea of going into the slums has a peculiar *fin-de-siècle* literary flavour reminiscent of Sherlock Holmes setting off in disguise from his flat in Baker Street to seek in some criminal slum the lost fact that will complete the case he is about to solve. Orwell too was seeking facts for a case, his case against society. But there seem to have been yet other motives behind his descent into the seedy underworld of tramps and beggars. The fascination of disguise, of putting on a new self, was undoubtedly one of them. One also detects a kind of *nostalgie de la boue*, a fastidious man's urge to submerge himself in a hideous and malodorous setting, rather as the decadent poets did in an earlier generation. Here there may well be a link between Orwell's attempts to discover his true self and his interest in Oscar Wilde, particularly in Wilde's florid masterpiece *The Picture of Dorian Gray*, a 'good bad book', as Orwell would have called it, which lodged in his mind when he was a youth at Eton and which he was still defending in the late 1940s. Dorian Gray also descended into the lower depths of London society, and if we adopt the device of uniting a group of sentences taken from three consecutive pages of Wilde's novel, we can establish the kind of image which, vivid at the time of first reading and living dimly in the memory, may well have helped to determine Orwell on his course of self-submersion in the slums.

As midnight was striking bronze blows upon the dusky air, Dorian Gray, dressed commonly, and with a muffler wrapped round his throat, crept quietly out of the house.... The way seemed interminable, and the streets like the black web of some sprawling spider. The monotony became unbearable, and, as the mist thickened, he felt afraid.... Ugliness was the one reality. The coarse brawl, the loathsome den, the crude violence of disordered life, the very vileness of thief and outcast, were more vivid, in their intense actuality of impression, than all the gracious shapes of Art, the dreamy shadows of Song. They were what he needed for forgetfulness.... Suddenly the man drew up with a jerk at the top of a dark lane. Over the low roofs and jagged chimney-stacks of the houses rose the black masts of ships ... he walked quickly in the direction of the quay.... In about seven or eight minutes he reached a small shabby house that was wedged in between two gaunt factories.

Dorian Gray went in search of opium, Orwell of another kind of forgetfulness, but each had his guilt, each picked a disguise, each set off with a touch of fear for the darknesses of London's dockland subworld, where, in the ugliness of misery, the diamond of reality might be found. The suggestion of a Wildean influence at this early period may seem far-fetched to those who think only of the later Orwell, with his plain man's stance and his undecorated prose. But it fits in with the aestheticist position which Orwell was defending in his *Adelphi* reviews during the early 1930s. It is true that he was already beginning to discipline the ornateness out of his own writing, but there

are still passages mingled with the generally spare and colloquial prose of *Down and Out in Paris and London* which might
have fitted very well into one of the decadent magazines of the
1890s; the interpolated tale of Charlie and his sadistic adventure
in the red-tapestried cellar is a striking example. But Orwell's
sustained interest in *The Picture of Dorian Gray* was most
probably due to the fact that it described a double life centring
around the creation of a new *persona*, and this was precisely
what concerned Orwell at the time he was making his expeditions into the slums.

These speculations lead one to the conclusion that a delayed
literary romanticism was one of the most important among the
motives that first started Orwell on the series of choices which
gave his life such a special and dramatic flavour for those
living in the generation after his death. He began with the
attempt to make life imitate literature, though he quickly turned
the paradox on its head and made his writing the distillation of
his life. Certainly his choice of action when he first descended
into the life of the slums appears, from all the evidence we
possess, to have been deliberate and premeditated, which means
that the account in *The Road to Wigan Pier* is factual, and that
in *Down and Out in Paris and London* at least partly fiction.

It is in France that the story begins. 'Poverty is what I am
writing about,' says Orwell in the first chapter of *Down and Out
in Paris and London*, 'and I had my first contact with poverty
in this slum.' The slum is a seedy quarter of the Left Bank in
Paris, and at first the reader is surprised that, after five years in
Asia, Orwell should make such a statement. But in Burma he had
seen poverty from the other side of the caste screen, as a ruler
observing the ruled; he had not been directly involved. It was
in Paris that he first actually lived among the poor, from whom
he had been insulated in England by his rigid middle-class upbringing; the culmination of the experience was his own sudden
and complete impoverishment through a burglary in his hotel
room.

Orwell devotes only a few pages to the relatively long period
in which he was an observer rather than a participant in the

life of the poor, and he emphasizes this spectator's role by describing just what he saw and heard: the strange raffish people in the bistros and the bugs marching in patterns over the walls of the hotel rooms; the coarse, noisy quarrels in the streets and the strange stories that the slum-dwellers told of themselves and each other. This period, he tells us, lasted eighteen months, which means that, after an obscure period following his return from Burma, he reached Paris about the beginning of 1928. Presumably he lived mainly on his savings, though he did sell some newspaper articles and he gave English lessons which brought him in thirty-six francs – about six shillings – a week.

The end of the eighteen months can be estimated fairly closely. 'How the Poor Die' tells us that in February 1929 Orwell underwent one of his rather frequent hospitalizations, this time for pneumonia, in the Hôpital X; this, he told me, was the Hôpital Cochin, a sprawling old-fashioned structure in the Boulevard du Port Royal which in the 1920s was still a stronghold of French medical obscurantism. It was in the Hôpital Cochin that Orwell first met Boris, the former tsarist officer turned waiter, and since the events described in *Down and Out in Paris and London* happened in the following summer, this places them – if we accept Orwell's guide-points – in the middle of 1929. It was in the company of Boris, fallen on equally bleak days, that Orwell tried to extricate himself from destitution.

At first, when Orwell (and now I am using the name to designate the possibly semi-fictional 'I' of the narrative) loses his money, he sinks into a mood of solitary resignation. Even before his room was robbed he had realized that his funds would not last long and had decided to find a job as a tourist guide or interpreter. But as soon as he really loses his money – all but forty-seven francs of it – he abandons his plans of finding work, for the curious reason that to live on a shilling a day is 'too difficult to leave much thought for anything else'. The argument is unconvincing, and all one can assume is that Orwell actually welcomed the idea of experiencing real destitution, of knowing at first hand what hunger meant. He describes the experience with the calm but involved interest which a physician might feel in observing the course of a sickness with which he has inoculated himself.

It is altogether curious, your first contact with poverty. You have thought so much about poverty – it is the thing you have feared all your life, the thing you knew would happen to you sooner or later; and it is all so utterly and prosaically different. You thought it would be quite simple; it is extraordinarily complicated. You thought it would be terrible; it is merely squalid and boring. It is the peculiar *lowness* of poverty that you discover first; the shifts that it puts you to, the complicated meanness, the crust-wiping.

At first Orwell endures poverty alone, and the shifts he does adopt reveal the reactions proper to his social position. For they are all designed to achieve what he elsewhere showed to be the special concern of the lower upper middle class – to keep up appearances on a totally inadequate income – and his life becomes a series of contrivances to prevent other people's getting to know about his poverty.

The situation goes from bad to worse; Orwell's English pupils leave him, his prospects of even a shilling a day vanish, and he cannot any longer avoid finding a job. But even now he does not go after one of the relatively good jobs he had originally contemplated. He decides to search out Boris in the hope that he can help him get work as a scullion in some hotel kitchen, one of the lowest-paid, most arduous and most despised of all the jobs available in Paris. Again one detects the touch of deliberation that marks all his encounters with the lower depths of society. Why pick this, of all occupations, without trying for anything better beforehand? The accident of his acquaintance with Boris is insufficient explanation. Orwell must have decided to make the best of his misfortune, at least in terms of gathering experience, by seeking an occupation in which he could find out by hard personal effort what it was like to become, as he later called it, 'the slave of slaves'.

But even this humble work is hard to get, and for days Boris and Orwell live mainly on luck. The experience gives Orwell the subject-matter for a series of fascinating disquisitions on such subjects as the cooking and shopping habits of the very poor, ways to deceive hotel landladies, the customs of Paris pawn-shops; in the process he gives us a glimpse into that mind packed with curious facts which in later years blossomed so extravagantly in his weekly essays for *Tribune*.

At last the two men find employment as *cafetiers*, the lowest grade of *plongeurs*, in one of the big international hotels in Paris. The chapters which recount their experiences form a classic piece of reporting on labour conditions in Paris during the bad old days of the 1930s, a study full of brilliant vignettes of the strange mixture of men of all types and nationalities who had found their way, almost like cockroaches, into the great dirty warren that lay on the other side of the soundproof and smellproof doors from the rich and often titled guests.

The most striking aspect of this earlier section of *Down and Out in Paris and London* is the model caste society which emerges as Orwell describes the organization of the hotel. Not only is the staff divided into a surprisingly complicated hierarchy of occupations, a microcosm of the social hierarchy outside, but there is also a gulf separating staff from guests as clearly as the rulers in Burma were separated from the ruled. The guests are flattered, defrauded, hated, but envied by the staff, in much the same way as the British by the Burmese; a genuine human relationship between the two sides is virtually impossible.

For the first time in his life Orwell now finds himself where he had long wished to be, among the exploited on the other side of the class barrier, working fifteen hours a day for a pound a week, and so far down the ladder that even his fellow workers can lord it over him. He has – so he believes – at last found a place among the disinherited, and when he comes to describe the life of a *plongeur*, the comparison he makes is significantly with some of the most exploited beings of Asia, the rickshaw wallah and the gharry pony. The three slaveries are, he feels, similar and equally unjustifiable.

These are instances of unnecessary work, for there is no real need for gharries and rickshaws; they only exist because Orientals consider it vulgar to walk. They are luxuries, and, as anyone who has ridden in them knows, very poor luxuries. They afford a small amount of convenience, which cannot possibly balance the suffering of the men and the animals.

Similarly with the *plongeur*. He is a king compared with a rickshaw puller or a gharry pony, but his case his analogous. He is the slave of a hotel or a restaurant, and his slavery is more or less useless.

At this point Orwell has succeeded, at least temporarily, in assuaging the gnawing guilt of Burma. He has become the European equivalent of the depressed coolie and the maltreated animal, the slave of slaves. And in judging the experience, he brings forward his own idea of the class struggle, of the gulf of misunderstanding between the poor and the rich, who choose to keep their inferiors in unreasonable bondage because in their minds lurks the fearful vision of the mob, the 'horde of submen' who have to be kept working for the safety of the upper classes.

A *plongeur* is a slave, and a wasted slave, doing stupid and largely unnecessary work. He is kept at work, ultimately, because of a vague feeling that he would be dangerous if he had leisure. And educated people, who should be on his side, acquiesce in the process, because they know nothing about him and consequently are afraid of him. I say this of the *plongeur* because it is his case I have been considering; it would apply equally to numberless other types of worker.

The statement has the touch of exaggeration with which readers were to become more familiar as Orwell's later books were published, but it does make a point essential to the world-view that inspires his writings – that men are divided between the ruled and the rulers, between the rich and the poor, between the educated and the uneducated, between the sahib and the 'native', and that fear perpetuates the division. The implication is that, having had the courage to descend into the depths, Orwell himself has shed his fear and can recognize the equality of all men. Let others do the same.

But there is one element of inequality left. Orwell can get away, and does so when the opportunity appears. His past and his English middle-class world draw him back through the mysterious B., who, after Orwell has left the hotel and worked for two weeks in the even worse drudgery in the kitchen of a chic Parisian *auberge*, writes from England to say that he can arrange a job 'looking after a congenital imbecile, which sounded like a splendid cure'. A magical reversal of roles takes place. Orwell goes back to the *auberge* where he had worked and drinks a beer in the bar. 'It is a curious sensation, being a customer where you have been a slave's slave.' And, though he does not seem aware of it at the time, the sensation brands Orwell as the middle-class man who because of his connexions has the privilege of escape, denied throughout their lives to most of his fellow *plongeurs*.

The same might be said of the experience which – if we follow the account given in *Down and Out in Paris and London* – awaits him when he gets back to London and finds that his imbecile charge has been taken abroad and will not be back for a month. 'I suppose you can hang on till then?' says B. With nineteen and sixpence in his pocket Orwell shows an almost unbelievable lack of forethought by neglecting to borrow from B. Instead, as we have seen, he drops down into the world of common lodging-houses, coffee shops and casual wards. This experience is as different from his life among the *plongeurs* as England is different from France – 'cleaner and quieter and drearier'. The narrative responds to the changed mood, and falls into a slower pace as Orwell endures the grime and smell of East London doss-houses and wanders with his tramp companions on the dreary begging circuit of casual wards.

The world in which he moves is less fierce, less cosmopolitan and possibly less individualistic than that of Paris; the one really strong character, Bozo the screever or pavement artist, 'has lived in France and despises the English'. Most of the tramps are wretched figures, little resembling the monsters which they appear to timid suburban housewives. Typical is Orwell's road companion, the Irishman Paddy Jacques:

He had the regular character of a tramp, abject, envious, a jackal's character. Nevertheless, he was a good fellow, generous by nature and capable of sharing his last crust with a friend; indeed he did literally share his last crust with me more than once. He was probably capable of work too, if he had been well fed for a few months. But two years of bread and margarine had lowered his standards hopelessly. He had lived on this filthy imitation of food till his own mind and body were compounded of inferior stuff. It was malnutrition and not any native vice that had destroyed his manhood.

Once again Orwell escapes, after a final hike to Lower Binfield, where the tramps sprawl on the village green waiting for the casual ward to open, and a clergyman and his daughter come and stare at them. We shall meet the clergyman and his daughter again and revisit Lower Binfield in Orwell's later works. Meanwhile we follow him back to London, where B. is waiting with a loan and a job, and back to the moral which he draws with almost Victorian conscientiousness from every experience. In the final chapters of *Down and Out in Paris and London* there is much discussion of why people despise beggars and tramps; it is complementary to his theory of why people force men to kill themselves doing worthless jobs like that of the *plongeur*. He rejects immediately the old argument that beggars are despicable parasites because they do not work.

A beggar works by standing out of doors in all weathers and getting varicose veins, chronic bronchitis, etc. It is a trade like any other; quite useless, of course – but then, many reputable trades are quite useless. And as a social type a beggar compares well with scores of others. He is honest compared with the sellers of most patent medicines, high-minded compared with a Sunday newspaper proprietor, amiable compared with a hire-purchase tout – in short, a parasite, but a fairly harmless parasite.

His final conclusion is that beggars are despised for one reason only – they do not succeed in earning a decent living in a world where to make a lot of money legally has become the criterion of respectability.

A beggar, looked at realistically, is simply a business man, getting his living, like other business men, in the way that comes to hand. He has not, more than most modern people, sold his honour; he has merely made the mistake of choosing a trade in which it is impossible to get rich.

This is an attempt to explain social standing by highly simplified economic criteria. Later Orwell came to realize that the class system, with its built-in standards of merit, was a great deal more complex, and by 1936, when he wrote *The Road to Wigan Pier*, he had reached the conclusion that the structure of class is not 'entirely explicable in terms of money . . . it is also penetrated by a sort of shadowy caste system', which is determined by a man's traditions rather than his income.

The impression one gains from a reading of *Down and Out in Paris and London* is that after his first descent into the underworld of extreme poverty Orwell felt that the establishment of contact with these great shadowy regions of society had been much easier than he first feared, and that he need only proceed on the same path in order to understand the lower classes completely. The book ends almost optimistically. 'Some day I want to explore that world more thoroughly. . . . At present I do not feel that I have seen more than the fringe of poverty.' This conclusion was in great part the result of the 'feeling of release, of adventure' to which he later confessed and which evidently resulted from a combination of his natural romanticism and his sense of having assuaged a guilt by making himself the nearest European equivalent of an Asian untouchable. On one occasion he encounters an Indian in a common lodging-house, and talks to him in Urdu; in replying the man calls him 'tum' – 'thou' – which, as Orwell remarks, would have made him shudder in India. 'We had got below the colour range,' he adds, with obvious satisfaction.

Only after the trip to the North Country in 1936 which is described in *The Road to Wigan Pier* does Orwell appear to have realized what an incomplete view even of working-class society is gained from a position below the colour and caste range.

6

In each of the three years following the appearance of *Down and Out in Paris and London* Orwell published a novel. The first, *Burmese Days*, made no reference to his experiences among European slum dwellers, and was undoubtedly planned before that interlude began. The remaining two, *A Clergyman's Daughter*, published in 1935, and *Keep the Aspidistra Flying*, published in 1936, were both concerned with characters who, like Orwell, slipped down for a period from the ledge of shabby gentility into the lower depths of society. Just as *Down and Out in Paris and London* is ostensibly a book about basic destitution, so *A Clergyman's Daughter* is ostensibly about faith and the loss of it, and *Keep the Aspidistra Flying* about money and the lack of it. But each in its own way fits in with the central Orwellian theme of personal alienation caused by the class system, and in each of them the central character, seeking to liberate himself, undergoes a metamorphosis which involves the substitution of a new *persona* for an old self.

As Orwell himself realized, *A Clergyman's Daughter* and *Keep the Aspidistra Flying* were his worst books, not necessarily because they were badly written, for both contain some good episodes and each marks an advance in the use of language towards the colloquial Orwellian style that was finally matured in *Homage to Catalonia* and *Coming Up for Air*, but because the material is in neither case completely assimilated into the literary form. The novels lack stylistic and structural homogeneity. They are marred by veins of self-conscious theorizing and social commentary which, however well they may suit Orwell's semi-autobiographical works, merely disfigure his fiction.

The principal reason for these weaknesses is undoubtedly that both novels are too close to the life Orwell was living and the anxieties he was experiencing at the time he was writing them. He was still unsure of his philosophical attitude and his artistic aims. He had not yet coped with that uneasy, tortured Eric Blair whom his acquaintances of that time remember as morose and often misanthropic, and who, if we are to accept Rayner Heppenstall's account, was liable to attacks of ferocious puritanism which his later friends find it hard to credit. His desire to create a plain and colloquial style of writing made him seem conservative and unexperimental, at least in terms of the early 1930s, so that his work was not readily accepted by avant-garde magazines and appeared in journals which were not quite in the swim, like the *Adelphi* and the *New English Weekly*. Afterwards he was reluctant to talk about his early failures, but he once admitted to John Atkins that *Down and Out in Paris and London* was turned down by several publishers before Gollancz eventually accepted it.

At the same time, he was trying to make ends meet without letting his friends know how poor he really was. Up to the early 1940s his income from writing was very slight. The magazines that published his work paid little more than token fees; even his books brought him relatively little before the publication of *Animal Farm*. Of *Homage to Catalonia*, published in 1937, nine hundred copies had been sold by the time of his death thirteen years later.

Sometimes, indeed, his writing income was so small that, even living spartanly, Orwell found himself obliged to alternate his periods of completely literary activity with interludes of employment, usually so badly paid that it can have offered little relief. He was still too proud to draw on the influence of his Etonian friends, but the peculiar dreariness of the jobs which he did accept and which he even endured for relatively long periods was probably due as much to inclination as to necessity. For example, the unhappiness of his own childhood in a preparatory school appears to have been the motive that prompted him to experience the process from the other end of the classroom when he taught for several months in a dejected private school at Hayes, one of the ugliest of West London suburbs. Later, he spent almost eighteen months as an assistant at the bookshop on South End Green in Hampstead. He detested both occupations, and became almost obsessed with the idea of poverty. His sister Avril tells how, while still a schoolmaster at Hayes, he suffered one of his recurrent attacks of pneumonia, and in his delirium talked always of money, and not merely money in general, but actual cash which he could keep under his pillow.

The preoccupations of those unhappy days are reflected in *A Clergyman's Daughter* and even more clearly in *Keep the Aspidistra Flying*. Not that these are in any literal sense autobiographical novels; neither Dorothy Hare, the heroine of *A Clergyman's Daughter*, nor Gordon Comstock, the anti-hero of *Keep the Aspidistra Flying*, was intended to be even a disguised self-portrait. Both of them, it is true, belong to Orwell's social class, 'the landless gentry' as he ironically called them, and each shares some aspects of his own experience and some fibres of his character. But this merely means that he is using the life he knew as the background against which to develop his characters in attitude and action, and that they start where he left off and go on their independent ways. Orwell did not lack imagination, but his inventive powers were not very strongly developed. He found it hard to construct situations entirely outside his own experience. In fact, he did so only once, in *Animal Farm*; in every other book, not excepting *Nineteen Eighty-Four*, there was a limitation of the roving fancy – a limitation closely linked to his peculiar type of intellectual honesty. Like Defoe, he had a passion for verisimilitude, and the best guarantee of verisimilitude is to rely on one's own direct knowledge to the very point where the imagination finally takes over and the characters glide on their own wings into their parabolic courses. The danger of such an approach is that the kind of work it produces does not always become fully detached from the writer's life or from his intellectual as distinct from his artistic preoccupations. This is notably the case with Orwell, and it mars even his late novels, where his characters are still liable to talk from the author's mouth. It is a fault which has led many critics to doubt if Orwell is a novelist at all, and on this point he was prepared to agree with them. 'I am not a real novelist . . .' he admitted to Julian Symons. 'One difficulty I have never solved is that one has masses of experience which one passionately wants to write about . . . and no way of using them up except by disguising them in a novel.' In considering his works we have always to remember this conflict between the desire to give some kind of expression to an experience which he apprehended with an unusual vividness, and the desire to create a work that would take on the autonomy of imaginative literature. Nowhere is the conflict more pronounced than in the two novels we are now considering.

A Clergyman's Daughter is, in its way, an Anglican novel, a twentieth-century descendant of *The Way of All Flesh*. It begins in the rectory of St Athelstan's Church at Knype Hill in Suffolk, a county which Orwell knew well because his family moved there in the year before he went to Burma. The adventures of Dorothy Hare, the Rector's daughter, follow a picaresque cycle of episodes, taking her to London, to the hopfields of Kent, to London again, and finally back to the rectory, where she resumes her old life, but not quite where she left it off, for the action of the novel is spiral rather than circular, and she returns to the point of departure a changed person, with a knowledge about the world and about herself which only her peregrinations have made possible.

The novel is schematically divided into five chapters, each of which recounts a phase in the heroine's progress. The first, and the longest, deals with a single day in Dorothy's life, beginning in the pre-dawn darkness as she awakens in extreme exhaustion from 'some complex, troubling dream'. The complexity and the troubles continue throughout the day. We realize very soon that Dorothy carries the burdens of a decaying parish for her selfish snob of a father, who is still living in the dreams of an 'imaginary golden past' of many servants and patient creditors. As she hurries about her day's duties, getting breakfast, waking the maid, attending Holy Communion, worrying about debts, visiting the poor and the sick, pleading with her father for housekeeping money, arguing theologically with Victor Stone the church-schoolmaster, avoiding tradesmen, fending off Mr

Warburton, the town satyr, and laboriously making cardboard armour for the Sunday-school play about Cavaliers and Round-heads, we learn a great deal about Dorothy, about the town in which she lives, and about the Anglican traditions that have dominated her world since childhood.

At twenty-seven, Dorothy is a pretty-plain girl with beautiful blonde hair and a thin face verging on the spinsterish. Some childhood trauma lives on in her mind, and she will never over-come her pathological fear of sexual relations; she is much more willing to plunge dutifully into her ice-cold bath each morning than to plunge into marriage. Her other fears are more typical of her class – fear of creditors, of financial insecurity in general, and, above all, of failing to keep up appearances. She is en-thusiastic in performing the obligations of religion, but what she takes for faith is really a combination of morbid religiosity, expressed in self-mortification (she sticks pins into herself as a punishment for blasphemous thoughts) and momentary flashes of a kind of ecstasy which really springs from an unusually strong response to the sensory beauties of nature but which she confuses with pious feelings. On the morning of that first day, for example, she is at the altar, trying to stifle her disgust at the thought of accepting the chalice after it has been slobbered over by the disgusting and senile lips of Miss Mayfill. She wishes to pray for forgiveness, but finds that she cannot, and then she is in agony as to whether she should accept the proffered wafer 'with such chaos in her heart'.

Then it happened that she glanced sidelong, through the open south door. A momentary spear of sunlight had pierced the clouds. It struck downwards through the leaves of the limes, and a spray of leaves in the doorway gleamed with a transient, matchless green, greener than jade or emerald or Atlantic waters. It was as though some jewel of unimaginable splendour had flashed for an instant, filling the doorway with green light, and then faded. A flood of joy ran through Dorothy's heart. The flash of living colour had brought back to her, by a process deeper than reason, her peace of mind, her love of God, her power of worship. Somehow, because of the green-ness of the leaves, it was again possible to pray. O, all ye green things upon the earth, praise ye the Lord! She began to pray, ardently, joyfully, thankfully. The wafer melted on her tongue. She took the chalice from her father and tasted without repulsion, even with an added joy in this small act of self-abasement, the wet imprint of Miss Mayfill's lips on the silver rim.

Here is a mind existing on a perilous razor's edge.

The day of Dorothy's labours and perturbations proceeds against the background of a typical English country town of the years of change between the world wars. Knype Hill is divided sharply in social terms between the would-be gentry and the godless workers who have come from the industrial areas to the new sugar-beet factory.

The great church broods over it all, as the past broods over England, 'much too large for the congregation, and ruinous and more than half empty'. The organ is unpaid for, the death-watch beetles are in the beams, and seven of the eight bells are unswung and splintering the floor of the belfry with their weight; one day they will come booming and crashing down into the church porch. The decaying church is the symbol of a decaying moral order; its condition poses the viability of ancient traditions in a modern world, and this is one of the novel's major themes.

With a zestful combination of knowledge and irony possible only to a lapsed Anglican, Orwell fills out the crowded day of parish duties, punctuating it with appropriate theological discussions, and convincing one that Dorothy is really a kind of upper-class *plongeuse*, a respectable drudge working a seventeen-hour day of alternating energy and exhaustion, one of the unlamented and uncomplaining slaves of genteel poverty. The only real relief that she gains during the whole day is when she walks down the street with Mr Warburton, who 'has over her the hold that the blasphemer and evil-liver always has over the pious', and from whom she gets 'without being aware of it, a species of sympathy and understanding which she could not get elsewhere'. The sympathy and understanding are, of course, for the feelings of rebellion which Dorothy cannot even admit to herself.

But Mr Warburton's sympathy is not without price, for before the day is out Dorothy has let herself be persuaded to visit his house, has stood up to an attack on her religion and resisted an assault on her virtue, and has fled with perturbation in her heart, observed by the town scandal-monger, Mrs Semprill.

Up to this point *A Clergyman's Daughter* might be a conventional if somewhat astringent novel about ecclesiastical life, a bit of modernized Trollope. But in the next part Orwellian idiosyncrasy takes over. Dorothy has suddenly abandoned her elaborately constructed life. Like Orwell in his tramping days, she is 'down and out', in the double sense of being destitute and removed from her own middle-class world. As the narrative proceeds we gather that she has already been missing for ten days in a state of amnesia from the rectory, where we had last seen her drowsily pasting together paper jackboots for Round-heads at midnight after her flight from Mr Warburton. At no point in the novel are we told anything about the lost ten days, but when her memory begins to return fragmentarily she is in the Old Kent Road, dirty and dressed in cheap, vulgar clothes; somehow during that ten days she has got from Knype Hill to London, and on the way she has been robbed, of her identity as well as her possessions. The golden cross she always wore around her neck is symbolically missing, and so is her name; when she is asked to identify herself, it is the word 'Ellen', the name of the rectory maid-of-all-work, that floats into her consciousness. She has, psychologically, been reborn, as Orwell wished to be, and reborn, as long as memory evades her, on the other side of the great gulf of class.

Having no recollection of her past, Dorothy is at first able to live without hesitation in 'the strange dirty subworld into which she was plunged'; it is only after several days that she begins to question whether she has always belonged to it. This ability to detach oneself from past and upbringing is what Orwell and his heroes have always striven for; only Dorothy, in an abnormal psychological condition, is able to attain it even for a short period. She falls in with a trio of young Cockneys belonging to the fringe world of petty crime, and with them she sets out to join the annual saturnalia of East Londoners, the hop-picking in Kent that marks the end of summer. The peregrinations of Dorothy and her companions as they wander erratically over the countryside, looking for work and robbing orchards and fields, sleeping under haystacks and wearing their feet bloody, are extraordinarily arduous, but Dorothy endures uncomplaining, and by the time she and the thief Nobby, having lost their two companions, find work, the novel has generated a joyfulness of feeling which in all of Orwell's books is rivalled only once, in the passage describing George Bowling's childhood fishing expeditions in *Coming Up for Air*.

In the green hopfield world, Dorothy is happier than she has ever been or ever will be again. The atmosphere of the fields, which Orwell knew directly from at least one season of hop-picking, is admirably evoked. The burning, scented afternoons in the plantations, the holiday atmosphere, the everlasting inane songs, and the warmhearted democracy that continues through the work hours and the scanty leisure; all these combine to create an unharassed feeling which Dorothy has not experienced since childhood. She does not need to be on her guard or to keep up appearances; in this world, unlike the past she remembers only in dim, puzzling images, everything is live-and-let-live. Looking forward into Orwell's novels, one realizes that these gypsies and transplanted Cockneys, working and larking in the Kentish hopfields, are the prototypes of the proles of *Nineteen Eighty-Four*, as amiable and obstinate, as doggedly down-to-earth and as totally unintellectual, as prone to be tempted by the shoddiest products of modern pseudo-civilization, and yet in their own unreasoning way as independent of that other world which claims to rule them.

Like the life of the Burmese in Orwell's earlier novel, that of the hoppers is represented as being far closer to nature than the life of the upper class to which Dorothy belongs. Many of these people are gypsies, furtive, animal-like little men, proud of their wandering life and of the illiteracy that marks them off from civilization. And even the Cockneys seem to make terms easily with the countryside, if not with its people, as their young men rove at night through the great unpicked orchards where the apples lie in golden heaps under the trees.

For Dorothy, whom the hopper accepts without curiosity, the interlude is rather like Flory's dip into the green jungle pool. It is a time of renewal through a descent, almost in a Jungian sense, into the soothing waters of half-consciousness. The experience, as Orwell says, is like one of those dreams in which 'one accepts everything, questions nothing. Dirt, rags, vagabondage, begging, stealing – all had seemed natural to her.'

But the dream ends; the waking world of her past claims her. Nobby is arrested for stealing apples and the shock of the incident sets Dorothy's mind working again. She remembers odd references she has heard among the hoppers to a rector's daughter and the scandal associated with her disappearance, and all at once she realizes who she is.

From this point joy drains out of the book, and vitality with it. There follows a dreary interlude while Dorothy, fearing to go home under the shadow of unjustified slander, tries to maintain her false personality as Ellen the housemaid and to find a job as a domestic servant. But outside the little democracy of the hopfields she finds that her class is against her. She cannot become a working girl, but she can become a beggar; Orwell here is approaching the complex view of the English caste system set out in *The Road to Wigan Pier*. It is to begging that she finally descends and, arrested for mendicancy, she is improbably rescued by the butler of her baronet cousin, a superannuated Edwardian masher, and is spirited away to teach in a dreadful little suburban private school. It is true that Orwell admirably conveys the atmosphere – the peculiar squalid deadness – of such establishments, and in Mrs Creevy, the proprietress of Ringwood Academy for Girls, he creates one of his best characters, an appalling figure of calculating ignorance and pietistic hypocrisy. But he is not content to employ the legitimate devices of fiction, and interrupts his narrative with long passages of authorial denunciation of the private-school system, introduced by the crudest of sleeve-pulling techniques.

There are, by the way, vast numbers of private schools in England. Second-rate, third-rate, and fourth-rate (Ringwood House was a specimen of the fourth-rate school), they exist by the dozen and the score in every London suburb and every provincial town.

Yet the experience – as experience – is important to Dorothy, since the attempt to create a valid pattern of life in this unpromising setting helps to bridge a chasm that has opened in her life. For with her memory she lost something else that would once have seemed very precious to her – her faith. After the first moment in the hopfields when she began to remember who she really was, there came a day of nostalgia for the rectory and the existence associated with it, for 'all the multitudinous, urgent details of a life that had alternated between work and prayer'. Then, undramatically, comes the realization that prayer means nothing to her. She remembers that she has not prayed at all since leaving home.

She recorded this fact as she walked slowly up the road, and she recorded it briefly, almost casually, as though it had been something seen in passing – a flower in the ditch or a bird crossing the road – something noticed and then dismissed. She had not even the time to reflect on what it might mean. It was shouldered out of her mind by more momentous things.

The loss of faith which is first revealed to Dorothy by a sense of the irrelevance of prayer is associated not only with the loss of memory, but also with the descent into that natural life which contains its own innocence and therefore demands not faith, but merely acceptance. The hopfields are Dorothy's Eden, and from them she is driven out to the bitter world of experience represented by Trafalgar Square and Ringwood Academy. With faith no longer there to provide a support from outside, she has to call up resources within herself; in Mrs Creevy's miserable school, where she is exploited and humiliated, she finds the challenge as she begins to awaken the dull minds of children whose personalities have been atrophied by years of unbelievably bad teaching.

Between them, Mrs Creevy and the narrow-minded Nonconformist parents of the pupils soon put an end to Dorothy's idealistic endeavours, and in the process they demonstrate the barrenness in pratice of narrow doctrines of salvation by faith as compared with broad beliefs that embrace and give importance to good works. Dorothy, born and bred in the Church of England, cannot begin to understand the Nonconformist mind in its arid twentieth-century form, and the lack of understanding is mutual. Clearly, if Orwell has any sympathies at all, they are, despite his own disbelief, with the Anglican position, and in the final pages of *A Clergyman's Daughter* we encounter for the first time in a strong identifiable form the conservatism that was the other face of his radicalism.

Partly out of boredom and partly under pressure from Mrs Creevy, who hopes to pick up a few Church of England pupils, Dorothy begins to attend the local church. Here she finds that every other aspect of the act of worship has become as meaningless as prayer. There is no doubt at all that her faith has vanished; she has undergone 'a change in the climate of the mind' which may not necessarily have been caused by her recent experiences, but which is certainly linked with temporary loss of memory and personality. Yet, despite her loss of faith, Dorothy does not feel in revolt against the way of life the church represents.

For she perceived that in all that happens in church, however absurd and cowardly its supposed purpose may be, there is something – it is hard to define, but something of decency, of spiritual comeliness – that is not easily found in the world outside. It seemed to her that even though you no longer believe, it is better to go to church than not; better to follow in the ancient ways than to drift in rootless freedom.

Dangerous as it may be to impute to an author the opinions of his characters, there is no doubt that the drift of *A Clergyman's Daughter* – and equally that of the succeeding novel *Keep the Aspidistra Flying* – suggests a turning away at this period from the rather unsystematic anarchism into which Orwell had plunged on his return from Burma. By all means go underground, both books exhort, by all means dip into the pool of irresponsible, elemental, unconscious life, but when you emerge you will probably value more than you have ever done before whatever is ordered and comely and decent in society, and you are more likely to find such things where sound traditions persist. There may seem to be a contradiction between this Tory desire to retain what is good in the past and Orwell's growing inclination at this time to line himself up with the Socialists, but the two trends have in common the desire for an orderly way of life. The real conflict in Orwell is always between the half Tory, half Socialist good citizen and the Anarchist ever suspicious that the good citizen may be trying to put something over on him. In both *A Clergyman's Daughter* and *Keep the Aspidistra Flying*, it is the good citizen who comes out on top in the end. The scandalous, amoral Mr Warburton is the nearest thing to a consistent voice of liberty in *A Clergyman's Daughter*, and when Mr Warburton has finally rescued Dorothy from the petty hell of private-school teaching and is taking her back home, he tries his best to persuade her not to return to her life of service in the rectory. Before his logic all her arguments fail, and she has not even the fire of faith to support her, and yet she does not give in because, however empty the cosmos may now seem to her, 'the Christian way of life is still the way that must come naturally to her'.

Later, in the last chapter of the book, Dorothy reflects on the question of faith, and lack of faith. With faith everything in life is woven together into 'a fabric of never-ending joy'. Without faith life is meaningless.

There was, she saw clearly, no possible substitute for faith; no pagan acceptance of life as sufficient to itself, no pantheistic cheer-up stuff, no pseudo-religion of 'progress' with visions of glittering Utopias and ant heaps of steel and concrete. It is all or nothing. Either life on earth is a preparation for something greater or it is meaningless, dark and dreadful.

Several years before Sartre published *La Nausée*, Dorothy was in fact undergoing the classic existentialist experience of horror at the realization that the absolute is in fact only the absurd, that man stands alone, without hope, in a universe unpopulated by God or gods. Orwell never claimed to be an existentialist; in fact, he had little use for popular philosophies, literary or otherwise, and was inclined to exaggerate the coterie elements in them. By 1934 he may have read the earlier novels of Malraux, the only absurdist who had published any important works of fiction by that time, but I have seen no actual evidence of this. Certainly by the later 1940s he had read not only Malraux but also Sartre and Camus, but he had very little to say about them; Malraux interested him most, but as a political novelist in the continental manner rather than as a writer of philosophical fiction. But, even if he wrote of Dorothy's experience with no knowledge of the way in which similar spiritual agonies were being treated by his French contemporaries, the revelation follows the customary pattern. What Dorothy discovers is that we give our own meaning to the world by patterns of order which we ourselves create and sustain.

She did not reflect, consciously, that the solution to her difficulty lay in accepting the fact that there was no solution; that if one gets on with the job that lies to hand, the ultimate purpose of the job fades into insignificance; that faith and no faith are very much the same provided that one is doing what is customary, useful and acceptable. She could not formulate these thoughts as yet, she could only live them.

Christopher Hollis suggests that in stating Dorothy's dilemma Orwell is really presenting his own, and *A Clergyman's Daughter* is such a chaotic mixture of genuine fiction and the thinly disguised experiences and opinions of the author that he may well be right, as he is certainly right in suggesting that Orwell could not accept a purely materialistic view of the human condition. Moral concepts like honour and decency were extraordinarily important to him, and he never supported either the Marxist view that human motivations are entirely economic or the Freudian view that they are entirely biological. He lamented more than once the end of the age of religious faith when men could believe in another life, and he regretted that the young people in the generation growing up around him had lost that knowledge of the Bible which at one time was one of the most precious possessions of Englishmen, and which had incalculably influenced English literature. He did not want to see the power of the church return; he detested bishops, Non-conformist preachers and Catholic intellectuals (collectively, that is to say, since he liked some of them personally and more than once defended Graham Greene and Roy Campbell against unfair attacks from the Left); he despised evangelism with its braying elders and hated any form of superstition, religious or political; if he had not disliked the professional atheists as much as any other type of evangelist, he would probably have declared himself one. Nevertheless, he realized that there was a natural cohesion and a common sense of purpose in every religious age which secular societies would be able to reproduce only with difficulty, and then probably in the wrong ways – the 'glittering Utopias and ant heaps of steel and concrete' to which he looked forward with nausea.

But even if we regard *A Clergyman's Daughter* as the novel in which Orwell had his say about religion, not to mention education and a good many other lesser matters of social con-cern, the very cyclic structure of the book emphasizes the recurrent major theme, presenting the fatally divided world of humanity, as Dorothy, the upper-class girl, drops out of her class, descends into the depths, loses her identity, finds it and returns to the point of departure wiser and sadder. Orwell's prodigals always follow the circular path, and always return, as Dorothy returned to the rectory and Flory to the bungalow and the secret life it sheltered. One's way of life – the elite, the party, the suburb, or the Church – always claims one back. And for these prodigals the return is no occasion for festival, since something is always destroyed in the process, life for Flory, faith for Dorothy, and, as we shall see, things equally important for the hero-victims who follow them.

7

LIKE many other writers George Orwell tended to be economical with his motifs, using them again and again until he had wrung every possible implication out of them. By the time he wrote *Keep the Aspidistra Flying* he had already used the aspidistra itself, that rather frayed symbol of middle-class English respectability, as a key image in his two earlier novels.

In *Burmese Days* it appears in malign guise at the end of the scene in which Flory feels mingled ecstasy and loneliness as he sits in the jungle pool and watches the green pigeon. He leaves the pool and walks away contented and at peace. But as with his dog he pushes on into the forest, the nature of his experience changes.

Soon they had lost their way in the jungle, and were wandering in a maze of dead trees and tangled bushes. They came to an impasse where the path was blocked by large ugly plants like magnified aspidistras, whose leaves terminated in long lashes armed with thorns. A firefly glowed greenish at the bottom of a bush; it was getting twilight in the thicker places.

The gigantic whip-bearing aspidistras blocking Flory's way in this darkening landscape of dead trees and tangled bushes have an obvious significance in the general context of his fate; they represent the forces of his past and his caste, the conventions of respectable England – grown monstrous in transplantation to an alien land – which will frustrate his attempts to escape from the role of the sahib and will in the end punish and help to destroy him.

In *A Clergyman's Daughter* the actual phrase 'Keep the aspidistra flying' is chanted by a defrocked clergyman in Trafalgar Square to the tune of 'Deutschland, Deutschland über alles' during the mock Walpurgis Night scene, and later the plant again appears as a malign image, when Mr Warburton, making his proposal of marriage to Dorothy in the train as she is returning to the rectory from her cycle of adventures, prophesies her fate should she decide to remain single. ' "Women who don't marry wither up – they wither up like aspidistras in back-parlour windows; and the devilish thing is that they don't even know they're withering"'

In *Keep the Aspidistra Flying* the plant becomes a more ambiguous symbol. On its comic level the novel might be seen as the record of the long, running battle which the hero, Gordon Comstock, carries on against this ubiquitous and almost indestructible plant. At first he lives in a miserable, narrowly respectable boarding-house for single men in Hampstead. The dining room is a chill place with a phalanx of clotted sauce-bottles on the table; its only glory is the multitude of its aspidistras:

They were all over the place – on the sideboard, on the floor, on 'occasional' tables; in the window there was a sort of florist's stand of them, blocking out the light. In the half-darkness, with aspidistras all about you, you had the feeling of being in some sunless aquarium amid the dreary foliage of water flowers.

Even in Gordon's own room stands a particularly mangy aspidistra, which he keeps unwatered, stubbing out his cigarettes on the stem and mixing salt in its earth. 'But the beastly things are practically immortal. In almost any circumstances they can preserve a wilting, diseased existence.'

Outside its comic aspect, the almost immortal aspidistra represents the stubborn sense of respectability which Orwell sees surviving everywhere in England except among the declassed – the intellectuals on one hand and the destitute on the other. Even when, in his desire to get deep underground, away from his friends, his family and his past, Gordon goes to live in a bug-ridden Lambeth slum room, he cannot escape the aspidistra. 'It gave him a bit of a twinge to see it. Even here, in this final refuge! Hast thou found me, O mine enemy? But it was a poor weedy specimen – indeed, it was obviously dying.'

The death of this last aspidistra coincides with the nadir of Gordon's descent into the underworld. But resurrection awaits hero and aspidistra alike. As the plant stands dead in the fetid room, Gordon's girl Rosemary at last becomes his mistress, and in this unpassionate act life is born again. Rosemary soon realizes that she is pregnant, and the idea of killing off through abortion the bud of humanity which he has planted shocks Gordon out of his crankiness. He returns to the world, takes up once again his respectable job, and insists that in the flat where he and Rosemary begin their married life, an aspidistra shall take the place of honour. Orwell has turned all the jokes about aspidistras on their head, though his intent is more ambiguous than at first appears.

Keep the Aspidistra Flying really belongs to the category which Orwell himself termed 'good bad books'. It has a verbose, repetitive style quite unlike that of any of his other books, and while there is often a genuine tone of ironic mockery, this frequently breaks down into an obsessive didacticism reminiscent of D. H. Lawrence at his worst. No doubt Orwell was deliberately evoking a paranoiac mood, and he represents fairly effectively the hypersensitivity to insult and the rooted sense of grievance which young men from insecure backgrounds develop when they find their way into environments – like the world of letters – where many of the inhabitants are more prosperous, more educated and better bred than themselves. One cannot entirely dismiss *Keep the Aspidistra Flying*, since every page shows an original mind at work, yet in the end it falls short of being a successful work of literary art largely because of its lack of restraint. Orwell was always tempted to overdo his effects, and this was why in later years he became so conscious of the need for self-discipline. His weakness appears to some degree in all his books except *Homage to Catalonia* and *Animal Farm*. But never again did Orwell allow a whole book to slip out of key almost from the first obsessive page to the last as he did in the case of *Keep the Aspidistra Flying*.

The nominal subject of *Keep the Aspidistra Flying* is, as I have said, money. Gordon Comstock, a young *poète manqué* who likes to have his moral cake and eat it, has condemned himself to voluntary poverty, leaving a good position in an advertising agency for a dead-end job at half his former wages in a suburban bookshop. Once he has taken this step he shows nis unfitness for the life of renunciation by perpetually bewailing his penniless condition. The book is heavy with those long, penurious calculations which Orwell always enjoyed compiling. In Gordon Comstock's case his obsession about money and his sense of inferiority play into each other's hands. ' "All human relationships must be purchased with money. If you have no money, men won't care for you, women won't love you; won't, that is, care for you or love you the last little bit that matters. And how right they are, after all! For, moneyless, you are unlovable." '

Almost to the end the relentless examination and denunciation of a society based on money continues. It is an extension to absurdity of Orwell's argument in *Down and Out in Paris and London* that the respect paid by the community to any task is proportionate to its remuneration. As Gordon's friend the wealthy Socialist editor Ravelston remarks, there is a superficial resemblance to Marxist doctrines in this habit of reducing all resentments against society to a purely economic discontent. But Gordon refuses to accept the facile comparison.

'You don't know what it means to crawl along on two quid a week. It isn't a question of hardship – it's nothing so decent as hardship. It's the bloody, sneaking, squalid meanness of it. Living alone for weeks on end because when you've no money you've no friends. Calling yourself a writer and never even producing anything because you're always too washed out to write. It's a sort of filthy subworld one lives in.'

Yet it is the subworld that Comstock has chosen, and, even though he admits to himself that 'the glow of renunciation never lasts', and that a life of voluntary poverty 'ceases to be a heroic gesture and becomes a dingy habit', he persists in clinging to his intentions and rejects indignantly both Ravelston's offers of loans and the efforts which Rosemary is constantly making to get him back into the advertising agency where she still works.

But, while Dorothy Hare could slip easily into the underworld of poverty by forgetting her identity, Gordon, who tries

to do it by a conscious effort of the will, finds the attempt to
lose his status as a member of the 'landless gentry' far more
difficult than he had imagined. In this respect *Keep the Aspidistra Flying* shows already the change in Orwell's attitude
which later became explicit in *The Road to Wigan Pier*, where
he revised the view expressed in *Down and Out*, and implied
in *A Clergyman's Daughter*, that it was easy to cross the lines
of class in Britain. Gordon is far more aware than the Orwell
who first went among tramps that, above the level of sheer
destitution, class lines remain almost impenetrable.

Gordon has not in fact become a pauper; a tramp would
consider his two pounds a week the passport to paradise. All he
has done is to go to the brink of the lowest ledge of middle-class
respectability. His employment, his friends, his girl Rosemary
are still genteel. So is his ambition to suceed as a rather pomp-
ous poet, and also is his resentment of the 'moneyed young
beasts' from Cambridge whom he sees cornering the publishers'
contracts and getting their poems printed because the editors
were college friends. In fact, the more difficult Comstock finds it
to maintain his precarious position, the more bitterly, despite
his proclaimed renunciation, he clings to it. Since he has thrown
away an income, his last vestige of gentility is his pride, which
forces him to buy the first drink even when he cannot afford
it and to refuse indignantly when Rosemary offers to pay for a
meal, even if this means that they have to tramp for hours in
the joyless London streets.

Gordon's anger – which is really directed as much against
himself as against others – springs, like Flory's, from the fact
that, though he has mentally resolved to cut away from his
class and his past, he has never had the courage to do so completely, so he lives in the limbo of the respectable poor, and
finds that his lack of money, far from morally ennobling him,
has merely intensified his sense of grievance and his aggressive-
ness. The whole of society seems to conspire against him, and
he returns its imagined hostility with hatred, so that he longs
for the war which (like Orwell himself from 1934 onward) he
foresees as inevitable, and which (unlike Orwell) he welcomes,

gloating over the thought of falling bombs, smashed towns and the end of the money-world.

As in every other development of the Orwellian theme of alienation, the problem of establishing contact with a more natural existence plays its part in Comstock's career. The money-world is death-oriented, hostile to life; it turns men into 'corpses walking'. Only when he passes through the street markets of the working-class districts does Gordon feel that he is really in contact with a way of living that has retained a reality of its own – the way of life of the working class, whose pride it is that they keep themselves to themselves. 'He liked the noise, the bustle, the vitality. Whenever you see a street market you know that there's hope for England yet. But even here he felt his solitude.'

Gordon's solitude is broken by his unexpected meeting with Rosemary in the midst of this island of proletarian vitality, and on that evening they decide on a trip to the country, to Burnham Beeches. Once again the pattern of repetition emerges; it was to Burnham Beeches that Dorothy Hare would go when she wished to escape from the deadly atmosphere of Ringwood House Academy, and it is to Burnham Beeches that Rosemary and Gordon go to escape from the sequence of frustrated meetings in the dark, dead streets of London.

At first, when they leave the train and begin to walk through the country roads, they feel 'shrunken and out of place', like men coming up from under the ground. But then, after they have walked themselves into trim, there is a flashing moment of revelation.

Suddenly, as they came out on to the road again, the dew all down the hedge glittered with a diamond flash. The sun had pierced the clouds. The light came slanting and yellow across the fields, and delicate unexpected colours sprang out in everything, as though some giant's child had been let loose with a new paintbox.

Thus, midway through the novel, comes the first moment of what might be described as real happiness, and when Gordon looks back on that morning he remembers 'the feeling of free-

dom and adventure', of a whole countryside, a world of nature,
awaiting them. But neither the happiness nor the sense of adventure lasts. The money-world has thrust its tentacles even
here. They leave the woods carpeted with golden leaves and
come down to the commercialized banks of the Thames, where
an expensive riverside hotel – the only place where they can
find a meal – consumes almost all Gordon's stock of money. He
consoles himself with the thought that Rosemary has at last
consented to become his mistress, and when, in the warm sunny
afternoon, they find a secluded copse, it seems that his desire
will certainly be fulfilled. But, at the very moment of pene-
tration, Rosemary thrusts him away; he is not using a contra-
ceptive. Angry, humiliated, Gordon blames his disappointment
on the money-system; the money-system makes women
scared of having children and puts a premium on what, with
Orwellian conservatism, he regards as the pernicious custom of
contraception. Obscurely he feels that it is an affront to the
concept of natural living which, in his own perverse way, he
is serving.

Gordon's disappointment after the disastrous trip to the
country contributes to the incident which finally pushes him
off the middle-class ledge into the void of the slums. He receives
an unexpected cheque from an American magazine, and spends
it in an evening of extravagance, in which he gets outrageously
drunk, insults Rosemary, is robbed by a prostitute, hits a police
sergeant, and passes a night in the cells, from which he is
rescued by Ravelston and Flaxman, a raffish commercial traveller, one of Orwell's Sancho Panza characters who plays a small
part in *Keep the Aspidistra Flying* but will later appear, meta-
morphosed and magnified, as the hero of *Coming Up for Air*,
George Bowling. Gordon's name gets into the papers, he loses
his job, and at last is forced to swallow his pride and accept
both the hospitality and the never-to-be-repaid loans of Ravelston. Eventually he takes an even more miserable job than the
last, and becomes the entire staff of a twopenny circulating
library for the semi-literate in the heart of the Lambeth slum.
Here at last, he feels, he has really got underground, away from

it all because he is beneath it all. He is away from his kind, away from the pretences of culture, away from the presumptions of wealth. He begins to feel accepted in this grey, characterless underworld. 'He was just the "bloke in the library", and practically one of themselves.'

But only practically; never completely. For Gordon finds that 'it is harder to sink than to rise'. The people from his past never let him alone. Rosemary in particular is driven to desperation by his acceptance of the life into which he has fallen. Now he is rejecting not merely money, but – she feels – life itself, and though she would never admit it, she proceeds to act Delilah – for Gordon's good of course – and to tempt him back to middle-class respectability by the bribe of fatherhood. It seems a happy ending. Comstock does not die like Flory. He does not see himself condemned to an eventual fate of loneliness without the consolation of faith, like Dorothy. Yet, like the others, he has to pay his own penalty as he is drawn back into his class. He pays it when he drops his vast uncompleted poem into the sewers, and returns to the advertising agency to write copy about 'Pedic Perspiration', which he does 'far better than anything else in his life'. And if we accept this as a defeat, then Rosemary, like all the women in Orwell's novels about men, is ultimately the enemy.

Keep the Aspidistra Flying, like every other Orwellian book, is heavily loaded with elements derived from the author's experiences. According to Rayner Heppenstall, Orwell was still working at the bookshop which provided part of the background while he was actually writing the novel. *Antichrist*, the review edited by Ravelston, is a caricature of the *Adelphi*. Comstock does some of the things Orwell did, and he obviously shares some of his frustrations; it is even possible to see his paranoia as a magnification of Orwell's own obsessions about the literary racket. But he has a little man's arrogance and viciousness which Orwell completely lacked, and possesses no share of his creator's generosity or compassion. These characteristics are given to another character, Ravelston, who also shares Orwell's tallness, his way of dressing, his public-school

background and his editorial ineptness. Absurd and tedious
though he is, Comstock emerges by the end of the novel as a
character in his own right, the prototype of the Lucky Jims,
those petty and petulant rebels of recent English fiction. The
image he leaves on the mind is rarely an Orwellian one, though
he is certainly linked with his creator and with the whole line
of Orwell's leading characters by the place he holds in the
grand exploration of the theme of alienation and the elite.

8

Books of reportage were in vogue during the 1930s; they
fitted in with the prevalent atmosphere of Mass Observation
and fashionable bolshevism. Somewhat high-keyed 'realistic'
accounts of their experiences by soldiers, sailors, miners and
convicts, often bound in the limp orange covers of the Left
Book Club editions, acquired a quasi-literary reputation because
of the self-conscious and artificial 'proletarianism' affected by
the intelligentsia of the decade. At the same time, owing to the
rigid class distinctions that prevailed even among the people
who regarded themselves as progressive, narratives of this kind
had a definitely exotic appeal, rather like that aroused by
accounts of the lives of remote and primitive tribes. Orwell's
enterprise in going among the tramps of London seemed almost
as daring as that of Tom Harrison, who had lived among the
head-hunters of the Solomon Islands and whose account of his
experiences was published by the Left Book Club within a few
months of Orwell's account of his further expeditions among
English primitives, *The Road to Wigan Pier*.

Today most of those documentaries, which seemed so ab-
sorbingly interesting thirty years ago, are completely forgotten,
and when we remember the Left Book Club it is, ironically,
usually for the book which the editorial committee, Victor
Gollancz, Harold Laski and John Strachey, published with the
greatest misgivings and the most profuse apologies for its heret-

ical ideas about socialism, Orwell's *The Road to Wigan Pier*. In a decade of documentary reportage, Orwell was in fact the only writer who gave permanence to what is normally the most ephemeral of literary crafts. Literate Englishmen of the 1960s gain their impressions of the almost extinct English tramp from *Down and Out in Paris and London*, and of the conditions of the unemployed of the 1930s from *The Road to Wigan Pier*, while those of us who have half forgotten the Spanish Civil War are likely to raise a more convincing ghost of that period from a reading of *Homage to Catalonia* than from any other book of the time. There are several reasons why these books have survived: their fresh and original style; their peculiar immediacy – the fact that each plunges us in its first sentence into a human situation which the rest of the book develops with fascinating variations; their strong projection of a perpetually interesting personality which infuses not only the narrative but also the highly idiosyncratic arguments; finally, their steady development of a philosophy of life and society which, for all its apparent contradictions, assumes self-consistency when one sees it in relation to the character of its creator.

The Road to Wigan Pier is by no means Orwell's best work, and some critics, notably Tom Hopkinson, have dismissed it as his worst. Faced with its complexity, and the apparent illogicality with which chapters follow each other in the manner of detached essays rather than as parts of a carefully planned work, Laurence Brander described the book rather aptly as 'a medley of documentaries and pamphlets', and one can in fact split the thirteen chapters into five groups which are united, not by the ordinary transitional devices of a linear narrative, as in the case of *Down and Out in Paris and London*, but rather by the fact that they all centre on a double problem, the problem of class in England related to that of socialism as a viable means of bringing to an end social miseries which an age of unemployment had made particularly evident.

The book opens with a mordant essay in description, a kind of English counterpart of the first chapter of *Père Goriot*, in which Orwell tells of his stay in a cheap Lancashire lodging-house, and of the depressed people he met there, trying to keep their heads just above the line of respectability that distinguishes old-age pensioners and newspaper canvassers from beggars and tramps. 'It is a kind of duty to see and smell such places now and again, especially smell them, lest you should forget that they exist; though perhaps it is better not to stay there too long.'

The phrase 'a kind of duty' is significant; Orwell at this point and in this book is taking on responsibilities. It was less a sense of duty than mingled feelings of guilt and adventurousness that had first taken him exploring the landscape of poverty, just as it was a sense of dedication rather than a sense of duty that made him, during the first eight years or so after his return from Burma to England, insist on rejecting the secure life and the good job for a career of writing. But 1936 was the year of his conversion to socialism and of his final decision to become a political writer. Up to the end of 1935, he had not yet made up his mind. Then Victor Gollancz, who had published his earlier books, offered him a commission to prepare a report for the Left Book Club on conditions in the depressed areas of northern England, and by the wintry early months of 1936 he was living among the coal miners of Lancashire. By April he was back in the south, and there still seemed little outward sign of a revolution in his outlook, for he had actually abandoned his working-class flat in Kentish Town and – like a Georgian poet – taken his country cottage in the tiny Hertfordshire village of Wallington; he was planning to reopen the general store, which he did almost immediately, and to marry Eileen O'Shaughnessy, which he did early in the following June. However, the writing of *The Road to Wigan Pier* appears to have greatly clarified his ideas regarding socialism, which I suspect he worked out as he wrote them down, and his commitment was sealed by the outbreak of the Spanish Civil War and by his decision to go to Barcelona, first as a journalist. He arrived there in December 1936, and immediately he decided to serve the Republic as a militiaman. By the end of the year, in other words, he was fully engaged politically, and engaged he remained to the end of his life. 'Every line of serious work that I have written since 1936 has been written, directly or indirectly, *against* totalitarianism and *for* democratic socialism, as I understand it.'

How Orwell understood democratic socialism was first adumbrated in the remaining four groups of chapters that form the body of *The Road to Wigan Pier*. First there are two chapters on miners, their working conditions and their way of life. Next come four chapters on various aspects of existence in the industrial districts of the north: the housing problem, the difficulties of making ends meet on the dole, the psychological effect of unemployment, the ugliness of the industrial districts, the virtues of the working class. These chapters doubtless adhere fairly closely to the commission which Gollancz originally gave Orwell. But the six chapters which form the second part of the book go far beyond anything the Left Book Club bargained for, and in retrospect one can only praise the editors – then more or less orthodox Marxists – for their intellectual honesty in publishing without alteration a denunciation of the left-wing establishment which must have been extremely disturbing both to them and to a large number of Left Book Club members.

In this latter part of *The Road to Wigan Pier* Orwell sets out his ideas on the nature of class distinctions in England, and proceeds to demonstrate that the Socialist movement has never realistically understood the durability of such distinctions on both sides of the glass curtain that divides the middle class from the workers. But time is running out, fascism is on the march, and unless the Socialist movement changes its outlook and finds some means of uniting the classes where their interests coincide, the middle classes will go over to demagogic reaction and all will be lost.

Much of what Orwell says here has been made irrelevant by events. Other passages are typical Orwellian pyrotechnics, as when, in Swiftian catalogue, he pictures the Socialist movement in Britain as consisting of 'vegetarians with wilting beards, of Bolshevik commissars (half gangster, half gramophone), of earnest ladies in sandals, shock-headed Marxists chewing polysyllables, escaped Quakers, birth-control fanatics and Labour Party backstairs crawlers'.

But behind the dying fireworks one perceives a serious attempt to state the problems regarding socialism which were – and remained – uppermost in Orwell's mind: its relation to class, to the concept of progress, to the prospect of mechanization. At the same time Orwell sketches his own view of a socialism based on the Marxist 'pea-and-thimble trick with those three mysterious entities, thesis, antithesis and synthesis', but on clearly stated ideals of justice and liberty.

This aspect of *The Road to Wigan Pier* I shall discuss later in considering the leading ideas embodied in Orwell's more openly polemical works. Here I am concerned primarily with the part which the book plays in the development of the central thematic structure of his fiction. In this respect it is perhaps the key work. Having fought his way through the difficult early years of his writing career, having worked off the undefined and rather emotional rebelliousness with which he returned from Burma, he was able at this point to see his own life and his relationship to society more clearly and more coolly than ever before.

I have already shown what valuable insights *The Road to Wigan Pier* offers on Orwell's Burmese experiences and on his subsequent adventures in the lower depths of society, but there are other aspects of the book which have an important bearing on the changing form of the personal myth that conditioned the themes of his novels. Except for slight encounters in childhood, this was the first time Orwell made any extended contacts with working people, as distinct from the derelicts who lived below all classes. The contacts were not of the intimate kind he had expected after the ease with which he made friends with tramps and *plongeurs*, and this perhaps explains the ironical title of his book. Wigan Pier is a standing joke in Lancashire. If a man cannot afford to go to Blackpool for the 'wakes' – holiday week – of his town, he will say that he is going to Wigan Pier. But Wigan, which is inland, has no pier, and so Wigan Pier means nowhere. Orwell makes a wry joke about his disappointment at not finding Wigan Pier, and he certainly did not find what he had expected when he reached the North Country.

What he did find made a variety of deep impressions, ranging from disgust – for the Bookers, who kept the lodging-house and preyed on those poorer than themselves – through compassion, to intense admiration, but always with the consciousness that here was a life in which he had and could have no part. This feeling is emphasized at the end of the first chapter, when the train is carrying him away from the lodging-house to the next hideous industrial town and he looks out from the window across the wintry scene of little slum houses.

At the back of one of the houses a young woman was kneeling on the stones, poking a stick up the leaden waste-pipe which ran from the sink inside and which I suppose was blocked. I had time to see everything about her – her sacking apron, her clumsy clogs, her arms reddened by the cold. She looked up as the train passed, and I was almost near enough to catch her eye. She had a round pale face, the usual exhausted face of the slum girl who is twenty-five and looks forty, thanks to miscarriages and drudgery; and it wore, for the second in which I saw it, the most desolate, hopeless expression I have ever seen.... She knew well enough what was happening to her – understood as well as I did how dreadful a destiny it was to be kneeling there in the bitter cold, on the slimy stones of a slum backyard, poking a stick up a foul drainpipe.

This is one of the most poignant paragraphs of a book that sets out frankly to stir compassion and anger. The image of that desolate face stays in one's mind as Orwell works out the implications of the scene, chapter after chapter, taking us through the industrial towns, presenting his bleak notations of rotting and crowded houses and occasionally superimposing some other face that tells silently of unspeakable degradation, and always a woman's face, for it is the women who bear the hardest brunt of poverty.

But we have also to place the scene in its context. Orwell catches sight of the woman from the window of the train, and the train is carrying him away. He is seeing her as an outsider who is going away because he cannot belong. And immediately afterwards, as the train gathers speed, it runs out into one of those gleaming countrysides which recur in Orwell's books and remind us of the lost world where men once lived in touch with nature. The sun shines, the stone fences wind darkly over the pure white snowy hills, and the rooks dance because they know that spring is not so far off. Orwell reflects: 'The earth is so vast and still so empty that even in the filthy heart of civilization you find fields where the grass is green instead of grey; perhaps if you looked for them you might even find streams with live fish in them instead of salmon tins.' There is no need for further comment; a civilization which creates such contrasts stands self-condemned.

If the women are the perpetual victims in the tragedy of poverty which Orwell writes in these early chapters, the men often appear as the heroes. Orwell admired energy and toughness, and in his case this was no mere adulation of the inactive intellectual for the man of action, since he was always ready, as he showed that same year in Spain, to tax his strength and his powers of endurance to the utmost degree. Yet when he talks of miners and describes them in their strange underground world, a peculiar intensity comes into his tone, and we realize that the experience of mingling with them has a special and personal meaning for him. They are the grimy caryatids on whose shoulders the economic life of society is supported; they look like 'hammered iron statues', they have the 'most noble bodies' and figures 'fit for a guardsman'. 'You can never forget that spectacle once you have seen it – the line of bowed, kneeling figures, sooty black all over, driving their huge shovels under the coal with stupendous force and speed.'

As we read further, we realize that these feelings are inspired by the miners only when they are underground. They appear 'strange and slightly sinister' as they emerge from the pit, and at such times their faces have 'a fierce, wild look', but as soon as they have gone home and washed, they sink into a tame ordinariness; 'there is not much to distinguish them from the rest of the population.'

It is the miner *in the mine* who excites Orwell, and we are not far off the reason for his excitement when we remember the words with which Gordon Comstock's life in the Lambeth slum of *Keep the Aspidistra Flying* is introduced. 'Underground, underground! Down in the safe soft womb of earth. . . . That was where he wished to be.' Gordon's idea of underground is the murky winter streets where the faces of the destitute float in the smoky gloom. But in the mine Orwell reaches the deepest underworld of all, and the most fearsome.

. . . When the machines are roaring and the air is black with coal dust . . . the place is like hell, or at any rate like my own mental picture of hell. Most of the things one imagines in hell are there – heat, noise, confusion, darkness, foul air, and, above all, unbearably cramped space. Everything except the fire, for there is no fire down there except the feeble beams of Davy lamps and electric torches which scarcely penetrate the clouds of coal dust.

And here, far below the subworld of the tramps, in the claustrophobic gloom that suggests not only hell but also those ancient cave-born myths that bring life out of death in the dark fissures of the earth, he encounters a race of men who are not degenerated by idleness and malnutrition like the tramps but work with an almost demoniac energy which few men above the earth can emulate. He has reached the farthest of the human underworlds, has mingled with its denizens, and has discovered that here – unlike the underworld above the ground – there is no place for him, for 'by no conceivable amount of effort or training could I become a coal miner; the work would kill me in a few weeks'.

Here is the point at which Orwell first senses his alienation from the workers, the feeling that, after all, he cannot flee from his own world and find himself in theirs. The rest of *The Road to Wigan Pier* is, if we follow one of its many threads, an exploration of this idea to its conclusion, which is that class shapes us far more than most men are ready to admit, and that in the West caste distinctions have a 'chasmic, impassable quality'. Political conversion, he argues, does not give a man the cultural attributes of another class, nor does any glib intellectual acceptance of the desirability of a classless society. For everything about us is shaped by the class to which we belong, as Orwell argues in a passage so important for the understanding of his viewpoint that I quote it at length.

All my notions – notions of good and evil, of pleasant and unpleasant, of funny and serious, of ugly and beautiful – are essentially *middle-class* notions; my taste in books and food and clothes, my sense of honour, my table manners, my turns of speech, my accent, even the characteristic movements of my body, are the products of a special kind of upbringing and a special niche about half-way up the social hierarchy. When I grasp this I grasp that it is no use clapping a proletarian on the back and telling him that he is as good a man as I am; if I want real contact with him, I have got to make an effort for which very likely I am unprepared. For to get outside the class racket I have got to suppress not merely my private snobbishness, but most of my other tastes and prejudices as well. I have got to alter myself so completely that at the end I should hardly be recognizable as the same person.

This is really the first open confession by Orwell that what he said fictionally in *Burmese Days* might be bitterly true in fact; that the rebel cannot escape his caste because the marks it lays upon him will always exclude him from any other. In terms of the specific recommendations for Socialist policy which are the overt concern of the final chapters of *The Road to Wigan Pier*, he makes it the text for a homily advocating a moratorium on attempts at artificial class-breaking. Only then, he imagines, the various classes may fight side by side for their common aims against 'the plutocracy', and in the moment of victory – Who knows? 'Perhaps ... we of the sinking middle class ... may sink without further struggles into the working class where we belong, and probably when we get there it will not be so dreadful as we feared, for, after all, we have nothing to lose but our aitches.'

I doubt if Orwell believed, even then, that this was a real possibility. England of the 1960s has certainly not fulfilled his prophecy. The unsinkable middle classes show every sign that they will defend their position to the last aspirate.

Yet there are times when life grants to those who long deeply enough for it the experience – no matter how remote it may seem – which they most desire, and to Orwell it was at last given to live for a brief period in something very close to the classless society of his dreams.

9

IF I were asked to pick the best of Orwell's books, I would immediately name *Animal Farm*. If I were asked which I liked most, I would select *Homage to Catalonia*. And this would not be merely because the book records a passage in history which has a peculiar emotional resonance for so many of us who were young thirty years ago. Many books do that, but from rereading most of them one gets little pleasure. The great virtue of *Homage to Catalonia* is not merely that it brings the period back to life in one's mind, but that it does so with such exceptional radiance.

This, indeed, is the book in which Orwell comes nearest to his ideal of writing 'good prose' that is 'like a window-pane'. He tells us how, when he was working on it, he tried 'very hard ... to tell the whole truth without violating my literary instincts'. And if *Homage to Catalonia* seems singularly effortless in comparison with, say, *Down and Out in Paris and London*, it has much more formal grace and cohesion than *The Road to Wigan Pier*, which appears to have been written in just about the same length of time. It is true that the narrative is broken by chapters of political discussion defending the POUM party against accusations of plotting with Franco, and putting forward an astute analysis of the role of the Communists in the Spanish Civil War. At the time of publication it looked as though these passages of very topical argument would spoil the book for later readers, and a decade after writing it Orwell seemed to agree with a critic who said to him, 'Why did you put in all that stuff? You've turned what might have been a good book into journalism.' He defended himself with the remark that he could not have done otherwise, because his anger at the thought of innocent men being falsely accused was one of his main motives for writing this particular book.

In fact, both Orwell and his critic were wrong. There are some rare writers, realistic by nature rather than by intellectual conviction, who can introduce argument or exposition into narrative writing without producing the usual shattering break of tone ; one of them was Tolstoy. There are also journalists who can write so truly for their own time that they raise journalism into literature and give it a permanent validity; one of these was Swift. Tolstoy and Swift were men of Orwell's own stamp, which possibly explains why he wrote long essays relentlessly analysing their faults. He, like them, was a moralist, and it was the moral passion that carried his best works to the level of high literary art. Even his concern for purity of style and language was a moral concern, springing out of his conviction that the real aim of literature was to tell the truth, in his case the political truth. Nowhere is this shown more brilliantly than in *Homage to Catalonia*, where a political passion – the quest for human equality – led him into the most meaningful and possibly – in spite of everything – the happiest experience of his life.

Orwell went to Spain with letters of introduction from the British Independent Labour Party. He had written rather scathingly of the members of that organization in *The Road to Wigan Pier*, and he himself – despite the fact that he was already a declared Socialist – belonged to no party; the connexion was possibly due to the fact that at this time the *Adelphi*, to which he still contributed regularly, was following the I.L.P. world-revolutionary line. His original intention was to visit the front as a war correspondent, but one can reasonably assume that he went there with some hope of joining in. In one of his columns in *Tribune*, dated 15 September 1944, he looked back on his journey to Spain and recollected how he quarrelled with a taxi driver in Paris and then took the night train towards the Pyrenees.

The train, a slow one, was packed with Czechs, Germans, Frenchmen, all bound on the same mission. Up and down the train you could hear one phrase repeated over and over again, in the accents of all the languages of Europe – *là-bas* (down there). My third-class carriage was full of very young, fair-haired, underfed Germans in suits of incredible shoddiness – the first *ersatz* cloth I had seen – who rushed out at every stopping place to buy cheap wine and later fell asleep in a sort of pyramid on the floor of the carriage. About halfway down France the ordinary passengers dropped off. There might still be a few nondescript journalists like myself, but the train was practically a troop train, and the countryside knew it. In the morning, as we crawled across southern France, every peasant working in the fields turned round, stood solemnly upright, and gave the anti-Fascist salute. They were like a guard of honour, greeting the train mile after mile.

To anyone who thinks of French peasants in normal times, that guard of honour seems like a sheer flight of fantasy. But the year 1936, the year of the Popular Front, of the great sit-in strikes in Paris, of the Spanish Civil War, did not belong to the normal times of European history. Remembering that season when the millennium did not seem an impossible dream, I can imagine that the peasants of the Languedoc did in fact salute the trains going down to the Spanish border. But I also think that Orwell himself was in the exalted and adventurous state of mind that gives an epic significance even to small actions.

Certainly he responded with intense feeling to his first sight of Barcelona, which in December 1936, when he arrived, still had the appearance of a citadel of resurgent anarchism. Going straight from England, he found the aspect of the city 'something startling and overwhelming'.

And it was the aspect of the crowds that was the queerest thing of all. In outward appearance it was a town in which the wealthy classes had practically ceased to exist. Except for a small number of women and foreigners there were no 'well-dressed' people at all. Practically everyone wore rough working-class clothes, or blue overalls or some variant of the militia uniform. All this was queer and moving. There was much in it that I did not understand, in some ways I did not even like it, but I recognized it immediately as a state of affairs worth fighting for. Also I believed that things were as they appeared.

In this atmosphere, to join the militia 'seemed the only conceivable thing to do', and Orwell, since his references were from the I.L.P., joined one of the units sponsored by POUM, the dissident Marxist party which, though he did not know it at the time, was the object of a particularly malignant hatred on the part of the Stalinists, rapidly gaining control in Republican Spain because Russia alone was sending appreciable supplies of arms to the Republican side. Orwell, still politically rather green, was actually sympathetic to the Communists because they seemed to have the most efficient plans for carrying on the war, and at one time he even contemplated joining the International Brigade. Not until he had been in Spain for five months did he get a glimpse, which stayed in his mind for the rest of his life, of the face behind the Communist mask.

Altogether Orwell served about four months on the Aragon and Teruel fronts. Owing to the stalemate which had been reached by this time in Aragon, he was engaged in comparatively little actual fighting, but he was nearly killed in May 1937 when a bullet went through his throat, miraculously missing the carotid artery, and gave his voice its characteristically monotonous tone by permanently damaging his vocal cords. On this occasion he imagined for a few moments that he was dying; the thoughts that flashed through his mind provide an excellent answer to those who have claimed that an urge to suicide drove him to the deadly Hebrides. His first thought, he notes, was 'conventionally enough' for his wife, now in Barcelona. 'My second was a violent resentment at having to leave this world which, when all is said and done, suits me so well. I had time to feel this very vividly. The stupid mischance infuriated me. The meaninglessness of it!'

From what I know of Orwell, he never felt differently to the day of his death, and I am sure that in the last moment of life, with whatever consciousness remained to him, he resented leaving it.

At the same time, though he admits to having been often

afraid, he never avoided the situations which were dangerous to life, and his observations have that vibrant clarity with which one perceives one's surroundings in the moments of peril when time slows down and everything takes on a preternatural sharpness of outline. He describes conditions at the front, the daily boredom, the occasional excitement of patrols and attacks, the filth and the cold, and does it better than most men who have written on war, but what he remembers with most warmth is the unique sense of comradeship and equality which he experienced in those early months of fighting on the government side. For this reason he saw his time at the front as 'a kind of interregnum in my life', different from anything that had gone before and probably from anything that would happen afterwards.

I had dropped more or less by chance into the only community of any size in Western Europe where political consciousness and disbelief in capitalism were more normal than their opposites. Up here in Aragon one was among tens of thousands of people, mainly though not entirely of working-class origin, all living at the same level and mingling on terms of equality. In theory it was perfect equality, and even in practice it was not far from it. There is a sense in which it would be true to say that one was experiencing a foretaste of socialism.

What Orwell had found was a little society in which, once and once only in his life, he could feel completely removed from a situation where there were ruled and rulers; a society which was not – like that of the derelicts – below the class line, but in which he could mingle, without any sense of caste, with men of every origin. He found it 'so different from the rest of my life that already it has taken on the magic quality which, as a rule, belongs only to memories that are years old'.

As Orwell saw afterwards, this was a situation which had happened almost by accident, and which probably owed a great deal to the fact that it had arisen 'among Spaniards, who, with their innate decency and their ever-present anarchistic tinge, would make even the opening stages of socialism tolerable if they had the chance'. It would not continue once the 'enormous game' of world-power politics moved into the Iberian Peninsula. Later events disappointed Orwell, but they did not disillusion him with what he had seen in the beginning. In June 1937 he could still write to Cyril Connolly, from the sanatorium where he was convalescing from his throat wound, 'I have seen wonderful things, and at last really believe in socialism, which I never did before.'

If Orwell's experiences in Spain brought him for the first and last time the kind of acceptance into a casteless comradeship of working men which he had always desired, they also introduced him to the kind of political caste system – the rule of the party elite – which in his later novels took the place of the socially organized caste system he had known in England and, on a more intensified scale, in Burma.

When the Spanish Civil War first broke out it seemed as though the class system had been given a geographical shape, so that the old ruling class was safely behind the Fascist lines, and the workers and their friends on the Republican side could proceed to create a society in which caste differences would no longer exist. Something like a social revolution did actually occur in Catalonia, when the industrial workers took over the factories and the peasants seized the large estates. But history has not yet produced any revolution that failed to create a new class system. In Spain a number of forces soon combined against the revolutionary society which Orwell had observed when he reached Barcelona in December 1936. Because of their peculiar relation to Russia, the only source of arms for the Republican side, the Communists moved towards a position of power; in order to ensure success they assumed an anti-revolutionary line which appealed to the remnants of the propertied classes. The result was a triple reconstruction of the caste system, militarily with the formation of an officer corps, politically with the consolidation of the Communist Party and its private police organization into a ruling elite, and socially in the re-emergence of the middle class, as Orwell found when he returned to Barcelona in April 1937, after several months on the Aragon front. 'The change in the aspect of the crowds was startling. The militia uniform and the blue overalls had almost disappeared; everyone seemed to be wearing the smart summer suits in which Spanish tailors specialize. Fat prosperous men, elegant women and sleek cars were everywhere.'

But more sinister things were happening in the political field. It is in the nature of any totalitarian party to eliminate its own heretics first, and so the Communist Party set out to make an example of the heterodox Marxists of the POUM by the double process of vilification and physical extermination. As we have seen, Orwell was by accident involved in this persecuted group. *Homage to Catalonia* takes on darker tones as he describes the internecine war in Barcelona, and particularly the period when he stood guard on the roof of a cinema above the barricaded streets in May 1937, during the fighting between the Communists and the police on one side and the Anarchists and the POUM on the other. After he had been sent to the Teruel front and had come back wounded at the end of May, he found the threat of political terror brooding over the city.

It is not easy to convey the nightmare atmosphere of that time – the peculiar uneasiness produced by rumours that were always changing, by censored newspapers and the constant pressure of armed men. . . . It was as though some huge evil intelligence were brooding over the town.

And then the storm broke, POUM was suppressed, its members and supporters were hunted down, and Orwell suddenly realized what Continental novelists like Koestler and Silone were writing about when he was forced, like one of their characters, to live for a short time the life of a hunted man, a secretive, double life. 'It was an extraordinary, insane existence. . . . By night we were criminals, but by day we were prosperous English visitors – that was our pose, anyway.'

The lessons about totalitarian police methods which he learned during those days on the run, and the lessons about totalitarian distortions of history which he afterwards absorbed when he came to study the Communist accounts of what happened in Catalonia during those early months of May and June 1937, stayed in his mind and helped to shape both *Animal Farm* and *Nineteen Eighty-Four*. From this point onward the organized political elite began to take the place of a socially defined upper class in the vision of a caste world which shaped his works of fiction.

Yet the final effect of *Homage to Catalonia* is, strangely enough, not sombre. The shadows of the latter days cannot overcome the radiance of clear colours that glow in the impressionistic prose, vigorous as Spanish revolutionary posters, which portrays the most dramatic moments. There are many such moments, but for Orwell the most vivid memory of all was that of the Italian militiaman who spontaneously shook his hand at the Lenin Barracks in Barcelona on the day before he joined the militia. He began his book with it and returned to it six years later in his essay 'Looking Back on the Spanish Civil War'.

When I remember – oh, how vividly! – his shabby uniform and fierce, pathetic, innocent face, the complex side issues of the war seem to fade away and I see clearly that there was at any rate no doubt as to who was in the right. In spite of power politics and journalistic lying, the central issue of the war was the attempt of people like this to win the decent life which they knew to be their birthright.

Homage to Catalonia is in its way an elegy on men like this once seen and never forgotten Italian, but it is not a lament for their ideals. In 'Looking Back on the Spanish Civil War' Orwell quotes a poem he wrote about that strange meeting. The last two verses, clumsy yet astonishingly tender, might be taken as a lyrical summary of all that he learned from the Spanish Civil War:

> Your name and your deeds were forgotten
> Before your bones were dry,
> And the lie that slew you is buried
> Under a deeper lie;
>
> But the thing that I saw in your face
> No power can disinherit;
> No bomb that ever burst
> Shatters the crystal spirit.

10

Homage to Catalonia ends on a vibrantly lyrical note, but its last words are not of Spain; they are of England, and they express all of Orwell's love for the country he had known in his childhood, and all his fears for its future. He describes crossing the Channel after his flight from Barcelona, and the impression – shared by almost everyone on returning from the Continent – of the extraordinary sleekness of the southern English landscape.

The industrial towns were far away, a smudge of smoke and misery hidden by the curve of the earth's surface. Down here it was still the England I had known in my childhood: the railway cuttings smothered in wild flowers, the deep meadows where the great shining horses browse and meditate, the slow-moving streams bordered by willows, the green bosoms of the elms, the larkspurs in the cottage gardens; and then the huge peaceful wilderness of outer London, the barges on the miry river, the familiar streets, the posters telling of cricket matches and Royal weddings, the men in bowler hats, the pigeons in Trafalgar Square, the red buses, the blue policemen – all sleeping the deep, deep sleep of England, from which I somtimes fear that we shall never wake till we are jerked out of it by the roar of bombs.

This final sardonic twist to the lyrical ending seems to contain all the dilemmas and agonies of Orwell's later years. For it was the very qualities which made England unconscious of its perils that were dear to him – the gentleness of its people, the sleepy beauty of its countryside, the decency of its traditions. On the other hand, his experience in Spain had made him aware for the first time of the kind of forces which were loose in Europe, and which had to be resisted if anything good from the past were to be retained in the new technological age to which humanity seemed irrevocably condemned. At the same time, he recognized that dangers might come from within as well as without; that, as he remarked in *The Road to Wigan Pier,* 'the machine civilization is *here*, and it can only be criticized from the inside, because all of us are inside it'.

The novel in which Orwell explores this whole territory of past versus present, or archaistic nostalgia versus a realistic acceptance of a world one does not particularly like, is *Coming Up for Air*. It was published only a few months before the outbreak of the Second World War, which its hero, George Bowling, prophesied as relentlessly as Gordon Comstock, though with none of Comstock's joy at the prospect of the falling bombs. It was written largely in Marrakesh during the winter of 1938-9. At the beginning of 1938 Orwell had been contemplating a trip to India, where, as in Spain, history was on the move during those late years of the thirties; but, doubtless as a result of the privations he had endured in Spain, he was taken seriously ill, and it was discovered that for the past decade at least he had been suffering from undiagnosed tuberculosis. He spent several months in a sanatorium in Kent, and then went for a winter of recuperation in Morocco. Apart from a disjointed impressionistic essay entitled 'Marrakesh' which John Lehmann published in *New Writing*, this interlude provided no experience that Orwell later used in his writing, and I cannot remember more than two or three passing references in his conversation, from which I gathered that he found the country extremely dull in comparison with Burma or Spain. Most of the time he appears to have been involved with the writing of *Coming Up for Air*.

This is the only one among Orwell's novels which appears to have been affected by an actual meeting with another writer. On his way to Spain at the end of 1936, he paid a visit to Henry Miller in Paris. Miller was then at the height of his form as a writer, and seemed more important as a literary artist than he appears thirty years afterwards. But it was less the character of his writing than his point of view, his philosophical irresponsibility, that fascinated Orwell.

What most intrigued me about him was to find that he felt no interest in the Spanish War whatever.... He could understand anyone going there for purely selfish motives, out of curiosity for instance, but to mix oneself up in such things *from a sense of obligation* was sheer stupidity. In any case, my ideas about combating fascism, defending democracy, etc., etc., were all baloney. Our civilization was destined to be swept away and replaced by something so different that we should scarcely regard it as human – a prospect that did not bother him.

Even Orwell's experiences in Spain did not dim the impression of his meeting with Miller, and just before the Second World War began in 1939 he started to write a long and rather rambling critical essay, 'Inside the Whale', which surveys most of the trends of the thirties, but all the time circulates around his own fascination with Miller's deliberate passivism. Miller was important and worthy of respect, he decided, because he neither ignored nor embraced what was going on in the modern world. 'He is fiddling while Rome is burning, and, unlike the enormous majority of people who do this, fiddling with his face towards the flames.'

The war began before Orwell had completed 'Inside the Whale', and there was a curiously fatalistic tone to his assessment, late in 1939, of the course of events. He saw the war as a stage in the break-up of the old liberal–Christian culture in which he himself had been reared, and he made a prophecy which later he was to work out in fictional detail in *Nineteen Eighty-Four*: 'Almost certainly we are moving into an age of totalitarian dictatorship – an age in which freedom of thought will be at first a deadly sin and later on a meaningless abstraction. The autonomous individual is going to be stamped out of existence.'

This was one of those characteristically extreme statements which reveal the contradictions within Orwell's point of view on such matters. His attitude resembled that of those advocates of determinism who always act as if free-will were a reality. He believed that any objective analysis of the world situation in 1940 could lead only to the most pessimistic conclusions, yet his actions negated his assertions. 'Everything one writes now', he remarked to Cyril Connolly while he was working on *Coming Up for Air*, 'is overshadowed by this ghastly feeling that we are rushing towards a precipice and, though we shan't actually prevent ourselves or anyone else from going over, must put up some sort of fight.' So, when the war began, he did not retreat into Miller-like passivism, but tried to enrol in any branch of the armed services that might take a man with ailing lungs, and eventually turned – at least for the duration – into a shrill critic of those who defended the attitude he had accepted as reasonable on Miller's part in 1940. Even *Nineteen Eighty-Four*, in this context, must be regarded as warning rather than prophetic acceptance, as an eleventh-hour call in the face of what its author regarded only as the possible.

The truth is that neither Orwell's quixotic nature nor his inherited Anglo-Indian traditions would allow him to take a passive view of the trends which he saw engulfing the world in the late thirties. Miller's philosophic irresponsibility had nevertheless the same kind of fascination for him as Mr Warburton's immorality for Dorothy Hare in *A Clergyman's Daughter*. *Coming Up for Air* is largely – though not entirely – devoted to a consideration of this question, and the hero, George Bowling, although he puts forward many Orwellian ideas, differs from his creator in being a kind of natural Millerite who has never read Miller, conscious of what is happening in the world but resolutely refusing to become engaged. To keep alive in war and in whatever horrors may come after war: that is George Bowling's innermost urge.

Coming Up for Air is a first-person novel, the monologue of an insurance man with a mind just a little too inquiring and perceptive for his own happiness. George Bowling is, as he puts it, a fat man with a thin man inside him. Externally he is one of Orwell's Panza-like figures, the final development of the succession represented by Mr Warburton and by the boozily cynical commercial traveller Flaxman in *Keep the Aspidistra Flying*. He is a big-bellied, red-faced man with a nagging wife and a dirty mind, a huckster's instinct and a taste for earthy pleasures; he seems to belong by nature to the postcard world of Donald McGill. But, like all of Orwell's heroes, he lives a double life, and it is the thin man inside him who starts looking at fat George Bowling's life and doubting its value, and who starts him off on the quixotic little journey which unites the rather fragile plot of the novel.

George Bowling begins life as a country boy in the Oxfordshire town of Lower Binfield, which figures in the tramps' peregrinations of *Down and Out in Paris and London*. His father is a small tradesman, a seed merchant slowly ruined by chainstore competition; in his case death just wins by a neck the race with bankruptcy. George starts out as a grocer's assistant, but in 1914 the earthquake of the war throws him up into the officer class, he becomes a low-grade executive in an insurance firm, improves his social position a little by marrying a rabbit-faced girl from a decayed Anglo-Indian family, and settles down to the dreary realities of suburban life in the kind of jerry-built housing estate that suits his income and his status. In other words, to all outward appearance he is a typical member of the British lower middle class, not quite a gentleman but by no means a prole. Yet underneath the bluff, corpulent exterior lurks the consciousness of the thin man, who is well-read, politically informed, and as much aware as his creator of the nasty things that are happening in the modern world.

As a character Bowling does not fit into the ordinary conventions of fiction. Sometimes he seems intended as a type of his class and period, at other times he is little more than his creator's voice, spouting the ideas Orwell has already expressed in *The Road to Wigan Pier*, and it would be easy for any critic to expose him – according to the rules of the game of novel-writing – as a kind of literary Frankenstein's monster whose various organs do not fit together particularly well, and whose history is somewhat artificially manipulated to explain the more puzzling features of his make-up. To give only one example, Bowling is lost for two whole years by the War Office while he serves as O.C. of a dump of fifteen tins of bully beef on the West Coast; this allows boredom to drive him into reading, and this in turn arouses his curiosity so that in the end he has absorbed, as well as a great deal of rubbish, all of Orwell's favourite books written up to 1918, including *The Picture of*

Dorian Gray. But the odd thing about Bowling is that, like Don Quixote, he soon wins his way into our minds as a kind of probable improbability, and once we have made that acceptance, his monologue immediately takes on a consistency of its own. We realize that we are in the mind of an original, who speaks to us in Orwell's most vividly colloquial and imagistic prose, and who has a love for the surface of the earth and an eye to the ulterior significance of its details.

One of Bowling's particular characteristics is his power to build up structures of associative thought out of visual images. He stops his car out in the country to look at the primroses on a March day. He takes in all the elements of the spring landscape. But it is the smoking embers of a tramp's fire that bring them into focus and create a meaningful experience out of them.

It's curious that a red ember looks more alive, gives you more of a feeling of life, than any living thing. There's something about it, a kind of intensity, a vibration – I can't think of the exact words. But it lets you know you're alive yourself. It's the spot in the picture that makes you notice everything else.

It is this experience that makes George Bowling finally decide on the journey into the past which is the subject of *Coming Up for Air*. But this is already two-thirds of the way through the novel, and the primary experience which sets the whole train of events going takes place the day before, when Bowling is walking down the Strand, thinking about the war which he is sure will start in a couple of years and about the unpleasant state of affairs it is likely to leave behind. He sees a newspaper poster announcing the postponement of the wedding of that forgotten monarch King Zog of Albania. By a positively Proustian train of associations, involuntary memory is released, and even as he strolls fatly down towards Charing Cross on a cold day in 1938, he is back in Lower Binfield on a Sunday morning thirty-eight years ago, a small boy listening to the choirmen in the church bellowing about Og the King of Bashan, with the musty smell of powdered corpses hanging in the air.

The second part of *Coming Up for Air*, which takes up

almost half the book, switches a telescopic focus on to the first conscious days of George Bowling's childhood, exploring a tiny shop world smelling of sainfoin and brings his life forward again to 1938, when 'in every shipyard in the world they're riveting up the battleships for another war'.

Lower Binfield is a place where, in memory, 'it was summer all the year round', and life seemed to go on 'like some kind of natural process'. Just as nature is not necessarily kind, so life in Lower Binfield was not all joy and happiness; people were poor, they died of avoidable sicknesses, they went slowly downhill in business, and if, like George Bowling's father, they tried to live according to some standard of decency in their dealings with the world, they were just as liable to suffer as the villains. But it was still a world with a different tempo from the 1930s, and if there were few water closets and fewer bathrooms and the dustbins smelt powerfully and the bluebottles buzzed around the house unmolested, well, 'Which would you sooner listen to, a bluebottle or a bombing plane?'

The most vivid of George Bowling's memories of childhood are all somehow connected with fishing, and the accounts of expeditions to farm pools and country-house lakes and to the Thames itself are the best pages of *Coming Up for Air*. To George Bowling the experiences they describe were so joyful and so intense that even thirty years afterwards they seemed symbolic of a vanishing and a better way of life.

As soon as you think of fishing you think of things that don't belong to the modern world. The very idea of sitting all day under a willow tree beside a quiet pool – and being able to find a quiet pool to sit beside – belongs to the time before the war, before the radio, before aeroplanes, before Hitler. There's a kind of peacefulness even in the names of English coarse fish. Roach, rudd, dace, bleak, barbel, bream, gudgeon, pike, chub, tench. They're solid kind of names. The people who made them up hadn't heard of machine-guns, they didn't live in terror of the sack or spend their time eating aspirins, going to the pictures and wondering how to keep out of the concentration camp.

Fishing not only provides George Bowling with his best and

freshest memories. It also gives him the focus of personal myth: a pool hidden in the woods and full of great dark fish seen once in boyhood. The second time he went near the pool he was tempted away by a girl and enjoyed his first sexual experience – a different kind of entry into darkness – in the long grass on the other side of the copse. Yet he never doubts that the pool and the fish are still waiting for him, and in an obscure way it seems that if he can only return to that dark glade and draw up whatever its waters offer, he will gain a fulfilment which his life has so far not provided.

George Bowling's rebellion against his world is a smaller one than that of Flory or Comstock. The plan of it crystallizes in his mind after he has attended a Left Book Club meeting in his suburb of West Bletchley and has looked into the mind of the anti-Fascist speaker and seen his vision of faces being smashed by hammers in 'the hate world, the slogan world' that lies in the future. And the next day, out in the country, watching the glow in the tramp's fire, he decides to make a small escape and spend a secret week in Lower Binfield, away from the modern world and fears of the future, away from the insurance office and the nagging wife, soaking up the peace he remembers, coming up for air. Above all, there will be the pool. 'I thought of it in the dark place among the trees, waiting for me all those years. And the huge black fish still gliding round it. Jesus! If they were that size thirty years ago, what would they be like now?'

As anyone who knows his Proust will have anticipated, the romantic journey back into the past is a disillusionment from beginning to end. 'Progress' has engulfed Lower Binfield as it has engulfed the rest of England. Bowling has difficulty finding the town of his childhood amidst the sprawling factories and housing estates. His old home, with its fascinating smells of seedsman's goods, has been turned into an arty tea-shop. The girl with whom he lay in the long grass has sagged away into a shapeless hag who, to his relief, does not recognize the fat man he has become. The dark pond in the secret copse has long been drained and turned into a dump for tin cans; what happened to the great fish nobody knows. Bowling's attempt to escape for even a week from his own world is totally frustrated, and his visit to Lower Binfield ends in a fine piece of Orwellian grotesquerie, when a British plane drops a bomb by accident on the town and causes ahead of time the first casualties of the coming war. Driving furiously back to the suburbs, he develops a mood of almost exalted pessimism:

The bad times are coming, and the streamlined men are coming too. What's coming afterwards I don't know. It hardly even interests me. I only know if there's anything you care a curse about, better say good-bye to it now, because everything you've ever known is going down, down into the muck, with the machine-guns rattling all the time.

The tunnel that leads to the nightmare world of *Nineteen Eighty-Four* is open already in Orwell's mind.

But for George Bowling even the dignity of philosophic pessimism is not possible. Returning home, he is accused by his wife of having gone away with another woman. Knowing that the story of his romantic attempt to escape will not be believed, he realizes that he will have to take his medicine. 'The old life in Lower Binfield, the war and the after-war, Hitler, Stalin, bombs, machine-guns, food queues, rubber truncheons – it was fading out, all fading out. Nothing remained except a vulgar low-down row in a smell of old mackintoshes.'

Like all his predecessors, the hero of *Coming Up for Air* has concluded that there is now no way out from the prison of one's class or one's time into the freedom of an idiosyncratic self. And, like them, he pays a penalty. The great dark fish will never swim again in the pool of his mind. *Coming Up for Air* has been called a conservative book. But conservatism implies a hope of preserving the good things of the past. Bowling sees them all being swept away in the tide of the future. At the same time, the book contains none of the Socialist idealism which had survived Orwell's Spanish experience to be recorded in *Homage to Catalonia*. Left without illusions about the past or hopes for the future, George Bowling seems to retreat into the narrow

present, where we can assume that, as he has persistently told
us, he will keep alive longer than most other people. Perhaps
it is this central toughness which we sense in George Bowling
that provides the equation mark in the Orwellian contradiction
which *Coming Up for Air* shows more strikingly than most of
his books, manifest in the contrast between its extraordinary
vitality of manner and its moral which implies the defeat of
life. Life is always defeated, because death exists. But it is
always there to pose the challenge anew.

II

ORWELL'S essentially didactic approach has always made it
difficult to establish in his case the kind of distinctions between
'creative' and 'non-creative' writing which literary scholars
pursue with such absurd assiduousness. Quite unashamedly he
used his novels to work out his political and moral ideas, and
he would have considered it dishonest to do otherwise. But at
the same time his imagination played just as lambently and un-
predictably over his journalistic and critical writings as it did
over his fiction. If he himself established any kind of hierarchy
within his own writing, it was one of quality and craftsmanship
rather than genre; he rejected those books, like *A Clergyman's
Daughter* and *Keep the Aspidistra Flying*, which he had written
in haste, and prized those, like *Animal Farm*, over which – as
he put it – he had *sweated*. Mere inventiveness, which in practice is what critics mean when they use the word 'creativity',
did not seem to him important in comparison with stylistic
purity, the exact arrangement of words, and he wisely took
much more pride in a good critical essay than in an indifferent
piece of fiction.

In two essays which contain some of the most astute critical
observations yet made on Orwell, John Wain has contended
that Orwell's work should be considered – as a Renaissance
critic might have done – according to its 'kind' rather than, as

modern critics are inclined to do of anything that comes their way, according to 'genre'.

The 'kind' to which Orwell's work belongs is polemic. All of it, in whatever form – novels, essays, descriptive sketches, volumes of autobiography – has the same object: to implant in the reader's mind a point of view, often about some definite, limited topic ... but in any case about an issue over which he felt it was wrong not to take sides.

Mr Wain proceeds to argue that, since Orwell's ideas meant so much to him, and really formed the central core of his work, we must do him the justice of taking them seriously; he upbraids those who have been so bemused by Orwell's extraordinary character and dramatic life that they have tended to judge everything he wrote in terms of his personal eccentricities.

It is a salutary warning, and later in this book I shall follow it to the extent of presenting Orwell's ideas as the products of a philosophy of life which, if not logically consistent, has at least a high degree of balance and cohesion. Yet it seems to me that even Orwell's philosophy is essentially personal, the rationalization of a series of highly idiosyncratic reactions to experience. When we consider his novels, or even those autobiographical works which, no matter how many masks they wear, still seem so intensely characteristic of the man who wrote them, we cannot escape from the close interconnexion between ideas and personality, and in this context the question whether it is the original Eric Blair or the new self George Orwell we are dealing with is not very important. With no author, in fact, do contemporary critical warnings against the personal heresy and the intentional fallacy seem more irrelevant than they do when one is discussing Orwell. It is always impossible to escape the intentions of a polemicist, which is why no New Critic has ever tackled either Swift or Dickens effectively, while one cannot evade the personality of a writer who is always intent, as Orwell was, on presenting his ideas in terms of his own experience. At times, indeed, his works obviously go, as all good literature does, past intention, and he would not be a successful polemicist if he were not able to see beyond his personal reactions and generalize from them. Idea – form – intention – emotional state: none of them can be ignored if we set out to achieve a balanced view of Orwell's writing, and particularly of any writing he did after 1936, the year when he acquired a political faith and at the same time – though not necessarily as a consequence – made a major advance towards literary maturity in *Homage to Catalonia*.

This digression into the nature of Orwell's writing may seem to belong more properly to the final part of this book, where I am concerned with questions of form and kind. I make it at this point because nothing less than a recognition of the importance of the polemical element in Orwell's later writing will explain adequately the course of his work and the development of his master theme after *Coming Up for Air* appeared, a few months before the war whose nearness had obsessed both George Bowling and his creator. It is not that there is any real breach of continuity. *Nineteen Eighty-Four* could very well be interpreted as the amplification of a vision of the future already adumbrated in *Coming Up for Air*. But there is a shifting of focus and direction in the later fictional works, *Animal Farm* and *Nineteen Eighty-Four*, which is related to the different nature of Orwell's experience after the outbreak of the Second World War and also, I think, to the changes of inner climate which made the Orwell one knew in the forties seem so different from the Blair his earlier friends remembered.

For more than six years, from the end of 1938 to early 1945, Orwell published neither fiction nor any important autobiographical writing, and even in terms of actual work there was a gap of more than four years between the termination of *Coming Up for Air* early in 1939 and the commencement of *Animal Farm* some time in 1943. Yet these were not wasted years for him, even as a writer. Nearly half the pieces in his *Collected Essays* were first published between 1939 and 1943, and almost all the others in this rather massive volume appeared between 1944 and 1947. To these eight busy years, in other words, belongs virtually all the critical writing Orwell considered important enough to preserve. All this he did, it must be remembered, while he was still working either at the B.B.C. or editorially at *Tribune* and while he was allowing at least part of his spare time to be consumed by a series of 'causes', from the Home Guard to the Freedom Defence Committee. His life was also expanding in other ways, for it was during this period that he ceased to be a real solitary, and though he never became a truly gregarious man, at least he now felt himself accepted on his own terms and built up that extraordinary variety of friendships which mellowed his final years. All these forms of action seemed to stimulate each other, and doubtless they were all stimulated by the atmosphere of the time, for the war years and the period immediately after peace, up to about the time when Orwell left for the Hebrides, were much more lively in literature and politics than the period from 1948 or 1949 down to the present day.

In the case of Orwell it was not merely that he worked with immense energy and produced a great quantity of writings of various kinds. There was an extraordinary change in quality, which had been foreshadowed by *Homage to Catalonia*, also the product of a period of life in a peculiarly stimulating atmosphere. Orwell's expository writing became steadily clearer and more flexible, and his critical powers, first demonstrated impressively in the long 1939 essay on Charles Dickens, were inspired and informed by an awareness which he would call political, but which – seen in the perspective of the years – seems rather to have been moral in essence. Orwell was always a moralist, even at Eton if one is to accept Cyril Connolly's account of him in *Enemies of Promise*, and when he acquired political opinions they merely channelled his moralism, but by no means tamed it. The test always came when political expediency or party interests clashed with his ideas of what might be true or decent; most often – and always in his later years – it was party interests that he let go in favour of decency.

The influence of this moral–political awareness can be seen not merely in an increased sensitivity to the social and ethical dimensions of a book or a situation he might be discussing, but also in the directness of writing it began to foster, even when he turned back again near the end of the war from essays to fiction. He tried to write, as he put it, 'less picturesquely and more exactly'. And he gave a more definitely political character than before to the theme of caste and alienation which re-emerges, in varying forms, in all his late works, beginning with *Animal Farm*.

'*Animal Farm*', said Orwell in 1947, 'was the first book in which I tried, with full consciousness of what I was doing, to fuse political purpose and artistic purpose in one whole.' He succeeded admirably, and produced a book so clear in intent and writing that the critic is usually rather nonplussed as to what he should say about it; all is so magnificently there, and the only thing that really needs to be done is to place this crystalline little book into its proper setting.

Conciseness of form and simplicity of language are the qualities which immediately strike one on opening *Animal Farm* after having read Orwell's earlier works of fiction. The fable is about a third the length of *Keep the Aspidistra Flying*, though the events of which it tells are much more complicated, and it is written in a bare English, uncluttered by metaphor, which contrasts strongly with both the elaborately literary diction of *Burmese Days* and the racy but sometimes over-rich narrative style of *Coming Up for Air*.

Mr Jones, of the Manor Farm, had locked the hen-houses for the night, but was too drunk to remember to shut the pop-holes. With the ring of light from his lantern dancing from side to side, he lurched across the yard, kicked off his boots at the back door, drew himself a last glass of beer from the barrel in the scullery, and made his way up to bed, where Mrs Jones was already snoring.

So it begins, and so it continues to the end, direct, exact and sharply concrete, letting events make their own impacts and stimulating the creation of mental pictures, so that one remembers the book as a series of lively visual images held together by a membrane of almost transparent prose.

There was no doubt in Orwell's mind about his intention in writing *Animal Farm*. He felt that the English in 1943 were allowing their admiration for the military heroism of the Russians to blind them to the faults of the Communist regime, and he also believed that the Communists were using their position as unofficial representatives of Russia in England to prevent the truth from being known, as they had done in Spain. *Animal Farm* was meant to set his compatriots thinking again.

The book succeeded because it created within the dimension of a fable a perfect and self-consistent microcosm. There was nothing very original about the basic idea of a community of animals acting like men, which had been used about fifteen hundred years before by the anonymous Indian author of that extraordinary collection of Indian political fables, the *Panchatantra*. But, like the author of the *Panchatantra*, Orwell gave his work freshness by introducing that peculiar blend of humour, incongruity and apparent candour which creates in the reader a willingness to suspend disbelief and to transfer himself in mind into the changed dimensions of a world where the pursuits of men can be seen dispassionately because it is animals which are following them.

Orwell liked animals, though he detested the sentimental British animal cult. In his world-picture animals, children, oppressed people stood on one side, and the oppressors, whether they were farmers, school-teachers, sahibs or party bosses, on the other. In *Burmese Days*, as I have shown, the relationship of Asians to animals is quite clear, and later on in *Nineteen Eighty-Four* there were to be several identifications of proles with animals. 'Proles and animals are free,' runs one of the Party slogans, and O'Brien, Winston Smith's tormentor, voices the dogma of the Inner Party when he says that 'the proletarians . . . are helpless, like the animals. Humanity is the Party. The others are outside – irrelevant.' On the other hand, for Winston in his rebellion, an inestimable power seems to lie in 'the animal instinct . . . that was the force that would tear the Party to pieces'.

In *Animal Farm* it is the outsiders, the helpless ones, who rise in rebellion and destroy the power of the oppressors, personified in the drunken Mr Jones. The idea of class division which in earlier books comes very near to the conception of two nations, rich and poor, is here modified to suggest two kinds – men and animals. 'All men are enemies. All animals are comrades,' says the prophetic old boar Major in his great oration shortly before the uprising.

The original division between man and animal corresponds to the old social division between hereditary upper and lower castes or classes which Orwell represented in his earlier works. But his experiences in Spain had led him to delve into the history of the development of power-structures during revolutions, and on this subject he was now as knowledgeable as anyone outside the ranks of specialist historians. He had learned that social caste could be replaced by political caste, and *Animal Farm* is a study in fable form of this process at work in a minuscule world which we can observe as closely as a community of ants under the glass lid of a formicarium.

The history of the revolution betrayed in the animal world is based, therefore, partly on what Orwell had seen of the Communist usurpation of power in Spain and partly on what he had read of the Russian Revolution and its abortion by the Bolsheviks. But his anti-communism does not mean that he is on the side of the traditional ruling class, represented by men. On the contrary, when the animals originally rise in revolt against the tyrannical Farmer Jones, he wins our sympathies for them, and we remain on their side throughout their subsequent struggles with humanity, accepting the fact that no matter what the pigs may do, no animal wants to be ruled again by Farmer Jones or his kind.

Yet from the very first day of insurrection it is evident that a new elite is replacing the vanished human rulers – the elite of the pigs, who are the equivalent of the Party. Immediately they arrogate privileges to themselves – first a monopoly of milk, then of apples. They become supervisors, while the other animals, with the sole exception of that arch anti-collectivist the cat, do the work. The pigs, it should be noted, are united when it is a question of defending their rights as an elite against the other animals. The struggle between Snowball and Napoleon is in fact a struggle within the party elite whose final result, whichever had won, would have been the increased consolidation and centralization of power in the hands of the pigs. This is what happens when Napoleon outmanoeuvres Snowball and immediately after his expulsion initiates the career of purges, atrocities and deepening tyranny that reproduces in minuscule the history of the Russian Revolution from 1917 to the 1940s.

At no point in *Animal Farm* does Orwell change his side. Though it is a third-person story, as all fables are, the point of view of the reader is always nearest to that of the unprivileged animals, and perhaps nearest of all to that of Benjamin, the sad and cynical old donkey who sides with no factions and always says that 'life would go on as it had always gone on – that is, badly'. Yet despite his exposure of the mounting iniquities committed by the pig elite, Orwell never falls into the error of suggesting that the farmers are any better. On the contrary, there is really nothing to choose, and the book ends in that fantastic scene in which the pigs entertain the neighbouring farmers in a social gathering, and the other animals, looking in, see a quarrel break out over cheating at cards.

Twelve voices were shouting in anger, and they were all alike. No question, now, what had happened to the faces of the pigs. The creatures outside looked from pig to man, and from man to pig, and from pig to man again; but already it was impossible to say which was which.

In other words, old and new tyrannies belong to the same family; authoritarian governments, whether they are based on the codes of old social castes or on the rules of new political elites, are basically similar and present similar dangers to human welfare and to liberty. For the interests of oppressors are identical; as Mr Pilkington jests at a more peaceful stage in the banquet, 'If you have your lower animals to contend with, we have our lower classes!'

By transferring the problems of caste division outside a

human setting, Orwell was able in *Animal Farm* to avoid the psychological complications inevitable in a novel, and thus to present his theme as a clear and simple political truth. In the process he left out one element which occurs in all his other works of fiction, the individual rebel caught in the machinery of the caste system. Not until he wrote *Nineteen Eighty-Four* did he elaborate the rebel's role in an *Animal Farm* carried to its monstrously logical conclusions.

12

BETWEEN *Animal Farm* and *Nineteen Eighty-Four* lies that painful document, *Such, Such Were the Joys*. This is the last of Orwell's autobiographical pieces, and the most difficult for the reader to accept, because the writer himself was dealing with those memories which in literary terms he found most intractable.

The exact date when *Such, Such Were the Joys* was completed has never, so far as I know, been revealed, but there is enough evidence to place it fairly closely, and this is important if we wish to relate it to Orwell's other writings. As late as 1938 Orwell found the memories of his schooldays so unpleasant that when Cyril Connolly was writing the chapters on boyhood in *Enemies of Promise*, he said to him: 'I wonder how you can write about St Cyprian's.* It's all like an awful nightmare to me, and sometimes I think I can still taste the porridge.' In *Such, Such Were the Joys* he refers to the events described as being more than thirty years in the past, which would suggest that he was writing at the earliest after 1945, and probably after 1947.

At this period there was a special reason why he should try to relive and to understand his own childhood. As his adopted son Richard developed from a baby into a small boy full of

* St Cyprian's was the actual name of the school which Connolly called St Wulfric's and Orwell called Crossgates.

character, he seemed to be reconsidering his own past, and to be facing the problems which he had left unanswered. He told me once that he did not want to send Richard to a boarding-school when he was very young, as had happened to him. On the other hand, in spite of his socialism, he was not impressed by the results of state education, and felt that while the present system lasted, there might be worse places to which a boy could be sent, when he was old enough, than a good public school. Interpreting these remarks in terms of his own past, I took them to mean that he found Eton more or less endurable, and what went before it unendurable, though he never went into detail with me about his experiences at Crossgates. Significantly, he does not appear to have made any attempt to get *Such, Such Were the Joys* published, and I think he may have felt that its value was therapeutic rather than literary. At last, by writing it all down, he had exorcized the childhood to which in the past he had referred only obliquely in *Burmese Days* and *Keep the Aspidistra Flying*, and more directly but very scantily in those pages of *The Road to Wigan Pier* in which he discussed the roots of the class attitudes he acquired from the environment of his youth.

In England the literature of boarding-schools is almost a genre of its own, and, as a document of ingenious tyranny bearing down on helpless misery, *Such, Such Were the Joys* is likely to remain among the classics of that melancholy form. How much of it was objectively true is hard to determine. Some of those who have written on Orwell found their own preparatory-school days relatively pleasant, and they are therefore inclined to doubt that life at Crossgates can really have been so bad as Orwell claimed; Christopher Hollis and Laurence Brander both take this attitude, but their evidence is useless, since they did not attend St Cyprian's. A closer witness was his sister Avril, who also believed that her brother was laying it on rather too thickly: 'It has been said that Eric had an unhappy childhood. I don't think this was in the least true, although he did give that impression himself when he was grown up.' But even Avril did not see St Cyprian's from the inside.

Cyril Connolly did. Connolly, a more ebullient and extroverted personality than Orwell, was ready to admit that 'St Wulfric's ... did me a world of good', but in factual terms his account runs very close to Orwell's, and suggests that the school was a place of relentless cramming, unashamed snobbery, capricious punishment, and pedagogic filthy-mindedness posing as moral vigilance. It was Orwell's peculiar sensitivity to his position as an impoverished boy among richer, stronger and more self-assured companions that made St Cyprian's the hell he describes. The picture is subjectively true.

Anthony West in his essay on Orwell (really a long *New Yorker* review of the first American edition of *Keep the Aspidistra Flying*) finds in *Such, Such Were the Joys* the sickly roots of *Nineteen Eighty-Four*. What West attempts in his study is, with patent malice, to cut the critical ground from under Orwell's achievement by suggesting that his works can mostly be explained in terms of neurosis. He does not use the actual word, but the persistent choice of adjectives like 'hysterical' and 'perverse' to describe various of Orwell's books, and the references to 'manic violence' and 'generalized sadism', to a relish for 'the murky and the horrible' and 'a remorseless pessimism', make West's meaning clear enough, particularly when he remarks that 'only the existence of a hidden wound' can account for all the features of Orwell's writing which he himself finds distasteful. According to West's interpretation, the clue to everything that is characteristic in Orwell's work is traceable to the reactions of an exceptionally morbid little boy to what may have been a perfectly good school of its kind.

This is carrying biographical criticism to an extreme which nowadays one rarely encounters. If the imputation of neurosis could kill a writer, we would have no further need to trouble ourselves with Swift, Dostoyevsky, Baudelaire, Kafka, Proust or Balzac. In any case, we have to observe once again the necessary caution in approaching a work which Orwell presents to us as autobiographical. For this is obviously an elaborately planned essay. Episodes are carefully constructed and highlighted for emphasis; incidents which took place over a number of years are brought together in obviously artificial arrangements to emphasize what seemed to Orwell in the late 1940s the significant aspects of this period in his life; and all is summarized in the usual passages of didactic reflection. The child experiences, but it is the mind of a man thirty years later which plays over the experiences, selects them and makes them give their message.

A great deal of what Orwell says is obviously imposed by hindsight. It is improbable, for example, that as a child he envisaged the school divided into three castes, with himself as a member of the lowest; he only began to schematize in this way during the last years of his life in Burma. And even when he presents his own thoughts on the subject of guilt at the age of eight, these appear not only exceptionally mature for a child of such an age, but also suspiciously near to the speculations about the awakening of feelings of guilt which he was pursuing at the time in connexion with *Nineteen Eighty-Four*, and which were much influenced by Koestler's *Darkness at Noon*.

He tells us, for example, that on the occasion of his first beating for bed-wetting at Crossgates (he was then eight), he cried because of a

grief which is peculiar to childhood and not easy to convey; a sense of desolate loneliness and helplessness, of being locked up not only in a hostile world but in a world of good and evil where the rules were such that it was actually not possible for me to keep them.... Sin was not necessarily something that you did: it might be something that happened to you.

Far from such thoughts being 'peculiar to childhood', they had been the stock-in-trade of sophisticated Continental writers for many years before Orwell wrote *Such, Such Were the Joys*, and I suggest that they are more important for what they tell us about Orwell's preoccupations with sin during the later 1940s than for anything they may reveal about an early 'hidden wound'. The same, I think, applies to the accounts of headmaster Sim's methods of impressing fragments of knowledge on his pupils' minds by frequent applications of physical punishment; such methods, of course, resemble the elaborate forms of mental conditioning by torture which are used in the Ministry of Love in *Nineteen Eighty-Four*. But I think that here again Orwell recollected them and gave them prominence in *Such, Such Were the Joys* precisely because in writing *Nineteen Eighty-Four* he was concerned with the techniques of teaching by painful experience, and it was natural that he should think back, as all of us do, to incidents within his own experience. The fact that we can find other parallels between Winston Smith's experiences and those of Orwell's childhood does not mean that the incidents in *Nineteen Eighty-Four* are, as Anthony West suggests, 'of an infantile character'; it merely shows that just as Orwell earlier saw the resemblance between the condition of animals and that of oppressed people, so now he saw the resemblance between the child facing the arbitrary rules of an adult world and the bewildered individual locked in the equally arbitrary system of a totalitarian society.

13

Nineteen Eighty-Four is a book that marks the end of a road; in that direction Orwell could have gone no farther, for it not merely culminates but also epitomizes all his earlier novels.

In *Nineteen Eighty-Four* the disciplined elite, which in *Burmese Days* Orwell first showed as a scruffy group of British colonial officials and traders, reaches its final terrifying form as the ruling Inner Party of Oceania, whose ideologues have stripped away all the moral justifications which the old imperialists and the totalitarians of the early twentieth century still maintained, all those at once lofty and despicable arguments that power must in some way be exercised so that a higher good may ensue. The Party now rules to enjoy power – and power alone. But power can only be enjoyed if it is expressed in cruelty and triumph. Says O'Brien, the Thought Police official:

Always, at every moment, there will be the thrill of victory, the sensation of trampling on an enemy who is helpless.... This drama that I have played out with you during seven years will be played out over and over again, generation after generation, always in subtler forms. Always we shall have the heretic at our mercy, screaming with pain, broken up, contemptible – and in the end utterly penitent, saved from himself, crawling to our feet of his own accord. That is the world that we are preparing, Winston. A world of victory after victory, triumph after triumph after triumph: an endless pressing, pressing, pressing upon the nerve of power.

This penitential state, which needs its sinners because it needs its sacrifices, is the final development of the Orwellian caste world. As in *Such, Such Were the Joys*, and as in Orwell's earlier pictures of the class society in England, the system is three-levelled, with the Inner Party at the apex of the pyramid, the Outer Party in the middle, fulfilling the same role as Orwell's own stratum in the English middle class, and the great mass of the proles, eighty-five per cent of the population, at the bottom. At last, the gulf that divides society has become complete and final. Any meaningful contact between Party member and prole has become impossible; they are members not merely of two different nations, but of two different races, for the Party is self-perpetuating even in a biological sense. The isolation of the elite is at last complete, because it is political rather than social, ideological rather than traditional. To destroy even the possibility of an urge to change this rigidly pyramidical society, the Party is rewriting history so that the past shall be dead for ever, and desiccating the language so that the very words which might describe such concepts as freedom, or justice, or decency will no longer exist.

If the structure of class which *Nineteen Eighty-Four* portrays is the ultimate development of the societies portrayed with acute caste-consciousness in Orwell's earlier books, the main character, Winston Smith, is a rebel in whose fate the experiences of the rebels in all the preceding novels are recapitulated. Like them all, he has that questioning turn of mind which his enemies regard as a flaw in character, and which makes him a dissident, at first only in thought, but later in action. Like

Dorothy Hare, he loses faith; like Flory, he is attracted towards what the Party regards as primitive; like Gordon Comstock, he rebels against a world of slogans; like George Bowling, he believes that the past is better than the present; and like the 'I' of the autobiographical books, he seeks in the alien culture of the lower depths a salvation which he cannot possibly find. Like all of them, he follows the *ignis fatuus* of a lost cause, is defeated and captured by his past, and endures the ultimate punishment of losing his inmost vision.

Of all these past anti-heroes, it is Gordon Comstock who comes most alive again in *Nineteen Eighty-Four*. Like Gordon, Winston is a small, sickly man engaged in the profession of manipulating words and ideas, in the service of a political fraud far more colossal than anything the advertising industry of the 1930s had ever dreamed of. Like Gordon, also, he rebels, though it is not against the money god, who has vanished in an age dominated by stark power, but against Big Brother, the Party personified. Like Gordon, he seeks salvation in the lower depths by trying to mingle with the proles, and like him he comes into fatal contact with a girl who stares at him in office corridors, as Rosemary stared at Gordon. He finally meets the girl – Julia – in a country setting which remarkably resembles the copse in which Gordon tried unsuccessfully to make love to Rosemary, and it is Julia who leads him, also by means of sex, into the course of folly which plays into the hands of the Thought Police, and so, unwittingly, she is the agent of the power god just as Rosemary was the agent of the money god in drawing Gordon Comstock back into the ways of conformity.

I emphasize these resemblances to demonstrate that *Nineteen Eighty-Four* is not, as some critics have suggested, a monumental nightmare explicable by the activities of tuberculosis bacilli during the last four years of Orwell's life. It is the culmination of twenty years of writing, and an authentic product, not of the tortured body registered at various sanatoria under the name of Eric Blair, but of the imaginative being who bore the name of George Orwell. Orwell himself said, writing of Dickens in 1939, that 'a writer's literary personality has little or nothing to do with his private character'. Perhaps we must qualify this so far as to say that the literary personality and the private character may share the same experiences, but often they make of them very different things.

What does distinguish *Nineteen Eighty-Four* from the earlier novels, though not from *Animal Farm*, is the imposition of a political framework which is merely foreshadowed in *Coming Up for Air*. This involves not only the transformation of the social class-structure of Orwell's previous novels into a political caste-structure, but also the construction of a negatively ideal political state. For *Nineteen Eighty-Four* is unique among Orwell's books in being a Utopia – a Utopia in negative. And here the basic experience lies not in Orwell's pathological condition, however much this may have darkened tones, but in his adventures in Spain and in the study of totalitarian politics into which this led him.

One of the most important documents in establishing the antecedents of *Nineteen Eighty-Four*, and particularly in showing the kind of reading which Orwell was doing while the novel was taking shape in his mind, is the essay 'Second Thoughts on James Burnham' which appeared in Humphrey Slater's magazine *Polemic* in 1946.

In this essay Orwell relates Burnham's *The Managerial Revolution* to his later book *The Machiavellians*. While Orwell has some shrewd and searching criticism to make of Burnham's general point of view (which I shall return to in attempting to determine Orwell's own attitude), he does present in *Nineteen Eighty-Four* the picture of a society which, in form if not in inner character, closely resembles that prophesied, in an approving tone which Orwell found distasteful, by Burnham in *The Managerial Revolution*. It is a society in which a self-perpetuating elite has taken the place of the older forms of political and social domination and rules over a great slave class, and in which the world is divided into three great states perpetually in conflict over the marginal areas of the earth, but never strong enough to conquer each other completely.

Orwell draws not merely on Burnham; indeed, the book that

influenced him most was Zamyatin's *We*, from which Huxley had already borrowed copiously in writing *Brave New World*. As I have said in my reminiscent introduction, it was after Orwell had obtained a copy of *We*, of which he already knew by hearsay and which he immediately discussed in *Tribune*, that he started work on *Nineteen Eighty-Four*.

In *We*, which appeared first in New York in an English translation, because publication in Russia was forbidden, Zamyatin envisaged an age, almost a millennium ahead, in which the majority of men are subjects of a United State which consists of a number of cities scattered over the earth and isolated by Green Walls and barriers of electrical charges from the rural spaces around and between them. This isolation from a natural environment is deliberate, since the rulers of the United State aim to turn man into a machine, to replace the organic by the inorganic, to provide a synthetic happiness by eliminating everything that can arouse natural passions or personal inclinations. Theoretically, man and woman have ceased to be persons, and, losing their names, they have become 'numbers' or 'unifs'.

All the 'numbers' wear similar clothes, and each carries on the metal plate that identifies him a watch to symbolize the rigid time-schedule to which daily life is subordinated; significantly, the most distinguished literary work that has been preserved from the past is the railway timetable. In the United State all the apartments are built with walls of glass, so that the actions of the 'numbers' are public, and really solitary activity is almost impossible. Only at times of sexual intercourse can the curtains be lowered for brief periods; such intercourse is strictly regulated by a Sexual Bureau, which issues tickets entitling the holders to the use of whatever persons they may choose, since, as a further denial of individuality, all 'numbers' are held to be available to each other. Mechanization enters into every aspect of life; the 'numbers' are nourished by synthetic petroleum foods, and even culture is dehumanized, music being composed by machines and university classes taught by robot professors.

This soulless society is ruled by a dictator called the Benefactor, whose government is periodically endorsed by elections held on the Day of Uniformity. He is supported by a political police, the Guardians, who hover above the city in planes equipped with observation tubes and whose task is facilitated by sensitive membranes which stretch across the streets and pick up conversations. Scientific tortures are used to extract confessions, and criminals are liquidated literally, by means of an electrical machine which reduces them to puddles of colourless water. Informing, even on one's relatives and friends, is considered a sacred duty. All these means are used to support 'the instinct of non-freedom', for, according to the prevailing philosophy of the United State, 'the only means to deliver man from crime is to deliver him from freedom'. Furthermore, loss of freedom is the only way to happiness.

In such a society it is logical that the past should be despised and, as far as possible, eliminated. Making explicit what is implied in almost all Utopian visions – even the positive ones – the rulers of the United State try to erect a perfectly 'crystalline' and immutable order. As D.503, the narrator, remarks, 'The ideal is to be found where nothing *happens*.' Yet the impulses of rebellion remain; even though every manifestation of nature has been eliminated within the Green Walls, the winds still blow clouds overhead, still bring pollen and gossamer to stir the atavistic feelings of the 'numbers'. 'Even in our day,' says D.503, 'one hears from time to time, coming from the bottom, the primitive depths, the echo of the apes.'

It is this lingering resistance to regimentation, shown also in his tendency towards passionate love, that leads D.503 into the sin of overt rebellion. Through a woman who insists on reliving the evil past in secret, who commits such cardinal sins as smoking, wearing skirts and drinking alcohol, he meets a group of conspirators who have established contact with the naked and hairy survivors of free humanity lurking in the forests beyond the Green Wall. The conspirators meet in an old house, from the centuries before the United State, which has been preserved as a museum; this is appropriate, since in

Utopia revolution reverses its process and turns into a movement towards the freedom of the past.

The Green Wall is blown up, and for a time it seems as though the unregenerate instincts of the 'numbers' will reassert themselves. But as *We* comes to an end the Guardians are winning, the leading rebels are tortured and killed, and those who escape death, including D.503, are subjected to a new operation which removes from them the unpredictable faculty of fancy and turns them into automata in human form, devoid of the last vestiges of individuality.

We is indebted in many ways to the Utopias and the somewhat rarer anti-Utopias of the past. One catches echoes of Plato and More, of Cabet and Campanella, of the Wellsian idea that science misused may atrophy mankind and of Dostoyevsky's idea that radical movements end paradoxically in slave societies. Yet *We* gains originality from the fact that Zamyatin was the earliest novelist to place all these fragmentary anticipations into the coherent context of actuality, the context of the very tendencies towards industrial regimentation, towards the closer regulation of daily living, which he saw emerging in the world of the 1920s. Thus *We* is the first novel of literary importance to present a relatively complete vision of the negative results of the realization of Utopia.

Between *We* and *Nineteen Eighty-Four* the resemblances are so close in both detail and structure as to leave little doubt of Zamyatin's direct influence on Orwell, who admitted it freely. Both authors see Utopia as a possible – even a probable – outcome of twentieth-century technological and political developments. Both assume that if this Utopian future ever arrives, it will involve the destruction of the very idea of freedom, the falsification or destruction of history and the sense of the past, and the reduction of culture to a rudimentary and mechanical function. Both envisage the economic structure of Utopia as collectivist and its political structure as a pyramid controlled by an exclusive elite with the help of an efficient police system. Both foresee radical interference in sexual life, and some form of conditioning to make the individual docile and obedient; such conditioning involves the destruction of privacy, the denial of a natural or spontaneous way of living, the systematic destruction of passionate relationships and of any association that might exist outside the state. In both states literature and music are produced by machine, life is run on strict time-schedules, men in helicopters look into windows. In Orwell's Oceania the telescreens in all the rooms enable the citizens to be observed as closely as the 'numbers' are observed through the glass walls of Zamyatin's buildings, and the place of the Guardians is taken by the ubiquitous Thought Police, who also operate by scientific methods of torture. Just as 'fancy' is the great crime in the United State, so 'thought-crime' is the unforgivable felony in Oceania.

Even when we go beyond the societies which Zamyatin and Orwell portray, there are close similarities between the plots of their novels. In each case the hero has, by some accidental circumstance, become conscious of his difference from the general depersonalized herd. D.503 has his hairy hands to remind him of the animal past, and Winston Smith stumbles accidentally on a piece of evidence which makes him aware of the deliberate and systematized falsification of truth in the state of Oceania. For each hero, rebellion is accompanied by a desire for possessive and passionate sexual relations and by a longing to reconstruct the past, symbolized in *We* by the old house where the conspirators meet and in *Nineteen Eighty-Four* by the antique shop in whose upper room Winston and Julia enact their furtive personal rebellion. Finally, each novel ends in defeat for the rebel, and in his punishment according to the spirit of the society in which he is trapped. D.503 is rendered surgically incapable of any further independent thought; Winston is tortured in the gleaming white cells of the Ministry of Love, betrays everything that is precious to him, and emerges a spiritual vestige of a man who waits for death in the cause of the state that has crushed him.

Yet in addition to these many points of resemblance, there are some important differences between *We* and *Nineteen Eighty-Four*. Zamyatin tended to be preoccupied with the mechanical problems which interested him as an engineer, and the statistical-mathematical outlook shapes both the attitude of his Guardians and the character of the society they construct, a crystalline, higher-mathematical order where men become merely figures in gigantic equations. Orwell, on the other hand, did not have a scientific mind, and the abstractions of mathematics made little appeal to him; hence his anti-Utopia is dominated less by technology than by predominantly cultural and psychological means of tyranny.

Again, there is a sharp difference between Zamyatin's calendar of the future and Orwell's. Zamyatin saw his United State a thousand years ahead. Aldous Huxley's 'brave new world', conceived approximately a decade after *We* was completed, lay only six hundred years in the future. Orwell, writing less than thirty years after Zamyatin, shifted his sights even more abruptly; finishing *Nineteen Eighty-Four* in 1948, he represented the final submersion of the human personality in the totalitarian nightmare as only thirty-six years ahead, and the scene as the familiar, shabby London of the immediate post-war years, in which only the vast pyramidal strongholds of the new governmental agencies tower up in menacing indestructibility.

It is this abrupt temporal foreshortening that gives much of its dramatic effectiveness to *Nineteen Eighty-Four*. But what distinguishes it even more strikingly from previous Utopias and even anti-Utopias is that the pretence of providing happiness as a compensation for the loss of freedom is not maintained. Even the synthetic pleasures and comforts promised by Zamyatin and Huxley no longer exist: life is shabby and austere; science is diverted to producing refined instruments of torture; industry feeds a perpetual war that engenders the hatred on which power rests.

The horror of the vision is not merely in its extremity, but also in its immediacy. For the feet that will stamp this vision on human faces, and the faces on which it will be stamped, belong, not to men bred – as in *Brave New World* – out of bottles or to men lobotomized out of consciousness like Zamyatin's 'numbers', but to physiologically unchanged human beings whose minds have become so dominated by mere cultural conditioning that they accept this travesty of existence without question; in a world where language itself has become so changed that the idea of freedom can no longer be expressed, they neither know nor imagine anything different. The elements of this horrific new world Orwell saw already existing in the world around him. His essays for the four or five years before he began writing *Nineteen Eighty-Four* were filled with discussions of the perversion of history and of language as part of a progressive deterioration of political morality throughout the world.

It is the peculiar immediacy of Orwell's vision, and its apparently complete negativeness, that lie at the base of much of the hostility it has aroused among critics who regard it as a kind of travesty of human nature, a statement of pessimism carried to perversity. Such critics tend to regard *Nineteen Eighty-Four* as prophetic in intent and realistic in approach, and they assume that its conclusion not only is unambiguously pessimistic, but also represents the actual opinions of the author. All these assumptions, I suggest, are incorrect; between them they have resulted in an interpretation of *Nineteen Eighty-Four* as crude and misleading in its own way as the widespread opinion that the book is intended merely as a tract against communism.

The first point to remember is that though the primary impulse for *Nineteen Eighty-Four* may have been the experience of politics in action, the urges that carried it forward were literary, and these we can only determine clearly when we determine Orwell's approach as a writer. That approach should by now have become obvious. He was a writer within the moralist tradition, and like all moralists – like Gide and Camus and Swift – he tended to write fables or parables rather than novels. In other words, he was not a realist in the ordinary sense, the sense of Dreiser or even Flaubert, even though his techniques at times appear realistic. In *Nineteen Eighty-Four*, as in his earlier novels, the natural tone of the writing and the verisimilitude of detail may at first mislead one, but Orwell has placed enough signs to put the observant reader very quickly back on the trail. One soon notices, for example, the part played by dreams. Winston is constantly dreaming uncanny dreams which are echoed in events. He has a recurrent dream of a 'golden country'; the spot where he and Julia first become lovers reproduces it down to the last detail of the big fish (descendants of those in *Coming Up for Air*) that swim in the stream across the fields. He dreams of the voice which says: 'We shall meet in the place where there is no darkness'; he realizes later that the voice was that of O'Brien, and not only discovers that O'Brien inexplicably recognizes the phrase, but also finds himself eventually in 'the place where there is no darkness' – the Ministry of Love, where the lights burn day and night in the white cells. The recurrent use of nursery rhymes helps to enhance the dreamlike quality of Winston's adventure, an adventure as fragile and vulnerable as the tiny bit of coral magnified within the glass paper-weight which he treasures as a fragment of the past.

But Winston is a dreamer within a nightmare, for the quality of the world of *Nineteen Eighty-Four* is precisely that, from the looking-glass absurdity of its slogans – War Is Peace, Freedom Is Slavery, Ignorance Is Strength – to the horrors out of recurrent dreams which are perpetrated in Room 101. The most terrifying nightmares are exactly of this nature, combining great verisimilitude with some monstrous dislocation of the world we know, and leaving us trapped and condemned in a setting that is at once completely familiar and abysmally strange.

Orwell, then, has constructed a nightmare which destroys a dream, and his intent in doing so, as Herbert Read has recognized, is satirical. *Nineteen Eighty-Four* is, first of all, a satire on the world of 1948, with its built-in Utopian tendencies, and as such it is often extreme to the point of caricature; the Ministry of Truth is on this level a caricature representation of the great propaganda agencies of the Second World War; Goldstein's account of Oceania a caricature of Marxist historiography; Newspeak a caricature of Basic English; and the beetle-like Party members caricatures of the Socialists whom Orwell had already flayed in *The Road to Wigan Pier*. But the great difficulty Orwell faced in writing *Nineteen Eighty-Four* lay in the fact that his intentions were not purely satirical; he also wanted to issue a warning about a danger in the future, and it is hard to be satirical about the future. One is tempted to be either optimistic or pessimistic; the first carries the danger of romanticism and the second that of melodrama, and it is the false light of melodrama that somewhat distorts the final chapters of *Nineteen Eighty-Four*. Yet even the quality of Grand Guignol that hangs over the doings in Room 101 cannot diminish the revelation Orwell makes at this point. He himself once said of Swift that he possessed 'a terrible intensity of vision, capable of picking out a single hidden truth and then magnifying and distorting it.' Orwell has picked on the hidden truth which Bakunin once knew and which the Marxists have obscured – that the love of power is stronger and more perverting than any material or economic motive. He has magnified and distorted the insight into a vision more frightening than anything in Swift.

But the acquisition of power is also a deprivation, since it cuts a man off from normal human joys and isolates him from his fellows. And so *Nineteen Eighty-Four*, when we have acknowledged and hence exorcized its melodramatic content, takes on a further satirical dimension. For O'Brien, telling the gospel of power, is not speaking merely for some hypothetical future Utopia. He is putting in an extreme and monstrous form the pretensions of all men of power; he is stating the logical consequences of the theory of elites which writers like Burnham and his Machiavellians have posed. In other words, he is a caricature, a monstrosity. We begin to see, as Winston does intermittently during his conditioning by torture, that O'Brien and the order he represents are insane, and our recognition of this fact lasts longer than Winston's. O'Brien's boast of an eternity of power reminds one of Hitler's boasts of the millennial Reich, which to victims in the concentration camps probably seemed at times tragically real. But only three years before Orwell wrote *Nineteen Eighty-Four* the millennial Reich had fallen away into ashes.

Furthermore, Orwell's own extra-fictional statements by no means suggest that he consistently believed, with O'Brien, that the rule of a power elite could in fact be permanent. The moments of unadulterated pessimism, such as he showed in 'Inside the Whale', are rare. By 1941 he was asserting that 'when it comes to the pinch, human beings are heroic', and despite the fact that he used Burnham's vision of the future as a suitable fictional frame, he denied it in 1946 as a literal portrait of the future. 'The huge, invincible, everlasting slave empire of which Burnham appears to dream will not be established, or, if established, will not endure, because slavery is no longer a stable basis of human society.'

Admittedly Orwell tended to be more self-contradictory on this question than on most others. Three years before, for example, in 'Looking Back on the Spanish Civil War' he actually referred to a feeling that 'a regime founded on slavery must collapse' as being 'mystical', by which he presumably meant 'unreasoning'. Yet in the same essay he made an equally 'mystical' statement of faith in humanity:

> No bomb that ever burst
> Shatters the crystal spirit.

I am convinced that this represented the true direction of Orwell's hopes, though he realized how far such hopes were imperilled, and foresaw that for long periods the things we have learned to value in the centuries of Western civilization may be submerged.

I suggest therefore that in the general scheme of Orwell's novels, *Nineteen Eighty-Four*, though it presents class in its ugliest political form and the fate of the rebel against the elite in its most tragic form, nevertheless poses a final question which is almost an assertion on the self-destructive nature of caste systems. For the Party elite consists of men who are dead within, who have sacrificed every human quality for the sake of power; they have destroyed themselves by divorcing their view of life from truth, from reality, from any natural impulse. The Party lives within its own doomed circle of fantasy from which even the rebel cannot escape. Winston and his Julia, meeting each other again at the end of the book like two ghosts, drained of mind, drained of character, drained of life, represent their world, whose mixture of ferocity and submission is a sign of its decadence. Life continues in the underground 'other world' of the proles, ignored, despised, but real and indestructible.

In *Nineteen Eighty-Four* Orwell has shown the ultimate conclusion of his vision of the evils of a class-divided society. Clearly he could see little future for his own caste, even in its changed form as the Party. But we should not leap too easily to the conclusion that he could see no future for himself. *Nineteen Eighty-Four* was, after all, a work of fiction, a satirical dream, and Winston Smith was no more and no less George Orwell than any of his predecessors.

PART THREE

THE REVOLUTIONARY PATRIOT

*Conservatism and Rebellion in
Orwell's World-View*

IN HIS novels and his autobiographical writings Orwell seems often to be posing his own version of the kind of dialogue between the hero and the absurd which from the thirties to the fifties dominated the literature of Western Europe. But his relationship with other writers who seem to fall into the same category is one of affinity rather than influence. Before the Spanish Civil War, when the dialogue was already in progress in his writings, he appears to have taken relatively little interest in contemporary writing in other languages. It was only after this experience that he began to recognize his own resemblance – a resemblance which few other English writers shared – to such writers as Ignazio Silone and André Malraux, Victor Serge and Arthur Koestler. He had declared himself a political writer, and these were men who had carried the art of political writing to a high point of intensity and clear-sightedness, largely because their history had been different from that of the English; they had been nurtured from youth in an atmosphere of brooding violence, and they had known the totalitarian world from inside its walls, had broken the law, fought in the streets, endured prison or concentration camp, and fled across frontiers. They were men who had, as Orwell said admiringly of Arthur Koestler, a special 'life-style', so that things did not happen to them by chance; their writing was shaped by the experience their life-style brought to them.

Orwell's sympathy for such men was bred of likeness. From the beginning he had avoided the kind of life lived by ordinary Englishmen. Even his decision to go to Burma had meant a turning away from the university career which his ability made appropriate for him, and from his return to England he took the shaping of his life even more deliberately in hand. By the time of the Spanish Civil War he was detached enough from his class and his fellow intellectuals to be able to enter into the situation on the Aragon front with the same kind of sensitivity as a Continental revolutionary. As a result, he developed a political awareness which enabled him, in *Homage to Catalonia*, to argue with an insight even shrewder than that which Koestler showed in *Spanish Testament*. Nevertheless, as late as 1944, he still believed that the experience of Continental writers made them capable of presenting the totalitarian world with an authenticity no English writer could rival. 'To understand such things one has to be able to imagine oneself as the victim, and for an Englishman to write *Darkness at Noon* would be as unlikely an accident as for a slave-trader to write *Uncle Tom's Cabin*.' In fact, the unlikely accident did happen. By a great feat of empathy, Orwell the Englishman imagined himself the victim of totalitarianism to such effect that *Nineteen Eighty-Four* now stands beside *Darkness at Noon* and *Fontamara* among the classic works of the age of concentration camps.

Orwell did not merely emulate the literary achievements of those Continental writers whom he admired. He also resembled them in recognizing the importance of a 'life-style', both for himself and for his heroes. Despite the special form which his novels took because of his peculiarly English preoccupation with class, one finds in them, as in the works of a whole group of Continental writers from Malraux and Silone to Camus, the central concern with the dialogue between the individual and his absurd or arbitrary environment. All his heroes are failures; indeed, he once said that every life, seen from the inside, was a failure. In just the same way the hero of every novel by Malraux and Camus and Silone is a failure, because the human condition condemns all men in the long run to defeat, if it is only the ultimate defeat of death. This does not really matter. The important thing is to have understood the truth about one's situation, and to have uttered the cry of rebellion that confirms one's humanity. This is what real heroism consists of. It does not consist of being perfect or good or pleasant or well-washed or even lacking in cowardice. None of Orwell's heroes is admirable in the ordinary sense of the word, and certainly none of them would have been as pleasant to know as Orwell himself. But, like him, each of them has a life-style which turns him into a rebel in the name of some kind of truth. The important thing about Winston Smith is not that he should have been defeated, but that he should ever have begun his private war against a regime that symbolized and contained all the anti-human and anti-vitalist forces which social man rears up to the detriment of individual man.

Temperamentally, Orwell was very different from most of the Continental writers he admired. He did not have that cold consistency, capable of instant inversion, which enabled Koestler, the complete Communist, to evolve with such extraordinary rapidity into the complete anti-Communist. The grand romantic arrogance of Malraux, the bookish aridity that underlies the dramatic gestures of Sartre – these I imagine he would have found repellent. On the other hand, he had a great deal in common with Silone, who tried to relate socialism to the traditions of the Italian countryside and who was not afraid to talk of the virtues that might have been lost in the process of a century of revolutionary politics. There are many passages of Silone's works, and particularly of *Fontamara* and *Bread and Wine*, which Orwell must have read with intense sympathy, for here was another man who believed in brotherhood, decency and justice as the foundations of socialism and who realized that in an age when the belief in immortality had vanished, much else that was important in religion – its whole ethical side – had begun to crumble away at the same time. It was these basic Christian qualities that Silone sought to preserve. 'Is a true and lasting revolution possible without them?' he asked. Orwell would have answered, like Silone, in the negative. He would also have found an echo of his own thoughts on the decay of language in the discourse which Pietro Spina makes, disguised as the priest Paolo Spada, to the young people at the Villa della Stagione in *Bread and Wine*.

To speak and to deceive (often to deceive oneself) have become almost synonymous. So far has this process gone that I, wishing to speak to you sincerely and fraternally, with no other object in mind than that of understanding you and making myself understood by you, if I begin to search for the right word, remain in perplexity, so false, equivocal, hackneyed and compromised are they.

But Orwell would not have accepted the sentence with which Pietro ends his remarks. 'Therefore it is better to keep silent and to trust the silence.' On the contrary, having decided that the English language was in a bad way, largely through its misuse by politicians, he immediately set about deciding how the situation might be put right, and in 'Politics and the English Language' he produced not only a most acute diagnosis of our linguistic maladies, but also a highly practical guide to what could be done to bring the language back into good health.

And here we see the difference between Orwell and so many of the Continental writers who in the past half-century have retreated from political into metaphysical rebellion. He did not think naturally in abstract terms; and in the broader philosophical sense he indulged in very little speculation. It was the concrete world, the surface of the earth, the actual texture of life that attracted Orwell; he might agree that the universe was meaningless in metaphysical terms, without attaching much importance to the conclusion, but he drew an extraordinary strength from enjoying that same universe's beauty. Similarly, when he looked at the dogged, seedy heroism of human beings he did not observe in it some metaphysical struggle against destiny out of an existentialist textbook; rather, he experienced a sense of wonder that the shoots of life could come struggling upwards, however pallidly, in the physical barrenness of megalopolis and in the moral barrenness of modern political life.

Of all the Continental writers, he was for these reasons perhaps closest to Camus, even more than to Silone. I suspect that Camus was more aware of Orwell than Orwell of Camus; his journals show that he had read not only *Animal Farm* and *Nineteen Eighty-Four* but also the books by Orwell such as *Burmese Days* which comparatively few Frenchmen would be likely to read. Mutual influence is unlikely, and in any case it is unnecessary to seek it, for these two great humanitarians, each of whom died unexpectedly in his forty-seventh year in the last January of a decade, were obviously born with a great deal in common. They shared the passion for clear, transparent prose; they both found more than enough beauty under the benign indifference of the heavens; they dwelt upon the heroism of unheroic men; they believed in the duty to fight against plagues, particularly the plagues that attack the human psyche, and to describe them with a stark fearlessness. In terms of world literature, Camus's great essay *The Rebel* is the work that most nearly complements – by means of its illuminated historical analysis of the inbred flaws of revolutionary movements – Orwell's imaginative projection of the totalitarian mind in *Nineteen Eighty-Four*. Camus's way of expressing himself is French and tends to be abstract, while Orwell's is English and tends to be concrete; but this kind of difference should not blind us to their essential similarity of outlook. Orwell was a rebel, not a revolutionary, and, in spite of verbal excesses into which his anger would sometimes lead him, he was, like Camus, a man of moderation.

2

IF Orwell found his peers among continental rather than British writers, this does not mean that his writing was any less English in character. On the contrary, his almost obsessive awareness of the concentration camp and the secret police as spectres looming over the whole modern world tended, if anything, to intensify his feeling for his country and its traditions. He was in no way attracted by the rather superficial cosmopolitanism which many English writers cultivated between the wars, and in his work one looks in vain for the French influences that played upon the poetry of the twenties or for the Central European elements – Marx, Freud, Kafka – which so deeply affected members of the 'orthodox' thirties school, like Auden, Isherwood and Rex Warner. In developing his prose style he sought an English purged of unnecessary borrowings from foreign languages. The very choice of the authors he discussed in his critical essays showed how thoroughly English were the roots of his literary art; Tolstoy and Koestler were the only foreign writers to whom he devoted major essays, and he discussed them not as novelists but as rival polemicists. Even among modern American writers he seems to have found little common ground; those who interested him enough to write about them at length were both expatriates – Henry Miller and T. S. Eliot.

But it was in his unsystematic way of thinking, and in his generally pragmatic approach, rather than in the limitation of his literary interests, that the national character of Orwell's work seemed to emerge most emphatically. Almost by instinct he shunned the intellectual scaffoldings, elaborate and consistent, which continental radical writers have always been inclined to construct around their works. One cannot imagine him attempting to compose, like Sartre, massive philosophical treatises to explain the themes which appear in another form in his novels. Even the rich and continuous flow of thought on artistic and moral and political problems which is revealed in Gide's *Journals* does not appear to have been part of his experience, at least if one can judge from the disappointing poverty of the diaries which he kept during the early war years and which were published after his death in the *World Review*.

Indeed, looking back through his writings one is impressed by the modesty of their origins. They were, in the best sense, occasional works, arising not out of philosophic deliberation or scholarly ambition, but from an urgent feeling of the need to give expression to certain thoughts and impressions. His nonfictional works were either autobiographical pieces of varying length, which related experiences and drew the appropriate conclusions, or the polemical essays which Orwell would write, often in white heat, when some idea had struck him forcibly and he wished to work out its implications. The formal critical or scholastic essay did not interest him, but he could write with freshness and interest on what seemed the most unpromising subjects. One can imagine what the ordinary political scientist or even the ordinary professional writer would have made of a subject like 'Politics and the English Language', but when

Orwell discussed it one was not merely convinced by the obvious common sense of his arguments, but also charmed – perhaps charmed too much – by the wit and brightness with which he carried on his examination of the monstrous perversions of the English language by politicians. 'Defoe', said Herbert Read, making the comparison with great perceptiveness, 'was the first writer to raise journalism to a literary art; Orwell perhaps the last.'

It is out of the mass of essays, out of the random thoughts of the articles in *Tribune* and other magazines, and out of the passages of argument embedded in the autobiographical works, that one has to piece together the philosophy of life which inspired Orwell's polemical writings and which complements the thematic structure of his fictional works. Like a great mosaic, it has more cohesion than its fragmentary nature might at first lead one to imagine.

What emerges is an attitude at once radical and conservative, and here again Orwell is taking a stance that is peculiarly English. Class divisions on the Continent may not have the same meticulous tenacity which they assume in Britain, but political divisions are much more sharply drawn along doctrinal lines. A politically conscious but eccentric writer of Orwell's type, who calls himself a Socialist and yet displays an extraordinary conservatism towards many aspects of life, is very hard to find there. Though the comparison might have been rather displeasing to Orwell, his nearest parallels probably exist among French Catholic radicals like Bernanos and Péguy.

Conservatism and socialism form the two poles of Orwell's political thought. What holds them together is the never wholly abandoned strain of anarchism. In Orwell's view a respect for the past was not inconsistent with socialism, which for him centred around simple ideas of liberty and justice and had little relation to Marxism or any other left-wing orthodoxy. Socialism, he felt, had to be built on what was there already; traditions should be not rejected, but used, and systems of ethics which had already served the people well should not be abandoned, at least until something better had grown up in their place.

Perhaps even the more distant past contained lessons, now almost lost, which socialism might with profit resurrect. Looking back in this way was nothing new in the English Socialist tradition. William Morris looked even farther back than Orwell, and saw his own particular kind of socialism leading in some distant future to that revival of the Middle Ages, with modern sanitation installed, which he described in *News from Nowhere*.

Orwell's conservatism can perhaps be seen most clearly if one follows one of his own polemical techniques and compiles a series of propositions which can be supported by evidence from his own writings. These propositions, it will immediately be evident, show Orwell on a number of important issues running counter to the accepted Socialist opinion of his time.

Progress. Progress is not necessarily good, nor is it even certain; the future will probably be worse than the past. A facile belief in the inevitability of progress makes one blind to the power of reaction.

Patriotism. Patriotism is an underrated virtue, and internationalism an overrated panacea.

Population. The birth-controllers are wrong. The people of England should increase and multiply. The childless should be subjected to penal taxation.

Imperialism. Imperialism is bad, but almost everybody opposes it for the wrong reasons. Anti-imperialists are often more despicable than imperialists.

Education. Education is a dubious blessing; the workers' instincts are often more reliable than all the reasoning of the intellectuals.

The State. Socialism is necessary, but state control is a dangerous expedient.

3

THE question of progress brings us immediately to the heart of Orwell's conservatism, since it is evident that his reservations are not those of the reactionary. He is not opposed to change; he merely questions, on the experience of his own lifetime, whether all change is good. Certainly he has no desire to see inequality, tyranny or aristocratic privilege returning, and in his essay on William Butler Yeats he states clearly his view that the desire to reconstruct a hierarchical medievalist past is not merely wrong but also – even in its own terms – doomed to disappointment. Yeats, he says, 'fails to see that the new authoritarian civilization, if it arrives, will not be aristocratic, or what he means by aristocratic. It will not be ruled by noblemen with Van Dyck faces, but by anonymous millionaires, shiny-bottomed bureaucrats, and murdering gangsters.'

At the same time, though he believed that aristocratic reaction could never gain its goals in the modern world, Orwell – with the experience of Spain behind him – recognized it as a powerful force that must not be ignored, and elsewhere he criticized H. G. Wells for an attitude which was really that of Yeats turned upside down. Because of his liberal optimism, developed in the non-military English nineteenth century, Wells did not understand the

tremendous strength of the old world which was symbolized in his mind by fox-hunting Tories. He was ... quite incapable of understanding that nationalism, religious bigotry and feudal loyalty are far more powerful forces than what he himself would describe as sanity. Creatures out of the Dark Ages have come marching into the present, and if they are ghosts, they are at any rate ghosts which need a strong magic to lay them.

The romantic yearning for the aristocratic past is thus condemned by Orwell as evil in its desire to reimpose injustice, sterile because it will never reconstruct the old hierarchical order, and dangerous because it opens the way for even worse tyrannies than those of the past.

At the same time it is significant that Orwell accuses Yeats of 'throwing overboard ... whatever good the past two thousand years have achieved', and that elsewhere he says, 'We live in the wreck of a civilization, but it has been a great civilization in its day.' This lament is echoed in 'Inside the Whale', where the mood shifts almost to melancholy resignation at the thought of 'the break-up of laissez-faire capitalism and of the liberal–Christian culture', with the consequent end of literature as we know it.

Orwell's yearnings towards the past are marked by a patriotism of time, just as his political loyalties are modified by a patriotism of space. At least one of the reasons why he appeared generally so antagonistic to the medievalist reactionaries was that he did not like what he knew of the Middle Ages. In fact the period which he liked most of all – unfashionably for a man of the thirties – was the nineteenth century, whose light, it seemed to him, was finally going out in the age between the great world wars. When he painted his picture of the ideal but vanishing working-class home in *The Road to Wigan Pier*, he emphasized that such a scene belonged only to the age that was coming to an end. Dip back into the Middle Ages, and you would find, not a brightly coloured little vignette out of William Morris's imagination, but 'a windowless hut, a wood fire which smokes in your face because there is no chimney, mouldy bread, "Poor John", lice, scurvy, a yearly childbirth and a yearly child-death and the priest terrifying you with tales of Hell'.

Leap forward a couple of hundred years, and you land in a future which Orwell appears to find almost as distasteful as the draughty dirt of the Plantagenet period. No coal fire; no racing news; dogs suppressed by the health fanatics and children by the birth-control fanatics; everyone 'educated', so that 'it is hardly likely that Father will still be a rough man who likes to sit in shirtsleeves and says "Ah wur coomin' oop street".' Thinking of the barbarian past and the sterilized future, Orwell concludes that 'our age has not been altogether a bad one to live in'.

If we seek to establish more closely the limits of this favourite Orwellian age, we can probably accept the evidence of *Coming Up for Air* that 1914 represented the beginning of the end; backward the age stretched through the manhood of Wells and Dickens to the confines of the brutal eighteenth century. The moral character of the era is personified in the imaginary portrait of its greatest novelist with which Orwell ended his essay on Dickens.

He is laughing, with a touch of anger in his laughter, but no triumph, no malignity. It is the face of a man who is always fighting against something, but who fights in the open and is not frightened, the face of a man who is *generously angry* – in other words of a nineteenth-century liberal, a free intelligence, a type hated with equal hatred by all the smelly little orthodoxies which are now contending for our souls.

The portrait, of course, might be a portrait of Orwell himself; he seems to be projecting on to Dickens and his age the qualities which other people recognized in him. But this does not mean that either the portrait or the identification is false; temperamentally Orwell was old-fashioned, as Richard Rees recognized when he first met him, and very often, in reading his works or listening to his conversation, one would think that this was precisely how an intelligent and percipient late Victorian might talk if he could be transported into our present age.

Orwell never contended that the nineteenth century was an ideal age. 'Society was ruled by narrow-minded, profoundly incurious people, predatory businessmen, dull squires, bishops, politicians who could quote Horace but had never heard of algebra. Science was faintly disreputable and religious belief obligatory.'

Yet these faults, it seemed to Orwell, were more than balanced by their accompanying virtues. The code of decent behaviour among the upper and middle classes – with its careful distinctions about what made a gentleman and what was or was not 'cricket' – did a great deal to mitigate the snobbish pretences and the predatory functions of the ruling caste. And if the truculence of the workers at times turned them into a 'mob', that was at least more dignified than being a mere 'flock', as Orwell believed the slum-dwellers had become in his own day – their old independence melted away into servility. Above all, there was still a sense of tradition, of continuity, and a realism about life and death, symbolized in *Coming Up for Air* by the churchyard in the centre of the town, where the living walk every day among the dead. It was, above all, a world where absolute concepts of good and evil still had meaning, where right and wrong were distinct and sharply defined.

One is struck immediately by the limitations of this world. It is England. It is the age from about 1830 to 1914, with a fraying remnant surviving into the 1940s. And what attracts Orwell to it is a peculiar combination of Christian and liberal virtues, or, to be a little more concrete, of a well-established code of fair behaviour with a recognition – however inadequately implemented – of liberty as a natural human right.

I do not suggest that in restricting his vision in this way Orwell meant to leave the impression that a decent society was the kind of freak which might emerge only at one time or place in human history. He was merely accepting the limitations of his experience and knowledge. He also found, as the earlier part of *Down and Out in Paris and London* shows quite clearly, something very vital in the working-class world of Paris; in Burma he obviously sensed that on the other side of the barrier between ruler and ruled there existed a society in which, as in Victorian England, monstrous abuses of power were mitigated by traditional balances – in this case the ethics of Buddhism and 'a sort of natural equality, an easy intimacy between man and man, which is simply unthinkable in the West'; and in Spain he encountered the fleeting but exhilarating vision of an egalitarian society in Anarchist Barcelona and among the militamen in Aragon.

There were times when Orwell felt that societies of this kind, in which some moral concept like liberty or equality or even decency still wielded a great influence, were doomed to disappear from the modern world, but there were other times, as in 1941, after the Battle of Britain, when he was astonished by the tenacity with which, under attack, traditional values might survive as active elements in the life of the community. At this time he wrote *The Lion and the Unicorn*, which caused a great deal of consternation among his left-wing friends because of its extraordinary mingling of conservative and revolutionary concepts. In this patriotic pamphlet he points out that while the goose-step is spreading over Europe (and here also, at least five years before starting work on *Nineteen Eighty-Four*, he brings in that obsessive image of 'a boot crashing down on a face'), in England 'the march is merely a formalized walk', and that this is indicative of a basic difference between British democracy, with its very patent faults, and continental dictatorships.

In England such concepts as justice, liberty and objective truth are still believed in. They may be illusions, but they are very powerful illusions. The belief in them influences conduct, national life is different because of them.... Even hypocrisy is a powerful safeguard. The hanging judge, that evil old man in scarlet robe and horsehair wig, whom nothing short of dynamite will ever teach what century he is living in, but who will at any rate interpret the law according to the books, and will in no circumstances take a money bribe, is one of the symbolic figures of England. He is a symbol of the strange mixture of reality and illusion, democracy and privilege, humbug and decency, the subtle network of compromises, by which the nation keeps itself in its familiar shape.

And as long as the shape is the familiar one of old England, as tenacious of life as a badger, one feels that for Orwell all is not yet by any means lost.

Yet within this old England with its slums and its hanging judges, its aspidistras and its coal fires, its lush countrysides and its orchards golden with Cox's Orange Pippins, its crude post-card humour and its love of decency and freedom, Orwell also sees what he calls 'the swindle of "progress"' already taking place, eating away like a monstrous ichneumon grub at the good life he remembers from childhood. He walks through the streets of England, watching the people and looking into the shops, and he sees how taste has been corrupted by 'a century of mechanization'. One of the dramatic revelation points in *Coming Up for Air* is when George Bowling goes into a milk bar in the Strand and orders a cup of coffee and a couple of frankfurters. He bites into one of the frankfurters.

The thing burst in my mouth like a rotten pear. A sort of horrible soft stuff was oozing all over my tongue. But the taste! For a moment I just couldn't believe it. Then I rolled my tongue round it and had another try. It was *fish*! A sausage, a thing calling itself a frankfurter, filled with fish! ... It gave me the feeling that I'd bitten into the modern world and discovered what it was really made of. That's the way we're going nowadays. Everything slick and streamlined, everything made out of something else. Celluloid, rubber, chromium steel everywhere, arc lamps blazing all night, glass roofs over your head, radios all playing the same tune, no vegetation left, everything cemented over, mock turtles grazing under the neutral fruit trees. But when you come down to brass tacks and get your teeth into something solid, a sausage for instance, that's what you get. Rotten fish in a rubber skin. Bombs of filth bursting inside your mouth.

Coming Up for Air stands beside Henry Miller's *The Air-Conditioned Nightmare* and Aldous Huxley's *Brave New World* as one of the great modern denunciations of the evils that grow out of an uncritical belief in progress, of an acceptance without discrimination of all, good or bad, that the machine age may have to offer. Nevertheless, it is well to remember that *Coming Up for Air* is a work of fiction, and that Orwell is using – as he pointed out that Huxley had done – 'the exaggeration of caricature'. George Bowling represents that side of Orwell's mind which reacted emotionally and with great revulsion against the modern mechanical world, which found manual work extremely satisfying ('Cease to use your hands, and you have lopped off a huge chunk of your consciousness,' he once said), which inspired his hatred of cities, and which eventually sent him off to find a fairly unassailable rural refuge in the Hebrides, where, if his health had not betrayed him, he might well have become more and more of a recluse from the twentieth-century world as time went on.

But outside fiction and private emotion, when he had to work in the rational world of polemical argument, his opposition to progress was less uncompromising, principally because it appeared to his reasoning, down-to-brass-tacks self that while an attitude like Bowling's is emotionally and aesthetically valid, it is nevertheless unrealistic because the machine has come to stay, and once it is there men will continue to use it. Yet the state of mind that produces the latter-day Luddite is one that he does not ignore; it has at least a cautionary value. 'The machine has got to be accepted, but it is probably better to accept it rather as one accepts a drug – that is, grudgingly and suspiciously. Like a drug, the machine is useful, dangerous, and habit-forming. The oftener one surrenders to it, the tighter its grip becomes.'

A great deal, Orwell points out, depends on what one means by progress, and in 1936 one of his principal criticisms of the Socialists was that they had committed themselves without proper thought to a concept of progress from which most sensitive people reacted with distaste. It involves the transformation of the world by machines until it has reached the point of dead mechanical order. It will be a 'prig's paradise'.

All the work that is now done by hand will then be done by machinery: everything that is now made of leather, wood, or stone will be made of rubber, glass, or steel; there will be no disorder, no loose ends, no wildernesses, no wild animals, no weeds, no disease, no poverty, no pain – and so on and so forth. The Socialist world is to be above all things an *ordered* world, an *efficient* world. But it is precisely from that vision of the future as a sort of glittering Wells-world that sensitive minds recoil.

Orwell sketches out some of the many dilemmas that cluster around both the concept and the fact of progress. He detects the inconsistencies in visions – like those of H. G. Wells – which portray Utopians as heroic and hardy when all the challenges that produce courage have been taken out of their lives and the elimination of manual work has forced them to invent artificial means of maintaining their strength. But it is not only courage and hardihood that mechanical progress threatens. Almost every meaningful human activity is endangered by the machine. To remain even mentally healthy, a man needs work and 'life has got to be lived largely in terms of effort'. But it is precisely the opportunity of effort that the machine steadily diminishes, cutting men off 'from the chance of working – that is, of living'.

That mechanical progress is inevitable seems then to be the main argument of the theoretical part of *The Road to Wigan Pier*. However, we may make the prospect a little less unpleasant, Orwell suggests, if we choose to accept progress-with-socialism rather than progress-with-fascism. By now he has talked himself into an impasse in which it is no longer possible to present socialism as anything more attractive than a lesser evil, and his arguments at this point become unusually feeble and obscure. He exhorts the sensitive man to accept the machine world because there is no alternative; the machine has got us in its grip. However, there may be a role as a 'humanizing' force, as a 'permanent opposition' within the machine world, for those who refuse to accept the full consequences of mechanization. What this will achieve, in view of Orwell's previous arguments that the machine will atrophy every kind of human initiative, it is hard to see; however, he does at this point appear to believe that one might be able to modify the concept of progress, and even the phenomenon itself, so that it would no longer be 'definable as making the world safe for little fat men'. As for his own inclinations, Orwell makes it clear that though his lower self as 'a degenerate modern semi-intellectual' may relish the comforts which progress will bring, in a different and somewhat deeper way he would prefer to see life becoming 'simpler and harder instead of softer and more complex'.

If this discussion reveals anything beyond a rather opinionated series of generalizations on the nature of progress, it is that Orwell was emotionally far removed from the majority of the middle-class Socialists, with their heritage of Wellsian Utopianism; he brought with him more than a vestige of the cold-bath Spartanism which in his day was automatically inculcated into members of the sahib caste. This Spartanism was unexpectedly gratified when, in the same year as he wrote *The Road to Wigan Pier*, he encountered in Spain an austere and libertarian type of socialism which was not linked indissolubly with the idea of progress. For the first time socialism appeared to Orwell not only as just, but also as congenial.

At the same time, he began to doubt whether 'progress' was

really so inevitable as he had at first imagined. In *Coming Up for Air*, written after his return from Spain, the leading character sees that the horrors imposed on life by the indiscriminate use of industrial developments may merely be the prelude to a collapse of society into a new barbarism as the wars sweep over the world and the civil wars follow in their path. And before the end of the war Orwell himself had begun to suspect that 'progress' might be a quite different 'swindle' from that which he had envisaged in *The Road to Wigan Pier*. Perhaps politics would be powerful enough to interfere with the direction of technological change – as great manufacturers had already done by suppressing inventions that threatened their interests. Perhaps 'progress' would not lead, after all, to the 'glittering Wells-world', but would be diverted and adapted to satisfy the needs of new power groups. The possibility is developed in *Animal Farm*, where the ordinary animals find that their material conditions are no better – and possibly worse – than they were before the revolution, and it reaches its logical climax in *Nineteen Eighty-Four*, where progress has virtually come to a halt except in one limited direction – the perfecting of the instruments of tyrannical government.

Orwell's final conclusion would seem to have been that progress based on modern technological developments is (a) undesirable and (b) unnecessary for the achievement of socialism, and that its inevitability is in doubt for the reason, which gives us no ground for rejoicing, that it may easily be diverted by politicians to serve the ends of tyranny. How much hope we do in fact have of 'humanizing' the course of progress he leaves in the end uncertain, but there is rarely any doubt of his conviction that we shall probably not in any foreseeable future experience a life as good as that of late-Victorian England. The only way we can hope to make the future more bearable is to carry with us as we march towards it, like the holy books that the Sikhs carried into battle, the codes of decency and justice that inspired men in the past. In all but name, this point of view is of course conservative; more truly conservative, indeed, than the policies of most Conservative parties.

4

'PATRIOTISM', said Orwell in 1941, 'is usually stronger than class hatred, and always stronger than any kind of international-ism.' This was not merely an accurate observation about the external world. It also expressed an important element in Or-well's own attitude. The words were written in 1941, after he had tried desperately to join up in the British armed forces and had found only the Home Guard open to him. By this time he had reconciled himself to working in other ways for the British war effort, and the pamphlet in which he made this statement, *The Lion and the Unicorn*, was at least in part a piece of high-class war propaganda. Yet there is no doubt that Orwell spoke with feeling, and meant everything he said about patriotism and about England.

In *The English People*, published after the war, Orwell took up the same theme, and here he remarked that the foreigner who studies the English people and their literature 'might end by deciding that a profound, almost unconscious patriotism and an inability to think logically are the abiding features of the English character'. This is probably true of the English, in so far as one can generalize for fifty million people; it was cer-tainly true of Orwell himself, whose logic was never perfect and who, when the war came, found himself articulating thoughts about his own relationship to his country which are only hinted in his earlier writings. Occasionally during the war years his patriotism took on a ranting, aggressive form, as in some of his London Letters to the *Partisan Review*, but towards the end of the war it seemed to recede into the half-conscious, like a fish sinking down into the depths of a pool; I cannot re-member any occasion during the period of our friendship, from 1943 onwards, on which he brought up the matter in an ob-trusive way, though one always recognized patriotism as part of his outlook and respected it just as he respected one's own particular quirks of opinion.

Orwell was highly conscious that his attitude in this respect marked him off from many of his fellow intellectuals, and particularly from the left wing which had established a strong position in the literary world during the 1930s. His shadow feud with the intelligentsia on this subject tended to be carried on in half-truths and immoderate generalizations, but a typical passage of Orwellian anti-intellectual sniping is worth quoting because it reveals not only the kind of man of straw which he habitually constructed to be knocked down with dazzling fist-play, but also the image of himself which he saw opposed to it in the ring. In *The Lion and the Unicorn* he declared:

In intention, at any rate, the English intelligentsia are Europeanized. They take their cookery from Paris and their opinions from Moscow. In the general patriotism of the country they form a sort of island of dissident thought. England is perhaps the only great country whose intellectuals are ashamed of their own nationality. In left-wing circles it is always felt that there is something slightly disgraceful in being an Englishman and that it is a duty to snigger at every English institution, from horse racing to suet puddings.

After imputing to the intellectuals far more influence than they actually possessed by laying on them a great deal of the responsibility for the weakening of British morale which tempted the Fascist nations to embark on war, he goes on to blame the Blimps (Mutts to his intellectual Jeffs) for the degeneration of the English intellectuals into 'purely *negative* creatures'.

Both Blimps and highbrows took for granted, as though it were a law of nature, the divorce between patriotism and intelligence. If you were a patriot you read *Blackwood's Magazine* and publicly thanked God that you were not 'brainy'. If you were an intellectual you sniggered at the Union Jack and regarded physical courage as barbarous.

From the very first sentence the argument is riddled with absurdities. English intellectuals, in their homes at least, were much less accustomed to French cooking than the moneyed class who could employ foreign chefs; when they ate out they were most inclined to frequent Italian rather than French restaurants, mainly because these offered well-cooked food at the cheapest prices. I know many writers who – at the time when Orwell wrote *The Lion and the Unicorn* – regularly followed horse racing, and I myself among others am addicted to suet pudding. These are trivial points, important only to illustrate the slashing inaccuracy with which Orwell would sometimes carry on his literary battles. When we come to the graver accusation that 'the English intelligentsia ... take ... their opinions from Moscow', it is easy to see why *The Lion and the Unicorn* was received among his fellow writers with an anger which rather took Orwell aback.

The Communist-lining group in the British literary world had always been a minority, even though it gained unwarranted prominence because three of the younger poets, Auden, Spender and Day Lewis, were associated with it, in addition to the hard core of dogmatic Stalinists centred round the *Left Review*. But by the time Orwell wrote *The Lion and the Unicorn* he must have known that visits to Spain had reduced Auden's Communist tendencies to silence and had ended Spender's fellow-travelling. Furthermore, almost the whole sub-generation of younger poets who appeared in the *later* thirties, whether they followed Dylan Thomas or belonged, as I did, to the group that gathered round *Twentieth Century Verse*, were anti-Stalinist in one way or another; they leaned towards personalism or pacifism, anarchism or Trotskyism, or were merely non-political. Finally, most of the leading figures in the English literary world had never even in the thirties been touched in any way by communism. How far – to quote only the names that come to mind as I am typing out this sentence – did Wyndham Lewis, T. S. Eliot, Herbert Read, Aldous Huxley, and Virginia Woolf take their opinions from Moscow? As for England being 'the only great country whose intellectuals are ashamed of their own nationality', if we are to consider this statement in terms of the proportion of writers who were willing to follow foreign gods, history shows that a far greater proportion of French writers succumbed to the attractions of communism or fascism than was the case in England.

Yet there is a way in which Orwell was not entirely wrong

when he accused the British intellectuals of being unpatriotic. British writers tended to adopt the critical view of patriotism which Wilfred Owen and Siegfried Sassoon took at the end of the First World War, rather than the heroic one which Rupert Brooke and Julian Grenfell took at the beginning. They were not prepared to accept the 'death or glory', 'theirs not to reason why', 'my country right or wrong' kind of attitude. Many of them – certainly a majority – supported the war, but they did so either (a) because they did not relish the possibility of living under foreign domination, which is at best a negative form of patriotism, or (b) because they took the particular type of internationalist view which regarded it as a duty to resist the spread of Nazism and to end the regime which had sent millions of innocent people to their deaths. Some of them – and one particularly remembers Keith Douglas, Alun Lewis and Sidney Keyes – died for these 'unpatriotic' reasons. As for the pacifist writers, most of them knew that their names were as high on the Nazi proscription lists as Orwell's, nor were they any more inclined than he to accept foreign domination. It was merely that they differed from him on the kind of resistance which they felt was morally justifiable. Their opinions, whether right or wrong, certainly did not come from Moscow; if they came from anywhere outside Britain, it was from India, from Gandhi. Perhaps mistakenly, the pacifists considered that Gandhi had given them a model example of how a struggle to maintain or regain one's freedom could be carried on without violence. Orwell talked a great deal of irrelevant nonsense about pacifists relying on the protection of the British navy to maintain their views (presumably he did not hear of the very successful passive resistance campaign carried on *behind* the curtain of Nazi occupation by the school-teachers of Norway in 1942), and he also amused himself by asserting that pacifism was really a disguised form of power-worship. It was, as so often in Orwell's campaigns, Don Quixote slashing out at self-created spectres. But here, once again, his built-in sense of fairness came to the surface before the end of the war, and he wrote in *Tribune* on 7 December 1944 a note deprecating the wholesale condemnation of pacifists: 'The important thing is to discover *which* individuals are honest and which are not, and the usual blanket accusation merely makes this more difficult. The atmosphere of hatred in which controversy is conducted blinds people to considerations of this kind.'

To be fair in turn to Orwell, there is no doubt at all that his patriotism was sincere. Some writers one might have suspected of currying favour with the general public or with the government by denouncing their fellow intellectuals of the Left. But Orwell felt that he had already cut himself off from the Establishment when he resigned his job in Burma, and now he was risking ostracism in the intellectual world; that he was not ostracized is perhaps the best disproof of his argument that the intellectuals had accepted their opinions from Moscow.

Orwell's patriotism, which he retained to the end of his life, was a complex state of mind which appears to have had many roots. His childhood in the Thames Valley had given him a passion for southern England, and he retained the memories of it throughout his life as his own 'golden country', though he had enough wisdom not to attempt to return there to live. His long periods away from home, in Burma and in Europe, heightened his feeling for England into a deep nostalgia, of which there are traces in *Burmese Days* and even in *Homage to Catalonia*. But these feelings did not coalesce into a clearly expressed sentiment of patriotism until the war actually came. There is even a distinctly ironic touch in the reference which Orwell makes to patriotism in *Down and Out in Paris and London* when he describes his return from France to England.

I was so pleased to be getting home, after being hard up for months in a foreign city, that England seemed to me a sort of Paradise. There are, indeed, many things in England that make you glad to get home; bathrooms, armchairs, brown bread, marmalade, beer made with veritable hops – they are all splendid, if you can pay for them. England is a very good country when you are not poor; and, of course, with a tame imbecile to look after, I was not going to be poor. The thought of not being poor made me very patriotic.

The implication here is clearly that patriotism is a luxury for those who can afford it. *Coming Up for Air* contains, at best, a kind of inverted patriotism in its angry outburst against what had been done to England, and 'Inside the Whale', finished after the war actually began, puts up no very convinced opposition to Miller's philosophic acceptance of the historic process which will destroy all that patriotism stands for.

It is obvious that the feelings which emerged a year later in *The Lion and the Unicorn* were the product of a developing internal struggle between conflicting impulses during the early months of the war, and that in the end Orwell's past triumphed. He went back to the loyalties of the colonial administrator caste, and in the process shed a great deal of the generalized bitterness against English society which had been implanted in him by his Burmese experiences. The very tone of his references to the civilization of England in *The Lion and the Unicorn* shows an intensity of feeling quite different from that expressed in his earlier works:

And above all, it is *your* civilization, it is *you*. However much you hate it or laugh at it, you will never be happy away from it for any length of time. The suet puddings and the red pillar-boxes have entered into your soul. Good or evil, it is yours, you belong to it, and this side the grave you will never get away from the marks it has given you.

In *The Lion and the Unicorn* and *The English People* Orwell has some very shrewd and some very odd things to say about England and its life. But he said even more interesting things in his other books when he was not straining so self-consciously to advertise his country. In terms of his general philosophy, the two most interesting points that emerge out of his patriotic preoccupations are his rejection of nationalism, and his contention that socialism and patriotism were both dynamic forces which could serve each other and, if combined, could not only transform England but also make the defeat of Germany more certain.

Nationalism is actually the subject of a separate essay, 'Notes on Nationalism', written at the end of the war, but supplementing what Orwell had to say in *The Lion and the Unicorn*. Nationalism and patriotism, he argued, are by no means the same thing, in spite of the fact that they are often regarded as identical, and here he gives what is probably his clearest definition of what patriotism means to him. 'By "patriotism" I mean devotion to a particular place and a particular way of life, which one believes to be the best in the world but has no wish to force upon other people. Patriotism is by its nature defensive, both militarily and culturally.'

Nationalism, on the other hand, is aggressive and exclusive in nature. It involves 'identifying oneself with a single nation or other unit, placing it beyond good and evil and recognizing no other duty than that of advancing its interests'. It is 'inseparable from the desire for power', not, of course, for oneself, but for the unit to which one belongs. By implication, if we accept these definitions, patriotism would allow room for individuality while nationalism would always seek to destroy it. The distinction certainly applied to Orwell's own attitude. He wished to defend his country at the cost of no other people; he was that extremely rare being, an English patriot who regarded the dismantling of the British Empire as one of the first items on the agenda for future action. But whether the distinction applies to patriotism in general is another matter, around which difficult questions cluster. How much territory does one need to defend the fatherland? Frontiers, historic, geographic and ethnic, being as muddled as they are, it is always hard to keep patriotic defence from turning into aggression which can develop into nationalism and end in imperialism, as happened to the patriots of revolutionary France, who began by defending the Rhine and ended finally outside Moscow. Chinese patriots believe the invasion of Tibet merely reinstated the wholeness of China; Tibetan patriots have a different opinion. Orwell in fact never faces up to the question of how local patriotism may be. Is he, in praising the English for uniting against German invaders, justifying by implication a Welsh patriotism which would seek to expel the English invaders? And if we talk of a Welsh patriotism, why not a Cornish one, and so on, until we come to the kind of situation imagined by Chesterton in *The Napoleon of Notting Hill*, where every parish is its own *patria*? Surely, in the long and distant run, the only solution must be an internationalism in which all loyalties, large and small, may find expression.

There are also peculiarities about Orwell's definition of nationalism, quite apart from its relation to patriotism. He uses it to mean the habit of identifying oneself with any kind of unit to the extent of 'recognizing no other duty than that of advancing its interests'. Pacifism, Zionism, anti-Semitism and Trotskyism are all, by this definition, forms of nationalism. So, if we carry on the argument on the lines of logical absurdity which Orwell has established, are vegetarianism, theosophy, and those strange excesses of partisanship which take place at the Boat Race and the Cup Final. No doubt nationalism does have certain elements in common with other forms of dedicated partisanship, but in itself it means something very specific, and one is surprised to find so strong an adherent of clear, unequivocal English as Orwell taking such a liberty with the language.

But when we return to the other point I have raised – the relation between patriotism and revolutionary socialism – we find Orwell trying to pass off another semantic trick. 'Patriotism', he tells us, 'has nothing to do with Conservatism. It is actually the opposite of Conservatism, since it is devotion to something that is always changing and yet is felt mystically to be the same.' The trick here is to use a capital letter, which identifies Conservatism as the creed of a particular party, and leads us adroitly away from the fact that in the generalized, small-letter sense the entire intent of English patriotism is to *conserve* that great agglomeration of people, places, traditions and customs which is known as England. Patriotism, when it surfaced during the Second World War like a great barnacled whale from the subaqueous sleep of the thirties, was conservative in this very sense, as well as – despite Orwell's wishes – being Conservative in the partisan sense as well, since it found its symbolic centre in the charismatic personality of Winston Churchill, the arch-conserver and leading Conservative.

This fact gives only a remotely historic interest to the unheeded proposals which Orwell made in *The Lion and the Unicorn* for the harnessing of patriotism to the social revolution. Almost certainly the idea arose out of his experiences in the Spanish Civil War, when he became attached to the losing faction in the internal struggle on the Republican side, the faction which contended that to defeat Franco one must carry out the revolution of social justice behind the government lines and so unleash a great flow of dynamic enthusiasm on the part of the poverty-stricken masses of Spain. As Orwell watched England, at the time when *The Lion and the Unicorn* was written, only slowly emerging from the apathy of the days of the 'phony war', he remembered Spain, and it seemed to him that nothing but a radical change in the social structure, an immediate establishment of economic justice, would galvanize the people into action. He deceived himself into believing that this was just what the majority of English people would want once they knew their own minds. The hope emerges when he discusses the effect of public opinion on the political fate of Chamberlain.

Only when the results of his policy became apparent did it turn against him; which is to say that it turned against its own lethargy of the past seven years. Thereupon the people picked a leader nearer to their mood, Churchill, who was at any rate able to grasp that wars are not won without fighting. Later, perhaps, they will pick another leader who can grasp that only Socialist nations can fight effectively.

In this paragraph there is one wild, unsupported statement — 'that only Socialist nations can fight effectively' – which sounds as if it had come out of a Trotskyist pamphlet, and one unfulfilled half-prophecy, which together show that Orwell was not very adept at assessing current political trends. His view remained that of a minority. Few even among the Socialists agreed with him on the wisdom of attempting a total social transformation in the mid-career of a world war, and the majority of the people were interested mainly in staying alive and staying uninvaded. Until the war was obviously won, they remained almost instinctively behind Churchill, who seemed much more able to guarantee survival than any of the Labour leaders.

Orwell was correct in realizing the importance of patriotism. Like all the great irrational mass impulses, it had been ignored by those heirs of the Age of Reason, the Socialists, and ignoring it they had neglected a powerful appeal which the Fascists and Nazis – and in Russia the Communists – had appropriated to their own great advantage. But there were at least two problems which Orwell never really faced. The first was how patriotism, even an enlightened form of it, could be related to the internationalism which, whether we like it or not, accelerated means of communication are making ever more necessary. The other was how one could find an effective substitute for the charismatic leadership which usually galvanizes patriotism into action. Patriotism and leadership as we have known them are both fraught with perils to the very aims of liberty and justice which Orwell made the basis of socialism.

5

PATRIOTS are usually interested in population. Population not merely ensures enough soldiers to fight for the fatherland. It is also an index of the vitality of the race, and sometimes, as in the case of the French Canadians, it can be a potent factor in preserving a national group from submergence by its neighbours. Orwell does not differ from other patriots in this respect, and the latter pages of *The English People* contain a rather long discussion of means to increase the English birth-rate. Orwell's proposals here are probably the most truly reactionary he ever made, including such familiar devices as the crushing penal taxation of childless people and a more rigorous repression of abortion. It shows Orwell at his most authoritarian, but it also shows an aspect of his thought which cannot be ignored.

For Orwell's concern with procreation went a long way beyond the merely mathematical calculations of the ordinary political patriot. As we have seen, he was concerned with life as an experience, with the vitality of nature, and at least one facet of his mind resembled that of D. H. Lawrence, without, of course, the gush and garrulity. It is his vitalism, even more than his patriotism, that explains the peculiar intensity of his attitudes towards birth and the family. It explains also the rooted and persistent hostility which he shows towards supporters of birth-control, and, indeed, towards any interference with sex as a natural function leading eventually to procreation. In *Keep the Aspidistra Flying* Gordon Comstock denounces contraception as 'just another way they've found of bullying us', and in *The Road to Wigan Pier* the birth-controllers are reckoned among the worst of the half-crazed fanatics who hang on the lunatic fringe of socialism. In the same book Orwell praises working people who get married and raise families on the dole.

Orwell may have been in many respects a solitary, but in his eyes the family was important for the health of society and the fulfilment of the individual. Although he wrote a great deal about the unhappiness of his childhood, it is significant that even in his melancholy work *Such, Such Were the Joys* he remembered his home as 'a place ruled by love rather than fear'. Whatever wounds his childhood may have given him, they did not deprive him of the desire to found a family himself, and he took a great pleasure in his adoptive parenthood. Turning to his works rather than his life, it is significant that two of his novels, *Keep the Aspidistra Flying* and *Coming Up for Air*, end right in the heart of the family, with the prodigal heroes returning home, and that one of the most unpleasant aspects of the Utopian society which Orwell stresses in *Nineteen Eighty-Four* is the shattering of family trust by turning children into spies against their parents.

At a time when apologies for the family were almost entirely the work of Catholic writers, Orwell's attitude was, here again, exceptional for a left-wing intellectual, but there is no doubt of the genuineness of his feeling that anything which threatened the family or interfered with the natural process of increase was an almost blasphemous attack on life itself. In *Nineteen Eighty-Four*, the Party pries into the sexual lives of its members and even runs an Anti-Sex League (successor to the birth-control organizations which Orwell detested in his own day), but the proles carry on their sexual life without any restraint except that imposed by their own moral code. The proles are in this way also the successors of the early twentieth-century working class whom Orwell admired for their lack of middle-class puritanism; in 'The Art of Donald McGill' he observed how robustly they jested about sex, but also how they approved only those sexual relations that led in the right direction, towards marriage well blessed with children. At the same time, in their jokes and songs, they celebrated the sexual act and the fertility deities, the mother goddesses, who appeared in comic modern disguise on the postcards which formed their most popular art.

By the curious underground ways of literary creation, 'The Art of Donald McGill' became one of the threads that led to Orwell's final novel. There are few really lyrical passages in *Nineteen Eighty-Four*, but one occurs when Winston Smith looks out from the room above the antique shop just before his arrest, and sees, hanging out her lines of washing, a woman who might have stepped from a comic postcard. His attention leaves Julia, the mistress doomed to be sterile who stands beside him, and he gazes almost worshipfully, as his thoughts grow into an ecstatic recognition of the indestructibility of life.

The woman down there had no mind, she had only strong arms, a warm heart, and a fertile belly. He wondered how many children she had given birth to. It might easily be fifteen. She had had her momentary flowering, a year, perhaps, of wild-rose beauty, and then she had suddenly swollen like a fertilized fruit and grown hard and red and coarse, and then her life had been laundering, scrubbing, darning, cooking, sweeping, polishing, mending, scrubbing, laundering, first for children then for grandchildren, over thirty unbroken years. At the end of it she was still singing. The mystical reverence that he felt for her was somehow mixed up with the aspect of the pale, cloudless sky, stretching away behind the chimney-pots into interminable distance. It was curious to think that the sky was the same for everybody, for Eurasia or

Eastasia as well as here. And the people under the sky were also very much the same – everywhere, all over the world, hundreds of thousands of millions of people just like this, people ignorant of one another's existence, held apart by walls of hatred and lies, and yet almost exactly the same – people who had never learned to think but who were storing up in their hearts and bellies and muscles the power that would one day overturn the world.

It strikes one as curious, on reading such a passage, that Orwell should ever have gained the name of a pessimistic writer oriented towards death. For the more often one does read it, the more natural and convincing the whole scene of Winston looking out at the prole woman in the yard appears in comparison with the melodramatic horrors in the Ministry of Love.

The prole woman, of course, is inaccessible to Winston, and here we are back in the frustrated caste world of Orwell's fiction. But, abstracted from that context, Winston's 'mystical' contemplation of a blowsy old trollop seems to set the crown on that wistful love for the fertility of nature which appears in rather different forms in the earlier novels. Translated into social terms, it involves reverence for the family as the unit of reproduction and growth, and also as the primitive collectivity, more fundamental and more natural than the state. Perhaps, having been sent from his home to boarding-school, like most boys of his class, at a much too early age, Orwell had an exaggerated sense of the joys of family existence. But his respect for the institution, and his desire to see it flourish to the end of renewing and multiplying the race, were strong and genuine, and formed yet another essentially conservative element in his view of life.

6

'I WAS a stage rebel,' said Cyril Connolly, describing childhood days at St Cyprian's. 'Orwell was a true one.' As Orwell observed more than once, lives look different when viewed from the inside, and Connolly's rebel became, in the subjective view of *Such, Such Were the Joys*, the everlasting victim, the predestined failure. Certainly, when Orwell left school and set off for a respectable post in the service of the Empire, the rebellion he may have shown at St Cyprian's and definitely showed at Eton seemed like a normal, passing phase in the life of a young man of the impoverished upper class. The years immediately after the First World War were a time of general ferment, when even public-school boys harboured revolutionary thoughts, but the world was simmering down by 1922, and Orwell with it. So, at least, it appeared when he departed from England.

Yet it was in the service of the Empire that Orwell was finally set on the course of rebellion that led him through anarchism to his very personal form of socialism. There is no need to go further than I have done already into the nature of his feelings by the time he returned from the East in 1927. It is sufficient here to say that his rejection of imperialism, emotionally and intellectually, was complete, and that the memory of having lived as a ruler in an alien country never ceased to trouble him.

At the same time, as the years went by, his attitude towards British imperialism changed considerably. Here there was no question of a conservative element supervening. Orwell never wished Britain to retain its imperial possessions or to continue the relationship, intolerable for nations as for individuals, of the conquerors ruling over the conquered. But he did want to make sure that the British people realized what might be involved in the abandonment of an empire, and he did develop a desire that justice be done both to the men who had ended the Empire and also to those who had made it, at worst, more tolerable than the totalitarian empires which might later take its place.

It was, Orwell felt, around the Empire that British hypocrisy clustered most thickly. The upper classes had developed a whole series of double arguments, of which they were barely aware, to justify their retention of the Empire; the working class acted as if it did not exist. Orwell did not attempt to defend this situation, and when Mulk Raj Anand published his fervently nationalist *Letters from India*, he wrote in reply a 'Letter to an Indian' which appeared in *Tribune*: 'On strictly political grounds, I cannot whack up any serious disagreement with you.... For a hundred and fifty years we have been exploiting you, and for at least thirty years we have been holding back your development.'

Yet – this was 1943 – he saw real difficulties in persuading the people that India should be freed, and some of these came, not from the nature of capitalism or the power of political conservatism, but from the promises of a steadily increased standard of living which were part of current Socialist propaganda. Orwell held the belief, which was current until quite late in the 1940s, that the abandonment of the Empire would diminish automatically the national income of Britain and in consequence the standard of living of the workers. 'And as long as socialism teaches people to think in terms of material benefit, how would the British worker behave if told that he had to choose between keeping India in bondage and lowering his own wages?' Fortunately the issue did not arise in this way. There was never any need for the British workers to go on to a diet of herrings and potatoes, for the European economy was transformed after the war in a way that anyone who had passed through the depression found it difficult to comprehend, and the abandonment of the Empire did not seriously interfere with the steady post-war rise of the British standard of living. When Orwell wrote, however, the problem still seemed genuine enough, and he felt that a great conspiracy of the press and the political parties 'of whatever colour' had united to prevent the people from seeing the situation clearly. But he also had enough faith in the innate decency of the British people to believe that with a full knowledge of the situation they might in any case act in the right way, even if it seemed to be against their material interests. In *The English People* he said :

We do know ... that they have sometimes championed the weak against the strong when it was obviously not to their own advantage. The best example is the Irish Civil War. The real weapon of the Irish rebels was British public opinion, which was substantially on their side and prevented the British Government from crushing the rebellion in the only way possible.

In the event, so far as India was concerned, Orwell was right. In general the British people approved of the Labour government's decision to leave India, regardless of the possible economic consequences to themselves. In large part, as Orwell admitted in the essay which he wrote on Gandhi after his death, this was due to the personal influence the Indian leader had established through his way of appealing to every man's sense of decency.

In my view the best pieces that Orwell wrote about India – which lies at the core of any discussion of British imperialism – were his essays on Gandhi and Kipling. He was enough of a novelist for even his essays to be best when they centred around the study of a personality, either through his life or his work; they were best of all when he picked an individual with whom he felt some kind of affinity. Gandhi and Kipling may seem poles apart, but Orwell had something in common with each of them. And both of them had for him the virtue that they belonged in the Indian scene and were not merely laying down the law from the outside.

If we look at the Indian side of the question first, it is evident that though Orwell was unreservedly in favour of Indian independence, he did not find the movement which aimed at its achievement entirely congenial. 'You know as well as I do', he said in his letter to Mulk Raj Anand, 'the element of mere nationalism, even colour-hatred, that enters into the Indian independence movement.' Of these things he did not accuse Gandhi. In fact, he admired Gandhi's entire lack of race or status prejudice, his uncompromising honesty, his willingness to take the trouble of discovering whatever was decent in an opponent and making that the basis of his approach. On the other hand he found him aesthetically rather unpleasing, distrusted his religious aspirations, and saw a disturbing anti-vitalist element in his teachings of asceticism.

I imagine these personal reactions to Gandhi remained fairly constant over a number of years. It was in his views of Gandhi as a pacifist politician that Orwell changed quite considerably in the years between 1942 and 1948. In 1942, when he, D. S. Savage, Alex Comfort and I were disputing in the pages of the *Partisan Review*, the question of Gandhi inevitably came up. Orwell reacted negatively, and took up the tough-speaking stance which he sometimes affected at this period:

As an ex-Indian civil servant, it always makes me shout with laughter to hear, for instance, Gandhi named as an example of the success of non-violence. As long as twenty years ago it was cynically admitted in Anglo-Indian circles that Gandhi was very useful to the British Government. So he will be to the Japanese if they get there. Despotic governments can stand 'moral force' until the cows come home; what they fear is physical force.

Two years later, again in the *Partisan Review*, Orwell bitterly attacked a book by Lionel Fielden, *Beggar My Neighbour*, which defended the Gandhian point of view. In this essay he makes at least one prophecy about India which was to be disproved only three years later. 'India is very unlikely ever to become independent' in a full sovereign sense, because 'she is unable to defend herself', and her fate is therefore likely to be bound up, with that of Britain and the United States; it is common decency rather than political reality which demands that India should be made 'formally independent'. Here again Orwell had somewhat misread the future. After the war the world did not divide into two or three great power blocs in exactly the way he anticipated as a result of his reading of James Burnham; the super-powers did emerge, but instead of losing by the situation, the lesser powers tended to gain by playing off one bloc against the other, and in consequence India has acted ever since independence as a sovereign state in every respect, even down to defying the United Nations whenever it saw fit.

Undoubtedly these unexpected circumstances helped to alter Orwell's estimate of Gandhi, whom he dismissed in the Fielden review with the cavalier statement that he 'has alienated the British public by his extremism and aided the British Government by his moderation'.

'Reflections on Gandhi', published shortly after the Indian leader's death in 1948, took the form of an extended review of Gandhi's autobiographical volume, *The Story of My Experiment with Truth*, which impressed Orwell with the honest commonplaceness of its approach. In his essay Orwell radically changes his estimate of Gandhi's influence and of his achievement. Where before he had stated flatly that Gandhi had objectively served the interests of the British, here he suggests that his impression may have been erroneous.

It was apparent that the British were making use of him, or thought they were making use of him.... How reliable such calculations are in the long run is doubtful; as Gandhi himself says, 'in the end deceivers deceive only themselves'; but at any rate the gentleness with which he was nearly always handled was due partly to the feeling that he was useful.

While Orwell brings up in this essay the familiar points about non-violence, he puts them as questions – and questions that need urgent discussion – rather than as objections. Perhaps even more than the fact of Indian independence, what stood between the Orwell of 1942-4 and the Orwell of 1948 was the yet harder fact of the bomb over Hiroshima. 'It is doubtful', he says, 'whether civilization can stand another major war, and it is at least thinkable that the way out lies through non-violence.'

Orwell was always more willing to make allowances for the errors of his opponents than for the faults of his friends, and though he declared himself a Socialist and an anti-imperialist, he very soon began to appear as a defender of imperialists against the more irresponsible attacks of the Left. As early as *Burmese Days* he made a plea for understanding on behalf of government servants in remote colonies, corrupted by isolation and idleness. 'Shooting an Elephant' is intended not merely as a parable attacking imperialist attitudes, but also as an explanation of some of the difficulties which the government servant encounters when he is placed in the artificial position – in relation to the people among whom he lives – of the agent of an alien power. There are moments in 'Shooting an Elephant' when we find ourselves not merely in Orwell's mind, but in that of a quintessential colonial policeman; we feel his exasperation at the sneering Burmese, we feel his lethargic resentment at being forced to wander about the town in a hot and humid climate searching for a mad elephant, we feel the compulsion to show off before the natives that makes him in the end, with the greatest reluctance, kill an animal he has no desire to destroy. This, Orwell is saying, is a human predicament like any other, and the fact that the central character is a policeman or an imperial official does not diminish his need for our understanding and our compassion.

Orwell's attitude towards the Empire, it has often been observed, became more ambivalent in the war years, as if he felt that crisis had brought about a situation in which not merely national but also class ranks would have to be closed. As Malcolm Muggeridge once remarked, there was 'a Kiplingesque side to his character which made him romanticize the Raj and its mystique', and Orwell began to regard as a heroic generation the old sahib class which had endured incredible risks and hardships in the days when sanitation was rudimentary and prophylactic injections were unknown. But, like everything else good, these great figures belonged in the past.

The middle-class families celebrated by Kipling, the prolific lowbrow families whose sons officered the Army and Navy and swarmed over all the waste places of the earth from the Yukon to the Irrawaddy, were dwindling before 1914. The thing that killed them was the telegraph. In a narrowing world, more and more governed from Whitehall, there was every year less room for individual initiative.... Few able men went east of Suez if there was any way of avoiding it.

By directing his admiration towards the Empire and the imperialists of the past, Orwell rather adroitly evaded assuming responsibility for the Empire of the present, which he had committed himself to opposing when he left Burma. Yet there is no doubt that he had a genuine admiration for the courage of the Empire builders, and also for their sense of responsibility, in which he found his fellow intellectuals of the Left completely lacking. This emerges particularly in his essay on Kipling which combines dislike for the man, appreciation of the 'good bad' writer and esteem for a peculiar integrity which shone through all the jingoism and the brutality.

In admiring Kipling, Orwell is in part demonstrating his own conservatism; the qualities he selects for approval are those which represent a bygone attitude. Men today, unless they are cowards or fools, believe – he tells us – in no 'sanction greater than military power'. By implication, he includes himself; the year is 1942, before the Bomb, before the death of Gandhi, and Orwell is feeling combative. Kipling, on the other hand, belongs to that enviable age when men believed in a 'law'. 'He still believes that pride comes before a fall, and that the Gods punish *hubris*.'

Kipling, as Orwell portrays him, is a rather odd figure, a kind of Flory who took the other fork of the road. Like Flory, he is a man of the elite standing on the very edge of his caste, regarded by the Blimps as a bit of a bounder; it is even said of him, as of Flory, that he must have 'a touch of the tarbrush'. But where Flory rebels, Kipling becomes the poet of the caste, celebrating its group-loyalties, and idealizing the Empire as a means of spreading civilization rather than of making money. In this role Orwell finds him more admirable than many of the people who condemn him, and he justifies Kipling in a paragraph which sums up all his own attacks on his fellow anti-imperialists and all his scattered defences of the imperial and military caste to which he once belonged.

But because he identifies himself with the official class, he does possess one thing which 'enlightened' people seldom or never possess, and that is a sense of responsibility.... All left-wing parties in the highly industrialized countries are at bottom a sham, because they make it their business to fight againt something which they do not really wish to destroy. They have internationalist aims, and at the same time they struggle to keep up a standard of life with which those aims are incompatible. We all live by robbing Asiatic coolies, and those of us who are 'enlightened' all maintain that those coolies ought to be set free; but our standard of living, and hence our 'enlightenment', demands that the robbery shall continue. A humanitarian is always a hypocrite, and Kipling's understanding of this is perhaps the central secret of his power to create telling phrases. It would be difficult to hit off the one-eyed pacifism of the English in fewer words than in the phrase 'making mock of uniforms that guard you while you sleep....' He sees clearly that men can only be highly civilized while other men, inevitably less civilized, are there to guard and feed them.

One's immediate reaction to a passage of this kind is to point out that Orwell too, living on his three pounds a week, was taking part in the racket he denounced. But he was always ready for the 'you're another' argument, as he called it. He would have answered that he was honest enough to admit the fact, while others were not. And here we get some measure of the role he saw himself playing – that of the disinfecting voice of decency in the Left. Let us be decent enough not to sneer at honourable opponents! Let us be frank enough to admit our own inconsistencies, to grant that we may not always be fine enough to live up to our principles! The unique thing about Orwell was that he managed to say such things and still seem, not a prig, but a plain man full of honest anger.

But there were deeper motives underlying Orwell's forays among the intellectuals than a desire to call them back to honest ways. Most of his friends were themselves intellectuals, as he was, and as individuals he liked them, but as a class the intelligentsia aroused his repulsion and even – one always felt – his fear. The irrationality of his attitude is particularly evident when we come to the question of education, and realize how consistently he elevated the half-educated working man above the intellectual.

In practice, Orwell had a kind of double standard where education was concerned. It was probably, he would tell one, desirable for middle-class people like himself to send their children to public schools. Where else, with their background, could they fit in while society remained the divided structure it was? Besides, schools like Eton had one great virtue, he said in an article in the *Observer* during 1948, 'and that is a tolerant and civilized atmosphere which gives each boy a fair chance of developing his individuality'. At the other end of the scale, however, he wrote in *The Road to Wigan Pier* an extraordinary passage of rabid anti-scholasticism in which he praises the workers because 'where "education" touches their own lives they see through it and reject it by a healthy instinct'. He goes on to paint the picture of the normal working-class boy, pining for the fourteenth birthday when he will leave school and 'be doing real work, not wasting his time on ridiculous rubbish like history and geography'. A working-class youth at eighteen, he maintains, is a man while a middle-class boy attending a public school is still a baby.

Education is thus revealed as one of the many swindles in the Orwellian racket-world, and the workers appear to make up for lack of it with a kind of instinct, an innate common sense, that makes them move forward cautiously and remain suspicious of 'modern ideas' which the intellectuals accept eagerly and without question. Thus, because of their conservatism, the workers have shown themselves less inclined than the intellectuals to fall for totalitarian creeds.

The common man is still living in the mental world of Dickens, but nearly every modern intellectual has gone over to some form of totalitaranism. ['Charles Dickens', 1939]

The intelligentsia are the people who squeal loudest against Fascism, and yet a respectable proportion of them collapse into defeatism when the pinch comes.... With the working class it is the other way about. Too ignorant to see through the trick that is being played on them, they easily swallow the promises of Fascism, yet sooner or later they always take up the struggle again. ['Looking Back on the Spanish Civil War', 1942]

The picture of the totalitarian intellectual is as unreal as that of the slow-moving, cautious but instinctively sane worker, as Orwell must have found almost every time he actually met a writer he had previously denounced in print for fascism or some similar sin. I can suggest only one reason for the obstinacy of Orwell's illusions on this point. The intellectual *par excellence* in his view was the college-trained writer of the type that controlled much of the London literary world, and among whom such doctrines as communism and a kind of Catholic neo-fascism were popular during the thirties. Such writers by no means represented the whole literary or intellectual world, which in England until very recent years has remained largely non-academic, but to Orwell, essentially a self-taught man and too proud to play the game of cliques, they did loom particularly large in his early unsuccessful days of effort. By the end of 1943 it was evident even to Orwell himself that his period of struggle had passed and that he was at least on the edge of the literary establishment. It is significant that just at this point his attitude towards the intellectuals began to change, swinging from abuse to defence, so that now, in 1943 and 1944, he began to publish in *Tribune* and elsewhere articles berating the leaders and doctrinaire theoreticians of the left-wing parties for their total failure to understand the part which writers might play in the achievement of socialism. Similarly, by the time he wrote *The English People* in 1947, he was willing to think in terms of an educational system based on ability rather than on class. But to the very end he retained, like Tolstoy, the haunting feeling that among those whose intelligences had not been shaped by learning there might lie ways of understanding life which were closed for ever to the intellectual mind.

7

IN the last few chapters I have presented some of the aspects of Orwellian polemics which demonstrate how difficult it is to fit him into any accepted political pattern. From the day he published *The Road to Wigan Pier* in 1936, until his death in 1950, not only the Communists, who frankly hated him, but also many doctrinaire Socialists within the Labour Party felt that their movement would have been better off without an advocate so given to prickly criticism and so liable to lapse into embarrassing bouts of conservatism.

Orwell accused left-wing intellectuals of being 'irresponsible', but this was precisely what he himself appeared to the men who were anxious to build up party discipline. Already, in 1936, Victor Gollancz complained about the 'strange indiscretion' of much that Orwell said about Socialists in *The Road to Wigan Pier*, and I am sure that many Labour Party supporters agreed with him. They probably agreed even more heartily in 1947, when Orwell remarked in *The English People* on the extent to which the distinctions between the Conservative and the Labour parties were becoming blurred, so that every year their mutual resemblance grew greater.

Orwell, in fact, wanted to speak as a Socialist, but at the same time to be free of any party discipline so that he could say at any moment exactly what he thought or felt without regard for the consequences. By 1943, he was beginning to find that the orthodox Socialists did not want him on these terms, and in that year he wrote in *Tribune* an article on the subject whose tone suggests that he was speaking from the bitterness of personal experience.

There is no knowing just how much the Socialist movement has lost by alienating the literary intelligentsia. But it has alienated them, partly by confusing tracts with literature, and partly by having no room in it for a humanistic culture. A writer can vote Labour as easily as anyone else, but it is very difficult for him to take part in the Socialist movement *as a writer*. Both the book-trained doctrinaire and the practical politician will despise him as a 'bourgeois intellectual', and will lose no opportunity of telling him so. They will have much the same attitude towards his work as a golfing stockbroker would have.

Any doctrinaire political group, from the Anarchists on the left to the Conservatives on the right, distrusts a free mind, but it is only by keeping his mind free that the writer can carry out his function. That this implies a division between literature and practical politics Orwell found it hard to admit, but in the end he did admit it, and one of his last essays, 'Writers and Leviathan', was devoted to exploring the implications. He still insisted that a writer who believed in socialism should be willing to take part in political activity, but as a citizen, 'not *as a writer*'.

Whatever else he does in the service of his party, he should never write for it. He should make it clear that his writing is a thing apart. And he should be able to act cooperatively while, if he choses, completely rejecting the official ideology. He should never turn back from from a train of thought because it may lead to a heresy, and he should not mind very much if his unorthodoxy is smelt out, as it probably will be. Perhaps it is even a bad sign in a writer if he is not suspected of reactionary tendencies today, just as it was a bad sign if he was not suspected of Communist sympathies twenty years ago.

Orwell was not recruiting residents for the ivory tower; on the contrary. He believed that the writer should be concerned about his world and his time; he should make it the subject of his writing; he should allow his political ideals to influence his literary style. Yet the very fact that he observes the world independently will make him suspect to the party bosses and the gramophone doctrinaires. He must reconcile himself to fighting 'as an individual, an outsider, at the most an unwelcome guerilla on the flank of a regular army'. This, in effect, is what Orwell had always done, with no scruples against sending an occasional burst of fire near enough to the ears of his fellow Socialists to keep them up to scratch.

Obviously, in Orwell's view, individual integrity and even, on occasion, individual caprice stand above political loyalty, and this fact alone makes one hesitate about regarding him as a politician at all. It is in the nature of the political animal to hunt in packs. The lone hunter belongs to another race – the race of moralists. The differences between politician and moralist are clear. The first is concerned with acquiring power in order to implement a certain programme (which may be merely the consolidation of power), and for him the means are always subordinate to the end. For the moralist the means are all-important; the quality of the act rather than its results is what he has first in mind. Yet the moralist does not go as far as the mystic and declare like Krishna in the *Bhagavad Gita* that we should be concerned only with action, never with its fruits. He would say rather that the action and its fruits cannot be divided, that one acts always to an end, but the end will be distorted and the fruit be evil if the action is wrong.

Here precisely, on this moral position, is where Orwell stood. Despite his frequent boasts of being more realistic and down to the bleak earth than any other Socialist intellectual, he was idealistic enough to believe that the political deeds of men could be governed by an austere rule which would preclude the deceptions and dishonesties usually associated with such activity. Politics, he admitted, was a dirty game. But his whole point was that it need not be dirty. And that was a moralist's point, not a politician's.

Spender once said that Orwell was 'really' the Socialist that 'hundreds of others only pretend to be'. If he meant this in ordinary political terms he was obviously wrong. If he meant it in the sense that Orwell saw socialism – unlike the politicians and the doctrinaires – as the social aspect of an all-embracing moral attitude, then he was right. Orwell was doubtless encouraged in this viewpoint by contact with the Spanish Anarchists and libertarian Socialists, for it is significant how much space he devoted in *Homage to Catalonia* to recording the moral rather than the political atmosphere of Catalonia in the winter of 1936-7 and to showing the heightened temper of individual morality in a society rejuvenated by a revolutionary spirit.

Orwell's vision of socialism could be stated as simply as Tolstoy's vision of Christianity. He did not often demand specific material improvements for the workers; he demanded instead the establishment of liberty and justice as the guiding principles of society, on the assumption that the rest would then automatically be added. But to achieve liberty and justice, and to keep them, we must not only be prepared to struggle – 'to deliver lectures in draughty halls, to chalk pavements, to canvass voters, to distribute leaflets, even to fight in civil wars'. We must also be prepared to do these things cleanly; to be honest with ourselves and others about the kind of acts we intend to carry out and their consequences; to behave decently and fairly.

All the elements of Orwell's view of life that must seem aberrant to the average orthodox Socialist (though few are honest enough to say so now fame has made him such an ornament to the cause) can be traced to the fact that always he based his stand on a personal morality rather than on a party programme. He feared material progress because it was morally softening, and he rejected excessive education for the same reason. The family he saw as a morally regenerating institution; and birth control and abortion as manifestations of moral degeneration. A great deal of sheer sentimentality entered into his attitudes towards England, the imperial tradition and the working class, but his upbringing and his family traditions made him perceive something virtuous in public service, even in a shabby cause like that of a dying empire, while his vision of working-class life was essentially that of the Spartan moralist, dwelling happily on the thought of the ideal working man who enjoys the comforts of sufficiency and is uncorrupted either by the evils of abundance which afflict the rich or by the naggings of ambition which disturb the peace of the genteel poor. Even Orwell's anxiety over the decay of history, and his passion for clean, exact prose, had moral roots in the desire to sustain truth.

It would indeed be hard to weld Orwell's attitudes into a clear-cut ethical system, and he certainly never attempted it. As I have already said, he was not philosophically inclined, at least in an academic sense. Like many writers who rely on the impressionist style and the free flow of argument, he never constructed an elaborate theoretical frame for his thought. Rather he enlarged the simple code of decency of a middle-class liberal into a rough-and-ready morality, extending it politically to include the basic elements of democratic socialism. It was a morality of austere virtues and wholesome life, bound up with a deep love of nature, and in large part reducible to the familiar phrases of proverbial wisdom. But it was sincerely, almost fiercely held, and it sustained him through twenty years of battling against hypocrisy, obscurantism and tyranny.

So much of Orwell's energy was spent on attacking the totalitarian tendencies which seemed to imperil the future of any kind of moral life for humanity that he did not devote very much time to elaborating Socialist plans or programmes. He never produced any work setting out clearly and concisely what he meant by socialism, and one has to search through his writings for the fragments that enable one to build up the picture for oneself. Partly, this was because of his anti-Utopian frame of mind; he shared the feeling of most libertarian Socialists that we have no right to plot the future which others may live, and he felt that excessive planning in any case carried the danger of creating a rigid society in which the evils of power would be inescapable.

He never returned in later life to his early rejection of the state as a basic framework of society. Indeed, he held that some system of law and compulsion was probably in the long run more conducive to freedom than none at all. For example, in his essay on Swift, 'Politics vs. Literature' (1946), he discussed the kinds of pressure exerted in the theoretically libertarian Utopia of the Houyhnhnms. This was the conclusion he drew:

In a society where there is no law, and in theory no compulsion, the only arbiter of behaviour is public opinion. But public opinion, because of the tremendous urge to conformity in gregarious animals, is less tolerant than any system of law. When human beings are governed by 'thou shalt not', the individual can practise a certain amount of eccentricity: when they are supposedly govered by 'love' or 'reason', he is under continuous pressure to make him behave and think in exactly the same way as everyone else.

Whether or not this is a valid criticism of the Anarchist position, the fact that the question troubled Orwell shows that at this period he was thinking very deeply on the nature of power in all its aspects; *Nineteen Eighty-Four*, of course, demonstrates that he did not minimize the corresponding danger that could come from a state too highly organized.

But we can only determine the kind of state or the form of government he would favour by a series of rather vague surmises, since what he did say on this subject was marred by inconclusiveness and even inconsistency. For example, he rejected the totalitarian state based on a single party, whether it existed in Russia, in Germany, or in the England of the future. Yet he also contended in *The Road to Wigan Pier* that socialism should broaden its appeal to induce the millions of the lower middle class to join the workers in overthrowing the 'plutocracy'; it is hard to see how such a development could result in anything less than the establishment of a single-party state. Again, he disliked the police, but he favoured heavy taxation of the rich and the childless, which would necessitate the establishment of an elaborate civil service of the kind that already – fifteen years after his death – governs the inhabitants of most modern countries as effectively as a secret police force, but even more insidiously, thanks to its network of forms, registrations and computers. He demanded, on occasion, the nationalization of all industry and of all land-holdings over fifteen acres, but he never stated clearly what kind of machinery should be created to administer the nationalized holdings; at times, as I have said, he talked as though he favoured a wide degree of workers' control of industry, but if this were the case he used the word 'nationalization' misleadingly, since what he actually meant was 'socialization'. That he may have intended something different from state control of industry is suggested by the fact that in *The English People* he adopted the libertarian idea of decentralization, arguing that the system of administration based on London should be broken down, that Wales, Scotland and the English regions should be given greater autonomy, that local universities, the provincial press and local cultures should be encouraged.

On the whole, there was nothing very revolutionary about any of Orwell's proposals for a Socialist society; many of the things he suggested were no more than liberal reforms which have since been carried out in countries that in no way consider themselves Socialist. But the details always struck him as unimportant. It was important, on the other hand, to make the people recognize the injustices that existed among them, and to make them aware of the dangers to liberty that might lie in the future. Then they might realize their own abiltiy to bring about changes, and develop within them the genius to create a good society. This was a vision of moral regeneration leading to political reform. But it was essential to Orwell's view of life that the change should begin with the inward recognition of the truth, about one's world, about oneself. Unless that took place, socialism could only be a mechanical process leading to the totalitarian nightmare.

PART FOUR

PROSE LIKE A WINDOW-PANE

Orwell as Critic and Stylist

JUDGED by the criteria of literary mandarins, George Orwell is a writer of monumental imperfections, who never produced a well-balanced novel or a critical essay devoid of some marring propagandist intent. Judged, on the other hand, by the standards of the avant-garde, his work seems conservative, obvious, at times even naïve. His interests and his tastes were limited: compared with Herbert Read he knew nothing of the visual arts; compared with Arthur Koestler he was a novice in the physical sciences; compared with almost any of the leading French novelists of his time he was a positive ignoramus in philosophy; and he had learned less psychology than many an intelligent undergraduate. Even his reading was limited, and few of the authors he read in later years engrossed his attention so much or left such a lasting mark on his mind as those great Victorians and Edwardians who had impressed him in his youth, Dickens and Thackeray, Gissing and Wells.

Yet the impression he has left is that of an open rather than a circumscribed intelligence. His prose was that of the plain, uncomplicated man, but he was far more protean than he chose to appear, and in the varied facets of achievement and personality he presented we can find the clues to the appeal he made to so many people of different types. 'I have always believed', said Julian Symons, a close friend, 'that what Orwell wrote is less important than what he was.' Others, who knew him less directly, have been attracted by the myth which he constructs in his novels, the myth of the rebel caught in the pressures of a society dominated and fatally divided by class. Yet others have taken the view that Orwell's ideas – his world-perspective – were far more important than anything else about him. And finally there are those, relatively uninterested in Orwell the man, and unimpressed by his themes or his ideas, who are still delighted by the quality of his literary style, its firmness, its colloquial vigour, its unpretentious vividness, and, above all, its limpid clarity.

Orwell would have regarded such distinctions as irrelevant. He was not indifferent to the impression he made as a man, since he valued friendships and was willing to make concessions in order to retain them; but he did not consider that this had anything to do with his vocation as a writer, except for the fact that his choice of a profession provided him with friends whose interests were literary and political like his own. As for the rest – the writer's literary personality and its projection in myth, the ideas the writer expresses, the language in which he expresses them – all these were, in his view, closely interlinked. Purpose could determine the character of prose, as he suggested in his late essay 'Why I Write': 'And looking back through my work, I see that it is invariably where I lacked a political purpose that I wrote lifeless books and was betrayed into purple passages, sentences without meaning, decorative adjectives, and humbug generally.'

But the purpose was not everything; otherwise many sincere men with sound ideas would be better writers than they are. In consequence, Orwell found himself forced, though somewhat uneasily, to include 'aesthetic enthusiasm' among the four 'great motives' for writing prose which he listed in the same essay; the other three were 'sheer egoism', 'historical impulse' and 'political purpose'. But the unsureness of his grip on aesthetic theory, one of those realms of abstract thought in which he felt least happy, is shown by the imprecision of his definition of the aesthetic motive.

Perception of beauty in the external world, or, on the other hand, in words and their right arrangement. Pleasure in the impact of one sound on another, in the firmness of good prose or the rhythm of a good story. Desire to share an experience which one feels is valuable and ought not to be missed.

While the first two items in this list are valid enough, the third is not, since all experiences are not aesthetic, and mere communication is not art. Yet the definition as a whole is valuable, since it does show what, apart from its didactic element, writing actually meant to Orwell.

The impulse to render his own experiences into some meaningful form was in fact much stronger in him than the impulse to invent original situations and sequences of events. This was largely because he felt that the political issues that pressed upon a writer in his day were too urgent to allow him to stray into other worlds than the familiar.

Flaubert could think himself into the stony cruelty of antiquity, because in the mid-ninetenth century one still had peace of mind. One had time to travel in the past. Nowadays the present and the future are too terrifying to be escaped from, and if one bothers with history it is in order to find modern meanings there.

Significantly, Orwell's only dip into the past – the past of Lower Binfield – describes a period, if not an actual place, which he remembered from his own childhood and which therefore forms a facet of his own experience. *Nineteen Eighty-Four*, is, admittedly, a novel about the future, but the future conceived as a degenerated present, extending along the lines of absurd logic the experiences of a contemporary Everyman. Only in *Animal Farm*, leaping into the world of fable, does Orwell let invention come into full play.

Orwell's other and more exact definitions of the aesthetic apply with equal force to his own writings. Beauty in the external world is an element in almost all his books; the descriptions of the jungle in the hunting sequences of *Burmese Days*, of the Kentish hopfields and orchards in *A Clergyman's Daughter*, the haunting evocation of the stark Spanish mountains in *Homage to Catalonia*, are unusually fine pieces of landscape writing.

But this is the outer aesthetic – what prompts the writer by its external beauty. The inner aesthetic comes with the 'perception of beauty ... in words and their arrangement', in the 'pleasure in the impact of one sound on another, in the firmness of good prose or the rhythm of a good story'. Farther on in 'Why I Write' (which, characteristically, Orwell wrote for his friend John Atkins to publish in a little magazine called *Gangrel* that made at best a token payment) he remarks that his aim since he returned from Spain has been to turn political writing into an art. The first impulse for whatever he has written in that period has been to expose a lie or to draw attention to a fact.

> But I could not do the work of writing a book, or even a long magazine article, if it were not also an aesthetic experience. Anyone who cares to examine my work will see that even when it is downright propaganda it contains much that a full-time politician would consider irrelevant. I am not able, and I do not want, completely to abandon the world-view that I acquired in childhood. So long as I remain alive and well I shall continue to feel strongly about prose style, to love the surface of the earth, and to take a pleasure in solid objects and scraps of useless information. It is no use trying to suppress that side of myself. The job is to reconcile my ingrained likes and dislikes with the essentially public, non-individual activities that this age forces on all of us.

Here Orwell fully exposes the particular duality that makes him almost unique among the writers of his time, the combination of a deep social indignation with the kind of autonomous and eccentrically curious mind that is proper to the artist, interpenetrating in such a way that it is really impossible to conceive one without the other. For one of Orwell's most significant characteristics, as a man and as a writer, was his almost complete lack of aesthetic affectation; though he was in fact one of the best prose writers of our time, he never sought to make any distinction between his imaginative work and the social criticism towards which he always felt impelled; such a distinction would have seemed unnatural to him. In this he differed profoundly from a writer like André Gide, who during his period of involvement in left-wing politics virtually ceased to write imaginatively, by implication conceding that there was something contaminating about the activity of social protest. The difference between the two writers lay, I suspect, in the fact that Gide came so late to the point of protesting against the nature of contemporary society that his indignation could not become the main core of his work, as it had been from the beginning for Orwell, who served his apprenticeship to writing with the guilt of an accomplice of imperialism burning in his heart.

Orwell was never a mere propagandist. 'All art is propaganda...' he said. 'On the other hand, all propaganda is not art.' He was, indeed, an engaged writer – though never in the narrow sense a partisan – but his engagement was no mere intellectual attitude; it was a passion born of experience and absorbed so completely into his personal philosophy that it became the inner subject of his books, around which the action played like a continuous allegory in various forms, and even of his briefest and most occasional essays.

It is for this reason that Orwell's critical writings have a peculiar importance in considering his work in general, since they show him developing his own attitude towards the relationship between the writer and the world, and an examination of them is the almost necessary prelude to a consideration of the more formal qualities of his writing.

There are very clear and self-imposed limitations to Orwell's critical scope. He denied the possibility of any genuine evaluative criticism, and it was in this denial – reiterated on several occasions – that his deliberate identification with the plain unintellectual man was most strongly expressed. In his essay 'Lear, Tolstoy and the Fool' he states his view of the only true criterion of literary merit.

In reality there is no kind of evidence or argument by which one can show that Shakespeare, or any other writer, is 'good'. Nor is there any way of definitely proving that – for instance – Warwick Deeping is 'bad'. Ultimately there is no test of literary merit except survival, which is itself an index to majority opinion.

At this point Orwell demonstrates that populist conservatism enters into even his attitudes towards literature. What is established in the minds of a sufficient number of people over a sufficient period of time is good. This, by implication, denies the value of mere experimentalism for its own sake, since it is only a generation ahead that we shall begin to know whether the avant-garde writing of today has stood the basic test of goodness; every writer works in the vacuum of his own esteem, condemned never to have a real idea – unless he outlives his main work as long as Hardy did – whether what he has done is 'good' or otherwise. It also, as Orwell suggests, demonstrates the ultimate futility of any kind of evaluative criticism.

Tolstoy was perhaps the most admired literary man of his age, and he was certainly not its least able pamphleteer. He turned all his powers of denunciation against Shakespeare, like all the guns of a battleship roaring simultaneously. And with what result? Forty years later Shakespeare is still there completely unaffected, and of the attempt to demolish him nothing remains except the yellowing pages of a pamphlet which hardly anyone has read, and which would be forgotten altogether if Tolstoy had not also been the author of *War and Peace* and *Anna Karenina*.

It is easy to point out the flaws in Orwell's contention that 'survival', considered as 'a test of majority opinion', is the sole genuine criterion of literary merit. Even as a general proposition one regards it with distrust. Very often a completely extraneous circumstance can change the nature of a writer's reputation. A hundred years ago Virgil and Horace were still much quoted writers in England, but since then a change in the British educational system has reduced their present readership to a tiny minority of even the literary-minded public; does this mean they have ceased to be 'good writers'? In dealing with contemporary writers Orwell in practice often ignored his rule, talking of 'the best writers of our generation' (most of whom he found to be fascistically inclined), and discussing writers like Yeats and Eliot in tones which left no doubt at all that he considered them superior to, say, Kipling or Noyes. Finally, it is doubtful if he would have continued to write with such dedication for the second half of his life, or would have resented the imperceptiveness of publishers so much, if he had not been convinced that he was, at least part of the time, a 'good' writer.

As for Orwell's point about 'majority' opinion, here he is

surely on the shakiest ground of all. It is doubtful if Shakespeare, even at the height of the Elizabethan period, was really the taste of the majority. And when we look at books which have survived over the centuries, and which seem very much alive to those who still read them today, we find that their appeal has often been to a relatively small number of people in each generation. Was the *Satyricon*, or *The Way of the World*, or *The Charterhouse of Parma* at any time the reading of the majority? Yet all of them have survived, and deservedly so.

At the same time one has to remember that many works have survived for long periods in the popular esteem despite the fact that by any kind of acceptable literary criteria they were inferior to other works which have almost vanished from memory; they make their appeal to the more spurious emotions – to sentimentality or that pale cousin of sadism which goes by the name of ghoulishness. Orwell realized the existence of this problem, and found a ready solution to it by inventing a class of 'good bad' writing. He makes the point particularly strongly in his discussion of Kipling, pointing out that at his worst 'Kipling is almost a shameful pleasure, like the taste for cheap sweets that some people secretly carry into middle life', and that even in his best passages 'one has the sense of being seduced by something spurious, and yet unquestionably seduced'. The answer to the problem, Orwell tells us, lies in admitting Kipling's badness.

One can, perhaps, place Kipling more satisfactorily than by juggling with the words 'verse' and 'poetry', if one describes him simply as a good bad poet. He is as a poet what Harriet Beecher Stowe was as a novelist. And the mere existence of work of this kind, which is perceived by generation after generation to be vulgar and yet goes on being read, tells one something about the age we live in.

There is a great deal of Orwellian whimsicality in this talk about survival being the only real criterion of good literature, about the majority being right, and about 'good bad writing'. It was one of Orwell's customary tricks in his long game with the intellectuals to try to startle them by suddenly assuming the mask of the philistine. Nevertheless, even allowing for shock tactics, these arguments have to be taken with a great deal more than a pinch of salt. Orwell's literary populism was sincere enough; he felt that there was a vitality in the life of the common people that could not be dismissed, and much of his time was devoted to examining the strange arts of this working-class culture, alien to his own. He was concerned deeply with the social roots of art, and particularly of literature, and when he came to a layer of society that nurtured types different from those cultivated in the greenhouses of the intelligentsia, he had to make the effort to judge them in their own terms. His literary criticism therefore covered a field a great deal wider than that of any other well-known contemporary critic, since it stretched from Henry Miller and T. S. Eliot at the top of the ladder to those venerable boys' magazines, the *Gem* and the *Magnet*, at the bottom.

This tendency to take notice of anything which appeared in print and which might affect the minds of other people was combined with a distrust of the methods of academic criticism in general. Not merely did Orwell reject evaluative criticism; he also doubted if there was any point in the formal analysis of writing. In his essay on Dickens he noted, rather sternly, that there are 'no rules in novel-writing', and nearly ten years afterwards, in one of his last essays, 'Writers and Leviathan', he remarked: 'I often have the feeling that even at the best of times literary criticism is fraudulent, since in the absence of any accepted standards whatever ... every literary judgment consists in trumping up a set of rules to justify an instinctive preference.'

One wonders how, with such a view, he could have devoted most of his writing time between 1939 and 1946 to a series of critical articles often monumental in scale and always serious in intent. The answer, I think, is that Orwell was attempting to create a type of criticism which he could regard as valid in terms of the nature of literature as he saw it, and valid also in terms of the historical period in which he lived. Against evaluative and formal criticism he practised descriptive and discriminative criticism. The important thing about any book and any author is what makes him individual, and so criticism has to be pragmatic; it cannot proceed according to set rules. And between writer and writer it is the differences in character and outlook rather than the differences in quality, which can never be determined exactly, that are important. Orwell brings this out in an admirable comparison between Dickens and Tolstoy:

Why is it that Tolstoy's grasp seems to be so much larger than Dickens's – why is it that he seems able to tell you so much more *about yourself*? It is not that he is more gifted or even, in the last analysis, more intelligent. It is because he is writing about people who are growing. His characters are struggling to make their souls, whereas Dickens's are already finished and perfect. In my own mind Dickens's people are present far more often and far more vividly than Tolstoy's, but always in a single unchangeable attitude like pictures or pieces of furniture. You cannot hold an imaginary conversation with a Dickens character as you can with, say, Peter Bezoukhov. And this is not merely because of Tolstoy's greater seriousness, for there are also comic characters that you can imagine yourself talking to – Bloom, for instance, or Pécuchet, or even Wells's Mr Polly. It is because Dickens's characters have no mental life. They say perfectly the thing that they have to say, but they cannot be conceived as talking about anything else. They never learn, never speculate. Perhaps the most meditative of his characters is Paul Dombey, and his thoughts are mush. Does this mean that Tolstoy's novels are 'better' than Dickens's? The truth is that it is absurd to make such comparisons in terms of 'better' or 'worse'. If I were forced to compare Tolstoy with Dickens, I should say that Tolstoy's appeal will probably be wider in the long run, because Dickens is scarcely intelligible outside the English-speaking culture; on the other hand, Dickens is able to reach simple people, which Tolstoy is not. Tolstoy's characters can cross a frontier, Dickens's can be portrayed on a cigarette-card. But one is no more obliged to choose between them than between a sausage and a rose. Their purposes barely intersect.

Which is about as pungent a statement of the autonomy of works of literature as I have heard anywhere expressed.

In further defining Orwell's criticism, we can say that it is eminently sociological, since he believes that not only the works of literature themselves, but also our understanding of them, are affected profoundly by the changing nature of society. Even being born into one class can make us read a novel or a poem differently from a man born into a higher or a lower class. Orwell's criticism is also historical in character, relating literature to political events and social changes. And it is personal, in almost every sense of the word. When Orwell writes on Yeats he is interested in the relationship between the poet's work and his semi-Fascist social theories. When he writes on Tolstoy he is interested in the novelist's attempt to renounce his social and financial advantages. When he writes on Dickens he disclaims interest in vulgar scandals about marital troubles, yet he searches deeply into the writer's mind and his world to find the clues to the behaviour of his characters. And when he talks of Gissing, he shows his realization that this tragic man's life cannot be dissociated from either the peculiar dingy tone or the gloomy subject-matter of his novels.

Finally – and I place this quality in isolation because it embraces all the others – Orwell was a moralistic critic. Just as his political doctrines were really moral doctrines in disguise, so, ultimately, literature also interested him for its moral implications, which is one of the reasons why he could become so deeply involved in sub-literature. Some of his critical essays, like 'Raffles and Miss Blandish' and 'Benefit of Clergy' (an analysis of Salvador Dali's autobiography), are written in overtly moralistic terms; in the other essays the moral purpose is more or less disguised, but search only a little and you find it informing and moulding the whole approach. It is a cardinal principle of Orwell's criticism that, as he remarked at the end of his essay on Yeats, 'a writer's political and religious beliefs are not excrescences to be laughed away, but something that will leave their mark even on the smallest detail of his work'. Literature influences the moral life and is inescapably influenced by it.

Within the moralistic framework Orwell's critical attitudes did change, and there are signs that at the end of his life, when he considered his phase of deep political involvement might be drawing towards an end, he laid more stress on formal criticism, on questions of structure and genre, than he had done before. This may well have been the result of a study of Conrad, on whom he was projecting an essay, but it appeared most noticeably in the late essay on Gissing which was completed not long before his death and which lay in the files of a defunct little magazine until it was discovered and published by John Lehmann in 1960 in the *London Magazine*. In the middle of this essay Orwell breaks out into what seems like a typically provocative statement, but the explanation with which he follows it up is extremely interesting:

I am ready to maintain that England has produced very few better novelists. This perhaps sounds like a rash statement, until one stops to consider what is meant by a novel. The word 'novel' is commonly used to cover almost any kind of story – *The Golden Asse*, *Anna Karenina*, *Don Quixote*, *The Improvisatore*, *Madame Bovary*, *King Solomon's Mines* or anything else you like – but it also has a narrower sense in which it means something hardly existing before the nineteenth century and flourishing chiefly in Russia and France. A novel, in this sense, is a story which attempts to describe credible human beings and – without necessarily using the technique of naturalism – to show them acting on everyday motives and not merely undergoing strings of improbable adventures. A true novel, sticking to this definition, will also contain at least two characters, probably more, who are described from the inside and on the same level of probability – which, in effect, rules out the novels written in the first person. If one accepts this definition, it becomes apparent that the novel is not an art form in which England has excelled. The writers commonly paraded as 'great English novelists' have a way of turning out either to be not true novelists or not to be Englishmen. Gissing was not a writer of picaresque tales, or burlesques, or comedies, or political tracts; he was interested in individual human beings, and the fact that he can deal sympathetically with several different sets of motives, and make a credible story out of the collision between them, makes him exceptional among English writers.

As usual, Orwell is exaggerating. But the passage is interesting because it shows a veering of his critical interest towards problems of form. And this veering of interest, I suggest, is connected with the change in attitude towards his own work which he was undergoing at the time. Even before he finished it, *Nineteen Eighty-Four* seemed to him the end of a progression.

2

POETS or fiction writers or dramatists who at some hiatus in their careers take to writing about the works of other men or about literature in general are usually the most interesting critics. Academic critics can tell us a great deal about the structure of literature, about its formal qualities, can dazzle us with symbolic pyrotechnics and astonish us with the follies of analytical methods carried to logical absurdity, but they are often left dancing like frustrated wasps around the work of art while the practising writer, with his knowledge of the real problems of creation, proceeds almost instinctively to its core. But such writer-critics have usually one limitation: they are interested only in writers towards whom they feel some affinity or some sharp antagonism or in aspects of literature which relate to their own present problems. It is a limitation that can, of course, be revealing to the critic who in turn writes on their work, since it provides one of the most fruitful fields of evidence on their general approach to writing, on their methods, and on their problems. And so, before proceeding to study Orwell's works in more formal terms than I have adopted up to the present, it will be enlightening to survey in at least some detail the field which his criticism covered.

Orwell's critical essays can be divided between the major pieces which, with the unaccountable exception of 'Rudyard Kipling' and 'George Gissing', were gathered into his *Collected Essays* published in 1961, and the minor pieces – short essays or review articles – which are still incomprehensibly uncollected and have to be sought in the back files of periodicals as varied as the *Adelphi*, *Poetry*, *Poetry Quarterly*, the *Observer*, and, above all, *Tribune*.

The major literary essays and the important minor ones fall into five groups, each of which indicates a particular field of Orwell's interests and also illuminates a corresponding facet of his attitude to literature and life.

The first group includes the essays on Swift ('Politics vs. Literature'), Tolstoy ('Lear, Tolstoy and the Fool') and Charles Dickens; the last is the longest of all Orwell's essays (about twenty thousand words). All three of these essays are written with a passionate involvement, which in the case of Dickens is blithe in tone, and in the case of Swift and Tolstoy rather angrily contentious. There are two reasons for the intensely personal quality which sets this group of essays off from the other literary pieces. They all concern writers whom Orwell admired greatly and whom he had read since his youth; Swift and Dickens, indeed, he had read since early childhood. In a literary sense he felt close to these men because each, in his own way, had devoted himself to translating a moral vision into fictional terms, which was the task Orwell had set himself by the time he wrote his major critical essays, so that his admiration for them had a more intimate quality than his admiration for, say, Shakespeare, whom he defended against Tolstoy.

There is, however, a further aspect of this group of writers which becomes particularly evident when we study 'Lear, Tolstoy and the Fool'. For the essay, we soon realize, is not really about Shakespeare, who is being defended; less than fourteen lines of his verse are quoted in twenty prose pages, and by the end of the essay he has become as shadowy as a *casus belli* at the end of a war. Nor is it about the Fool, who is allowed to speak only one line, nor even about Lear. It is, overtly, about Tolstoy and his motives for selecting King Lear for special assault. Tolstoy attacks the play on critical grounds, for its manifest absurdities; Orwell suggests that underlying this attack is a deep resentment, perhaps not entirely conscious, of the multiple resemblances between what happens in the play and what in real life happened to him.

There is a general resemblance which one can hardly avoid seeing, because the most impressive event in Tolstoy's life, as in Lear's, was a huge and gratuitous act of renunciation. In his old age he renounced his estate, his title and his copyrights, and made an attempt – a sincere attempt, though it was not successful – to escape from his privileged position and live the life of a peasant. But the deeper resemblance lies in the fact that Tolstoy, like Lear, acted on mistaken motives, and failed to get the results he had hoped for.

This tells us why Tolstoy chose *King Lear* as the special object of his anti-Shakespearean campaign. But it leaves open the question why Orwell himself, when he wrote an article on a novelist whom he admired and whose masterpieces he found extremely sympathetic, should have chosen to focus it upon a pamphlet which he regarded as one of Tolstoy's failures and which he found antipathetic. As in the case of Tolstoy and *King Lear*, we are led to speculate on the hidden reason for the antipathy; it seems certain that Orwell, in his turn, was fighting against a half-recognized similarity. For he too – in his youth if not in his old age – followed the example of Lear and Tolstoy in attempting a major act of renunciation. He gave up his career in the Indian service, which was probably no great sacrifice, but he followed it up by his deliberate descent into the lower depths of destitution. Afterwards, like Tolstoy, he realized that he had acted on mistaken motives, and that the impression he had first gained of having crossed the great gulf of caste was an illusion. The history of Orwell was as 'curiously similar' to the history of Tolstoy as Tolstoy's history to Lear's, and what appears to be violent disagreement is really an unwilling and unadmitted recognition of moral affinity.

Apart from attacking Tolstoy's views on *King Lear*, Orwell attacks his Christian anarchism as, in 'Politics vs. Literature', he attacks Swift's Tory anarchism. But the attack on Swift is sustained on a number of other levels as well. It is directed at such things as his disbelief in progress, his impatience with opponents, and his distaste for humanity, which culminated in a strong conviction that man stinks. Once again, one detects the unadmitted similarities between the critic and his subject; Orwell devoted a large part of *The Road to Wigan Pier* to an extensive criticism of the concept of progress; he was impatient with opponents, at least when he encountered them typewriter in hand; he lived, as he confessed, a large part of his life with the conviction that he himself smelt and that the working class smelt even worse.

Orwell's relationship to Swift was even more complex than his relationship to Tolstoy, largely because he and Swift belonged to the same literary tradition, that of English Tory dissent. Not only did Swift embarrassingly express opinions which he himself had once expressed but had since to some degree abandoned, but he also displayed qualities of which Orwell could only approve. Curiously enough, those which he most admired, to the extent of emulation and even imitation, he hardly mentions in his essay: Swift's clean, vigorous, unadorned prose, and his extraordinary satirical power. What he does concentrate on is the inexhaustible fascination which *Gulliver's Travels* holds for him and many others despite the fact that it presents what seems to him a diseased and negative view of humanity and of life in general.

Swift falsifies his picture of the world by refusing to see anything in human life except dirt, folly and wickedness, but the part which he abstracts from the whole does exist, and it is something which we all know about while shrinking from mentioning it. Part of our minds – in any normal person it is the dominant part – believes that man is a noble animal and life is worth living; but there is also a sort of inner self which at least intermittently stands aghast at the horror of existence.

The inner self in Orwell not only allowed him to underestimate the satirical intent in Swift's more violent passages, so that he seems to take for an actual physical stink what Swift means to be understood as a moral stink, but also to ignore the strong humanitarian element that lies behind even such apparently ghoulish essays as *A Modest Proposal*. The fury and obscenity to which all satirists are prone usually mask an idealistic view of humanity and an agonized disappointment that this view has not been lived up to. The bitterness of the satire in *Nineteen Eighty-Four* suggests that in this respect Orwell himself was in the same mental situation as Swift, and explains his failure to look with a more balanced eye upon the intention of *Gulliver's Travels*. He attacked Swift's tendency to go to extremes precisely because he shared it and feared it in himself. It was ironic justice that Orwell's detractors should have accused him of the same anti-humanitarian bias as he exaggeratedly imputed to Swift.

This brings us to the common feature of 'Politics vs. Literature' and 'Lear, Tolstoy and the Fool': the attack on anarchism – a doctrine which both Tolstoy and Swift maintained in varying forms and which in each case Orwell criticized on the grounds that it would substitute for the tyranny of the law the more dangerous because less definable tyranny of public opinion. As far as it goes, Orwell's point is a good one; but it is necessary to ask why, in both essays, he should have left out the positive aspects of anarchism and painted a one-sided picture of it as a rather barren doctrine dominated by the urge to moral censorship. He had enough experience, gathered in his Spanish days, to know better. And when we come to the roots of his attitude we realize once again that he was criticizing a tendency within himself. On questions of authority and government Orwell showed two sharply divided attitudes. One side of him belonged to the imperial tradition, defended the sahibs, and talked toughly about the realities of force. The other side of him, represented by the rebel at school and in Burma, reacted against imperialism, rejected all partisan disciplines, and saw that those who believed in the realities of force became the addicts of power. Clearly, in making a special point of criticizing Swift and Tolstoy for their anarchistic attitudes, he was trying to discipline his own strong emotional feeling for a doctrine which his realistic and rational self recognized to be, at least in its pure form, impractical in any foreseeable future. Anarchism remained a restless presence in his mind right to the end; it was one of the themes he hoped to develop in the novels after the manner of Joseph Conrad which, when he died, he was planning as his programme for work in the 1950s.

It will be seen that a great deal of the passion that inspires the essays on Swift and Tolstoy is really a disguised cry of agonized recognition as the critic sees himself in the mirrors of his subjects. I am not, of course, suggesting that Orwell is carrying out deliberate distortion; very little that he actually says about either Swift or Tolstoy is factually untrue or, in detail at least, unjust; it is the selection of statements and the tone of presentation that creates the bias.

The essays on Swift and Tolstoy are in fact exceptional in the degree of bias they reveal. The longer piece on Dickens is not nearly so confined to narrow moral issues, largely because Orwell did not feel the same agonized involvement with Dickens as he did with the other two writers. Dickens was not a man with extreme views, at least of the kind that touched in Orwell the raw nerves of passionate discussion. Moreover, he represented, perhaps more intimately than any other writer, the radical, unmilitaristic English nineteenth century, Orwell's ideal period; he gave expression to all those virtues of decency and fairness and peacefulness in which Orwell delighted; the mirror he held up reflected a consoling and pleasing image, for in Dickens Orwell recognized those qualities of himself, the honourable qualities of a nineteenth-century liberal at his best, which he could accept without any desire to perform the rites of exorcism.

Consequently the study of Dickens is far broader and more comprehensive than those of Swift and Tolstoy, far less marred by anger, and only biased enough to give a pleasant touch of idiosyncrasy to the interpretation. It is probably Orwell's best piece of criticism. It examines Dickensian morality, centred around its simple message: 'If men would behave decently, the world would be decent.' It places Dickens in his time and his class, discusses the limitations of his world-view, puts into perspective his horror of revolutions and his proposals for social reforms, and praises his 'lack of vulgar nationalism'. Occasionally the sharp brilliant definitions of aspects of Dickens send quick facets of Orwell flashing into one's vision – for example: 'It is hopeless to try and pin him down to any definite remedy, still more to any political programme. His approach is always along the moral plane.'

Almost certainly one of the reasons why Orwell could regard Dickens more affectionately yet more dispassionately than either Swift or Tolstoy was the fact that in a literary as well as in an emotional sense he was more distant from him. The clear, undecorated prose and the sharp satiric vision of Swift, the extraordinary Tolstoyan power of representing the surface of the earth with impressionistic authenticity and of rendering characters so naturally that one's mind seems to fit into theirs – these were achievements which Orwell not merely admired, but sought also to emulate.

On the other hand, though he enjoyed reading Dickens, he never really wished to imitate him, and so he could settle down to describe Dickens's way of writing, as well as what he wrote about, with a detail which he never attempted with any other writer. He discusses the limitations of Dickens's characterization, the monstrosity of his caricatures, the variety of his types, the shapelessness of his construction, the wild abundance and irrelevance of his imagery.

The outstanding, unmistakable mark of Dickens's writing is the unnecessary detail.... Everything is piled up and up, detail on detail, embroidery on embroidery. It is futile to object that this kind of thing is rococo – one might as well make the same objection to a wedding-cake. Either you like it or you do not like it.

Orwell did like it. It is true that his essay was written when he had just finished his own single experiment in a heavily detailed and rather exuberantly colloquial manner, *Coming Up for Air*, but I doubt if, even when he developed the spare and simple style of *Animal Farm*, he thought any less of Dickens. For he tended to see such matters historically; a sprawling manner was appropriate to the nineteenth century, a spare and functional manner to the twentieth. Besides, Dickens had the virtue of being an undeniably 'good' writer who was also popular, though Orwell certainly overestimated the extent to which Dickens was actually read among the working class.

On the whole the essay on Dickens is, though the earliest, one of the best of Orwell's major critical pieces, humane, informed, pleasantly discursive and unusually balanced between the sociological, the historical, the personal and the aesthetic. If anything jars, it is the recurrent discussion of class, though at times this is admirably done, taking the form of that kind of brilliant close analysis of caste gradations and their implications in all kinds of social and political directions whch only an English critic or a Hindu pandit can carry out satisfactorily.

3

BESIDE the core of major essays on authors with whom Orwell felt special affinities stands a somewhat larger group of essays relating to writers who in one way or another played an enlightening part in his mental development. These include 'Rudyard Kipling', 'Wells, Hitler and the World State', 'In Defence of P. G. Wodehouse', 'W. B. Yeats' and 'George Gissing' among the major essays, as well as lesser pieces on Thomas Hardy, Mark Twain, Thackeray, Oscar Wilde, Havelock Ellis, D. H. Lawrence and Osbert Sitwell. Curiously enough Orwell never seems to have written anything of even trivial importance on Bernard Shaw, Galsworthy or Arnold Bennett, all of whom were formative influences; he had every intention of writing an elaborate study of Conrad, but death prevented him.

All the major essays in this second group were first written as occasional pieces. 'Wells, Hitler and the World State' emerged out of Orwell's rather shocked response to a series of newspaper articles which Wells had written early in 1941, fantastically underestimating the power of the military forces which Hitler had at his disposal after the collapse of France; it seemed to Orwell a tragic example of how a man who had been a leader of the intellectual vanguard a generation ago could lose touch with the changing world. The excuse for writing on Kipling was the publication in 1942 of a selection of his verse edited by T. S. Eliot. 'W. B. Yeats' was a long review article on Narayana Menon's excellent but now forgotten ilttle book *The*

Development of William Butler Yeats, which appeared in 1943. 'In Defence of P. G. Wodehouse' was a characteristic example of Orwellian chivalry, written in 1945 to protest against the attempt to victimize Wodehouse for foolishly allowing himself to become the tool of Nazi propagandists while he was an internee in occupied Europe. 'George Gissing' celebrated the reprinting after the war of two of that neglected novelist's out-of-print works. From 1941 onwards an increasing number of Orwell's critical essays and articles were of this occasional kind, a fact which marked his emergence during these years as a busy journalist who in times of health had little leisure to produce long critical set pieces like 'Charles Dickens', 'Inside the Whale', and 'Boys' Weeklies' which he wrote at the beginning of the war in 1939 and 1940.

I have already discussed the implications, in terms of both Orwell's social ideas and his views on writing, of the pieces on Kipling, Wells and Gissing. 'In Defence of P. G. Wodehouse' has a double interest, since it shows admirably how well Orwell could combine the discussion of a current political issue with literary criticism of a sociological type. Even during the war, Orwell had been concerned over the occasional injustices which had crept into the treatment of people rightly or wrongly suspected of being Fascists, and when a British writer who had blundered into a situation that made him look like a collaborator was in danger of being sacrificed to the post-war lust for revenge, he immediately stood out in his defence. The fact that he was a popular writer whom the intellectuals were inclined to despise was undoubtedly a further count in Wodehouse's favour so far as Orwell was concerned. Certainly he never went to the same amount of trouble over Ezra Pound.

'In Defence of P. G. Wodehouse' is an excellent piece of pleading, in which Orwell begins by stating the background of the case – how Wodehouse was overtaken at le Touquet by the German advance in early 1940, and was immediately recognized by astute German propagandists as the kind of naïve man who might be put to use. He made some five broadcasts from Berlin, one of which was an interview with an American (C.B.S.) correspondent. The talks described his experiences in internment camps, truthfully said that he had been well treated, and made a few rather inanely Wodehousean comments which showed the kind of decent feelings it is sometimes tactless to express during a war. According to Orwell, who was connected with the B.B.C. at the time of the broadcasts and therefore probably had some inside knowledge of reactions, the passage which caused most offence was one that in peacetime would doubtless be regarded as conveying vacuously laudable sentiments: 'I never was interested in politics. I'm quite unable to work up any kind of belligerent feeling. Just as I'm about to feel belligerent about some country I meet a decent sort of chap. We go out together and lose any fighting thoughts or feelings.'

Orwell had to disinter and repeat these elementary facts because as the war went on the content of the original broadcasts had been forgotten, and the legend had developed that Wodehouse had acted as a kind of lowbrow Pound, and had expressed ideological sympathy for the Nazi cause. It was even suggested that his books contained 'Fascist tendencies', and they were banned by many English libraries.

Having shown that 'the events of 1941 do not convict Wodehouse of anything worse than stupidity', Orwell went on – in order to show how innocent of any Fascist taint Wodehouse's books actually were – to present a study of the man as writer. In doing so he inset within the essay of defence a brilliant essay of criticism, almost three thousand words in length, analysing the content and the mentality of one of the leading popular novelists of the traditionally educated English middle class.

Orwell confesses to having first read Wodehouse – as well as Swift – when he was eight. Since that time he had followed his work closely, and he claimed to have read more than two-thirds of the fifty novels which P. G. Wodehouse had written. The reasons why Orwell should have kept on reading such a writer are even more interesting than the comments from which we can deduce them.

For Orwell the most significant fact about Wodehouse, which explains his total failure to understand the situation in which he was placed when the Nazis laid their hands on him, is that he lived still in the past of which he wrote. And, contrary to general assumption, Orwell contends, this past is not the silly age of the twenties and thirties, but the decade between the first appearance of Psmith in 1909 and the first appearance of Jeeves and Wooster in 1919. Wodehouse, in other words, is really writing, mainly between the wars, of a pre-1914 world of public schools and country houses, so that his characters appear out of date even in relation to the early 1920s. Orwell further remarks on the 'public-school morality' that infuses all Wodehouse's works, on the classical allusions which show that Wodehouse wrote, snobbishly, for a readership 'educated along traditional lines'. Wodehouse went to an unfashionable school, Dulwich, and, after he left, worked in a bank. But the minor schools of England are even more intense in their snobberies than the major ones, and Wodehouse, as Orwell tells us, 'remained "fixated" on his old school and loathed the unromantic job and the lower-middle-class surroundings in which he found himself'.

All these points about Wodehouse are true enough, but Orwell missed what is really Wodehouse's great virtue; that he abstracted *out of time* the world of snobs and bounders and knuts, so that even today, his books are still read, rather in the way that people read Congreve and Sheridan, not because they are period pieces, but because, in his own trivial but quite authentic way, Wodehouse has presented certain social attitudes which, for the English at least, belong outside the accident of history.

Orwell is significantly anxious to date Wodehouse's world, to place it, very clearly, before 1914: in other words, within that idyllic period when everything was, to his mind, if not better, at least more ordered and decent than it had since become. In the same way, he makes a particular point of Wodehouse having been 'fixated' on his old school. Orwell too, as *Such, Such Were the Joys* showed quite clearly, was 'fixated' in a similar way, and the fact that he remembered the worst of St Cyprian's while Wodehouse remembered the best of Dulwich should not make us lose sight of the sense of affinity which the common obsession about boyhood experience encouraged. It would probably not be unfair to suggest that Orwell defended Wodehouse rather than Pound because Wodehouse evoked his own past in all its pleasant and unpleasant aspects, and Pound, that alien, raucous mid-Westerner, did not.

By Orwellian definition Wodehouse was a 'good bad writer' whose interest is sociological rather than literary. His work – particularly his public-school stories – forms a bridge in subject-matter leading to a third group of Orwellian essays, those which have formed the foundation for a whole branch of con-temporary British criticism – represented particularly by Ray-mond Williams and Richard Hoggart – devoted to the study of popular culture at various social levels. There are three major essays in this group: 'Boys' Weeklies', 'The Art of Donald McGill' and 'Raffles and Miss Blandish'; and they are among the best Orwell ever wrote, mainly for the very reason that they are about sub-literature. No question of evaluation comes in here, because the works Orwell is discussing are below the value level, and no dominant authorial personalities are involved to arouse uncomfortable feelings of antipathy or resemblance; in such works the almost anonymous craftsman takes the place of the conscious artist.

On the other hand the works of popular literature and art are full of interest as soon as one takes them out of their familiar contexts and examines them in the same way as a natural his-torian might examine a new species of bird or animal. But, by 1939, when Orwell wrote on boys' weeklies, this had not been done. Everyone, indeed, was familiar with the little backstreet newsagents' shops which he described in the first paragraph of his 'Boys' Weeklies'.

The general appearance of these shops is always very much the same; a few posters from the *Daily Mail* and the *News of the World* outside, a poky little window with sweet-bottles and packets of Players, and a dark interior smelling of licorice all-sorts and fes-tooned from floor to ceiling with vilely printed twopenny papers, most of them with lurid cover illustrations in three colours.

But few educated people, since boyhood at least, had read many of the papers sold in such shops or had looked, except with furtive and embarrassed interest, at the gross and sometimes obscene picture postcards displayed prominently in their windows. Orwell did both. Some of his lore of little shops went into *Coming Up for Air*, but he reserved his most serious consideration of the subject for his essays.

All of these essays share with each other and with the defence of P. G. Wodehouse a nostalgia for things outdated. The world of the *Gem* and the *Magnet* is a static world where 'nothing ever changes, and foreigners are funny'. It has never caught up with the horrors that haunt the minds of intelligent men in the 1930s. 'The clock has stopped at 1910. Britannia rules the waves, and no one has heard of slumps, booms, unemployment, dictatorships, purges, or concentration camps.' Similarly, in considering the subject of comic postcards, Orwell finds that though contemporary events or activities which have comic possibilities are quickly made use of, the 'general atmosphere' of the postcard fantasy world is 'extremely old-fashioned'. 'The implied political outlook is a radicalism appropriate to about the year 1900.' Again, in 'Raffles and Miss Blandish', the comparison is between 'the 1900 version' of glamorized crime and the 1939 Americanized version, much to the latter's detriment.

In the case of the papers which he discusses in 'Boys' Weeklies', it is true that Orwell detects a sinister influence behind their unmoving conservatism; he attributes it to the fact that they are operated by a large newspaper combine which has a vested interest in fostering the politics of the Conservative Party, and ends his essay with the rather whimsically presented suggestion that left-wing intellectuals should turn their attention to 'popular imaginative literature' and that Socialists should enter the field of boys' magazines. Yet even in making this political criticism, he is still impressed by the fact that 'the moral code of the English boys' papers is a decent one. Crime and dishonesty are never held up to admiration, there is none of the cynicism and corruption of the American gangster story.'

A similar comparison is the whole point of 'Raffles and Miss Blandish', which is concerned with fashions in crime fiction.

Raffles is a hanger-on of the upper class in pre-Boer-War England, and the values E. W. Hornung gives him are those of the world in which he moves. He has nothing so un-Englishly systematic as 'an ethical code', and lives by a few socially acceptable rules of behaviour, at best a code of manners.

But it is just here that the deep moral difference between *Raffles* and *No Orchids* becomes apparent. . . . Certain things are 'not done', and the idea of doing them hardly arises. Raffles will not, for example, abuse hospitality. He will commit a burglary in a house where he is staying as a guest, but the victim must be a fellow guest and not the host. He will not commit murder, and he avoids violence wherever possible and prefers to carry out his robberies unarmed. He regards friendship as sacred, and is chivalrous though not moral in his relations with women.

With the appropriate remark – 'Now for a header into the cesspool' – Orwell compares this pattern of behaviour with the total nihilism that inspires the action of *No Orchids for Miss Blandish* and other books by James Hadley Chase, a British author who in the 1940s pioneered the imitation of American sadistic fiction.

Their whole theme is the struggle for power and the triumph of the strong over the weak. The big gangsters wipe out the little ones as mercilessly as a pike gobbling up the little fish in a pond; the police kill off the criminals as cruelly as the angler kills the pike. If ultimately one sides with the police against the gangsters, it is merely because they are better organized and more powerful, because, in fact, the law is a bigger racket than crime. Might is right; *vae victis*.

This, of course, is moral criticism in its purest form. It is the type of criticism which is uppermost in this whole group of essays, for, as I have already shown, the real theme of 'The Art of Donald McGill' is not the formal qualities of popular art, but the moral attitude of the working class and the half-conscious myth on which it is based. Only in 'Boys' Weeklies' does Orwell direct any even half-serious literary criticism towards his subject, describing the repetitious plot-structure of the stories, commenting rather superficially on the recurring characters (Billy Bunter is a 'really first-rate character'), and analysing the outdated language and the 'extraordinary, artificial, repetitive style, quite different from anything else now existing in English literature' in which they are written. Clearly, apart from a certain boyish enjoyment, the main interest which Orwell took in sub-literature of this kind was sociological; he regarded it as symptomatic of the moral health of society.

4

THE comparison which forms the central theme of 'Raffles and Miss Blandish' is not merely a comparison between two types of crime fiction. It is a comparison between two different moral landscapes – that of England before 1914, that of the world as a whole after 1933. It opens the way for the last two groups of Orwell's major critical essays, those dealing with contemporary writers and those dealing with the relationship between literature and politics in the 1940s. And if in all his essays about writers of a past generation – with the sole exception of the very late piece on Gissing – Orwell portrays the English nineteenth century as an island of relative goodness in the evil ocean of history, when he comes to consider contemporary writers he never ceases to be conscious that the bad old ghosts from before the nineteenth century have begun to march again, and that they have been joined by a tribe of evil spirits peculiar to the twentieth century.

To the group dealing with contemporary writers belong 'Inside the Whale', the study of Henry Miller which contains embedded within it a survey of typical literature of the 1920s and 1930s; 'Arthur Koestler', published in 1944; and 'Benefit of Clergy', the review article on Salvador Dali's autobiography that was written in 1944 and literally cut out of every copy of *Saturday Book* (though it still appeared on the contents page) because the publishers feared legal action. The progress shows – in terms of Orwell's critical writings – the same intensifying alarm at the political–moral state of the world as mounts up in his fiction when we go on from *Coming Up for Air* through *Animal Farm* to *Nineteen Eighty-Four*. The essays in the second group – those dealing with the relationship between literature and politics – were written and published after those I have just listed, in the period immediately before the writing of Orwell's last novel; they are 'The Prevention of Literature', written in 1946 as a protest against the lukewarmness about freedom of the press demonstrated at the PEN International Congress on *Areopagitica* in that year; 'Politics and the English Language', also published in 1946; and 'Writers and Leviathan', published in 1948. Dealing explicitly and generally with the problems of writers in a world becoming yearly more totalitarian, they sketch out the main ideas on which Orwell based his vision in *Nineteen Eighty-Four* of a totalitarian language and literature as part of a completely totalitarian world.

In 1939, when he started writing 'Inside the Whale', which is his second largest essay, Orwell still felt free to produce a rambling and rather discursive piece, discussing many aspects of the literature of his time from the viewpoint of a writer resolutely independent of schools and movements. Miller's passivism in the face of disasters which he knows to be inevitable is of course the overriding moral–critical theme of the essay, and this I have already discussed in relation to *Coming Up for Air*, but 'Inside the Whale' also contains many insights of a more purely literary nature.

Of Miller himself Orwell probably writes a more intelligent appreciation than anyone has done since 'Inside the Whale' appeared. Miller, he decides, has something in common with Joyce – the ability to give life and meaning and interest to the commonplace – but he is not an artist in the same at once monumental and meticulous manner as Joyce. Rather he is an ordinary, somewhat hard-boiled man, an American businessman, talking about life with a gift for words. Orwell admires Miller greatly as a natural prose writer.

[In his books] English is treated as a spoken language, but spoken *without fear*, i.e. without fear of rhetoric or of the unusual or poetical word. The adjective has come back, after its ten years' exile. It is a flowing, swelling prose, a prose with rhythms in it, something quite different from the flat, cautious statements and snack-bar dialects which are now in fashion.

It is even possible that reading Miller had an influence on the style of *Coming Up for Air*, which contains Orwell's most exuberant writing, as well as on the philosophy of its hero.

What in the end attracts Orwell most to Miller is the sheer happiness that emerges from his books, books that describe hardship, failure and frustration, but in the end leave an almost unique expression of the uninhibited enjoyment of life. 'So far from protesting, he is *accepting*.'

Miller's vitality, the basic optimism that runs through all his works, Orwell contrasts with the 'pessimism of outlook' which seemed the keynote of the English twenties, that physically comfortable age whose leading novelists and poets, moved by cosmic despairs, produced the best writing of the century. Purpose, political purpose, returned – without joy in life – in the 1930s, but, Orwell points out, the Marxization of literature was a failure in so far as it sought to bring literature to the masses, while for the writers themselves it produced only disillusionment for the better men and an enslavement to party hackwork for many of their inferiors. 'On the whole,' Orwell concludes, 'the literary history of the thirties seems to justify the opinion that a writer does well to keep out of politics.' Even at this time in 1940, politics still provided Orwell with most of the subject-matter of his writing, and it is clear from the context that what he means by 'keeping out of politics' is an avoidance of party orthodoxies. During the decade that followed he tried to find some means by which he, a writer interested in politics, might work with politicians; but by 1948, when he wrote 'Writers and Leviathan', he had returned, with the force of added experience, to the same position as he sustained in 'Inside the Whale'. The direction of thought in the last years of his life suggests that, had he survived, his withdrawal from political interests would have been almost complete.

The intensive reading of Henry Miller which Orwell undertook to write 'Inside the Whale' inevitably brought him up against the question of literary obscenity. In the case of Miller, Orwell was willing to accept 'a seeming preoccupation with indecency and with the dirty-handkerchief side of life' as a necessary part of a philosophy that took all life joyously, without discrimination. 'To accept civilization *as it is*', he remarks, 'practically means accepting decay.'

But to accept what is obscene and evil in the world one finds is one thing. To nurture it within oneself is another. And this explains the contrast between Orwell's tolerant treatment of Miller and his ferocious condemnation of Salvador Dali in 'Benefit of Clergy'. This essay looks at high art as 'Raffles and Miss Blandish' looked at popular literature. Its subject is Dali's autobiography, and the criticism, despite the introduction of a little amateur psychology, is almost entirely moral. It is clear that what raises Orwell's anger is not the sexual but the sadistic element in Dali's writing and painting. Dali's autobiography is 'a book that stinks', Dali himself is 'a symptom of the world's illness' and his paintings are 'diseased and disgusting'. Orwell knows what he thinks of Dali; the problem he faces is what can be done about an artist who is obviously 'as antisocial as a flea'. And here he proposes a division between the artist and the citizen. Crime for art's sake cannot be tolerated. But as an artist, Dali must be defended. He is not a fraud, and his works, which technically have the kind of merits Orwell appreciates, should be diagnosed rather than being suppressed. Why an artist of undoubted ability should act in this way is the question we must solve. For '*wickedness*' (and the italics are Orwell's) is in an artist only an escape from some hidden frustration.

The essay on Koestler shares with that on Dali a preoccupation with violence, but this time it is not the violence of the individual sadist that concerns him, but the much more terrifying – because much more impersonal – violence of the totalitarian state. Koestler, one of Orwell's personal friends, aroused his interest for several reasons: he had developed, like Orwell himself, a 'style of life'; for a long period he had worked in the secret heart of the Third International and was therefore one of the most informed of anti-Communists; and, in Franco's prisons and in the refugee camps of France, he had lived out the drama of the political fugitive in the Europe of the thirties.

The real heart of Orwell's essay is his interest in Koestler's novel of Stalinist Russia at the time of the Moscow trials, *Darkness at Noon*. Superficially, there is a considerable resemblance between the central situations in *Darkness at Noon* and *Nineteen Eighty-Four*, between the sufferings of Rubashov in the Ogpu prisons and those of Winston Smith in the Ministry of Love, but Orwell's criticisms of Koestler's book illuminate the differences rather than the similarities. As he points out, *Darkness at Noon* centres round one question: 'Why did Rubashov confess?' Much mystery still hangs over the Moscow trials. Were the accused men guilty? That they were not guilty of the crimes actually attributed to them seems evident. Were they tortured and blackmailed with threats to their relatives and friends? Orwell considers this the commonsense explanation. Koestler, however, incorporates a strong element of willingness in Rubashov's final confession; it arises out of 'mental bankruptcy and the habit of loyalty to the Party'. Underlying Koestler's choice of this least likely of three possible alternatives, Orwell suggests, is a judgment on the whole revolutionary tradition, a suggestion that the very process of revolution is corrupting. Given such a conclusion, which seems to be a fair reading of Koestler, Orwell assumes that one can only become either a complete pessimist or, as Koestler had described himself, a 'short-term pessimist', who feels that the present is doomed to be unpleasant and that all one can do is to withdraw from action and try to remain sane in the hope that in a century the storms will have blown over and the world will be a better place.*

Orwell did not accept pessimism. He felt, like Camus, that we must build our dikes against the storm and try to mitigate its

---

* I consider this a false assumption, since it ignores the alternatives to violent action. In Orwell's essay on Gandhi, written four years after that on Koestler, he first gives consideration to the possibility of non-violent action.

effects. This is why the tone of *Nineteen Eighty-Four* is admonitory whereas that of *Darkness at Noon* is fatalistic. To begin, Winston Smith does not represent, as Rubashov does, the last flickers of bourgeois decency dying out in the twilight of revolutionary tyranny. On the contrary, he represents the flame of human decency, of the love for liberty and truth, springing up in the depths of an established darkness. He does not carry Rubashov's share of guilt for founding the regime that destroys him; on the contrary, by our standards he is as totally innocent as by the standards of his society he is totally guilty, merely for having had the thought of opposition. And when Winston confesses and submits it is not through any rot that springs from within himself, but entirely because he has been submitted to physical tortures and relentless psychological conditioning. That Winston resists in his own way until the moment when all his possible defences have been destroyed provides the core of hope in *Nineteen Eighty-Four* – a core which is entirely absent from *Darkness at Noon*. Once again, the essay on Koestler brings its own evidence that *Nineteen Eighty-Four*, dark though its tones and lurid though its Gothic lighting may appear, was not the product of an ultimately pessimistic attitude. Revolutions indeed go wrong if we do not take care, Orwell is saying, but perhaps one of the reasons why they do so is that men always tend to link the revolutionary process with the dream of Utopia. It is the deadly illusion of perfectionism that Orwell attacks, here as in *Nineteen Eighty-Four*. In its place he sets up a humane stoicism. 'Perhaps some degree of suffering is ineradicable from human life, perhaps the choice before man is always a choice of evils, perhaps even the aim of socialism is not to make the world perfect, but to make it better. All revolutions are failures, but they are not all the same failure.'

WHAT makes almost all of Orwell's essays still so fresh and fascinating, long after the occasion for their writing has lost its original interest, is the informality, the sense of linear development, which gives one the feeling of being inside the author's mind as he is developing his thoughts. In the essays on individual writers the sense of participation is deepened by the fact that Orwell can never resist thinking of another writer as a person and trying to see him in his mind's eye, and as it is the literary rather than the everyday personality that he reconstructs, we get from his criticism a kind of imaginative satisfaction analogous to that induced by certain elusive types of fiction. And if, as usually happens, Orwell unconsciously reveals as much about himself as he does about his subject, the interest is further deepened.

The essays that deal with general literary questions have not quite the same personal intimacy, and in this they rather resemble his purely political essays. We no longer feel that we are inside the author's mind. Instead, we can imagine ourselves sitting in a London lecture-hall of the 1940s, one of those decrepit, grey, draughty places dating from the days of Marx and Morris and frequented by small political parties and vegetarian groups. But for once the speaker is better than we had ever hoped for, combining, in the great radical tradition, strong opinions, pungent heresies, brilliant reasoning, great scholarship, contempt for scholars, and a colloquial delivery that does not despise the advantages of rhetoric. Occasionally the speaker passes off on us a bit of logical legerdemain, occasionally he shows prejudice or paranoia, and sometimes his jokes are rather threadbare, but it is all in the spirit of the performance, and we go away with the general impression of sensible things well and sincerely said.

In these essays, Orwell is dealing with topical questions – What has happened to the old traditions of free speech? Where is the English language going? What can writers expect if they get involved with the Labour Party? – but he uses these issues to state some permanent truths about literature. In 'The Prevention of Literature', for example, he is concerned about the growing tendency in the post-war world to depart from the old equation of rebellion with intellectual integrity. In the West, he points out, it is the majority group of rebels against the existing order, the Communists and their supporters, who are most inclined to claim 'that freedom is *undesirable* and that intellectual honesty is a form of antisocial selfishness'. He sums up the immediate problem in this statement: 'What is really at issue is the right to report contemporary events truthfully, or as truthfully as is consistent with the ignorance, bias and self-deception from which every observer necessarily suffers.'

At this point Orwell might merely be defending the freedom of journalists, but he rapidly expands the field to include *all* prose writing, and it is here that the essay takes on its real interest, since it tells us what Orwell considers the necessary prerequisites for the flourishing of his art, and so, indirectly, the conditions he himself needs in order to write effectively.

He denies, for example, that in this matter there is any real distinction between the needs of 'imaginative' and 'polemical' literature. The polemical writer deals in fact; the imaginative writer deals in 'subjective feelings, which from his point of view are facts'. But when the novelist is expected to adapt what he says to the requirements of political orthodoxy, he is falsifying his subjective feelings, and when he has done that he has 'destroyed his dynamo'. Literary inventiveness – even more than inventiveness in the other arts – is dependent on free ranging over the fields of thought, and when liberty of thought perishes, literature is doomed. So, by implication, the defence of literature must begin as soon as the freedom of the journalist is threatened. Freedom of the press, like other freedoms, is indivisible. 'Writers and Leviathan', written two years after 'The Prevention of Literature', carries the same idea into the narrower field of political action, warning the author to beware of offering his talents even to those parties which evoke his sympathies, for the good reason reiterated that orthodoxy and imaginative activity are incompatible.

'Politics and the English Language' deals with another aspect of the danger which politics, and particularly totalitarian politics, poses to literature. Orwell points to the generally accepted opinion that 'the English language is in a bad way', but, unlike most of those who lament this fact, he believes that if we act resolutely, the decay can be stopped. The essay was written in 1946, at the end of a period during which Orwell had been consciously working on his own style to achieve the spare and direct form of *Animal Farm*; he was speaking from experience and a sense of involvement. In his view, politics has been one of the principal causes of the decay of the language, because 'political speech and writing are largely the defence of the indefensible'. Politics – on the Left as on the Right – has become steadily more insincere, and 'the great enemy of clear language is insincerity'. But the position might easily be inverted, for a return to clear language could, by exposing insincerity, help to bring about a 'political regeneration'. Orwell advocates a return to simplicity, freshness and economy of writing, to a general abandonment of stale images and meaningless jargon.

When we consider how well Orwell handles the question of language and verbal form on this occasion, and how able he shows himself in the analysis of bad writing, we are inclined to regret that he did not devote himself more seriously to stylistic criticism. As it is we are left with a single brilliant statement on some of the most important causes of bad writing, and an indication of Orwell's own attitude as a practising writer, summed up admirably in the sentence: 'If you simplify your English, you are freed from the worst follies of orthodoxy.' Setting out to express through literature his vision of the truth, Orwell was led to a progressive simplification and clarification of his own language. But simplification does not mean impoverishment, as we realize when we listen to the voice of Orwell's prose.

WHAT is above all needed is to let 'the meaning choose the word'. This phrase, which provides the keynote to Orwell's recommendations for the regeneration of the English language, might also be taken to summarize the attitude towards literary form which he developed during the part of his writing life that is known to us. The thought he had to express always came first into his mind, and the form was selected, in so far as an artist ever does select deliberately, to present with the greatest effectiveness the message he wished to convey. In 'Why I Write' he explains:

My starting point is always a feeling of partisanship, a sense of injustice. When I sit down to write a book, I do not say to myself, 'I am going to produce a work of art.' I write because there is some lie that I want to expose, some fact to which I want to draw attention, and my initial concern is to get a hearing.

At the same time form and style were, for him, no mere mechanisms for the achievement of clear expression. One need only compare *The Road to Wigan Pier* with reports on slum conditions prepared by trained sociologists to realize that what Orwell has produced is something very different from ordinary competent expository writing. In the selection of words, in the shape of sentences, in the arrangement of incident and argument, there is an individual sensibility at work, a mind that operates by other rules than those of mere utility. As Orwell himself remarked, he could not write even in an expository sense if he did not find it also an aesthetic experience.

Nevertheless, Orwell's 'partisanship' significantly affected the nature of his approach to the art of writing. Always he wrote to a purpose outside writing itself, so that the form of the work of literature was never, for him, an end in itself, and he never indulged in stylistic experimentation for its own sake. Even in discussing other writers, he soon tired of the formal aspects of their work, no matter how deliberately and effectively these may have been cultivated. His essay on Yeats, for example, begins with a singularly feeble attempt at verbal analysis, noting an affected use of the word 'that' ('Or that William Blake'), remarking that certain phrases 'suddenly overwhelm one like a girl's face across a room', commenting that Yeats 'does not flinch from a squashy vulgar word like "loveliness"', and showing the lack of seriousness with which he approaches such analysis by lazily confessing that he is merely quoting from memory. But as soon as he begins to chew on what for him is the meat of the subject, the ideas and the moral impulses that underlie Yeats's poems, his essay suddenly takes on pace and authority, and the schoolboyish ineptitude of the opening stylistic discussion completely vanishes.

If we can accept what Orwell tells us in 'Why I Write' about his literary development it seems evident that the extra-artistic impulse was always the starting-point of his writing. As a child, he tells us, he began to make up stories and to write poems because he recognized within him 'a facility with words and a power of facing unpleasant facts' that enabled him to compensate for a feeling of 'being isolated and undervalued'. As we have seen elsewhere, Orwell is inclined to impute to himself at a very early age (he is now talking of the time when he was less than five) the kind of self-analysing propensity which seems improbably adult for even the most precocious child. We must reserve judgment on this information, and pass to the period of Orwell's later schooldays and early manhood, on which his statements are likely to be more objectively reliable.

This is what he describes as his 'non-literary' period, extending – he tells us – up to about the age of twenty-five, but clearly it was the time when the characteristic features of his attitude as a writer were first established. He did in fact carry on a certain amount of sub-literary activity on a rather trivial level; he edited school magazines ('the most pitiful burlesque stuff'), and produced 'made-to-order' poetry and semi-comic *vers d'occasion* 'quickly, easily and without much pleasure to myself'. When we remember the atrocious quality of most of the poetry which Orwell wrote and even published during the early

1930s, we can accept the implication that this early work was intrinsically valueless. More interesting is the pattern it seems to prefigure, since Orwell remained always an occasional writer. With the exception of his two worst novels, *A Clergyman's Daughter* and *Keep the Aspidistra Flying*, he appears to have produced hardly anything out of the mere decision to write a book. In almost every other case there was an 'occasion', a particularly interesting experience, or an argument or fear nagging in his mind, that gave him the first impulse to write.

But the fact that writing was Orwell's special way of reacting to experience, and that he felt impelled to give his argument – no matter how much preliminary conversation there had been – a final shape in prose, is something that still has to be explained. And here he tells us that from early childhood down to his days of inner solitude in Burma he had carried on a habit of creating unspoken and unwritten literature, first by inventing crude adventure stories of which he was the hero, and afterwards by keeping running a mental narrative of 'what I was doing and the things I saw'. 'Although I had to search, and did search, for the right words, I seemed to be making this descriptive effort almost against my will, under a kind of compulsion from outside.'

The feeling of being compelled, of writing against one's will, is a common one among writers; indeed, it seems to be an essential aspect of any creative activity that much is given and motivated by some source outside reason, and the activity of the artist consists largely in shaping and controlling this element consciously and rationally. This 'outside' or unconscious element remained strong in Orwell's work. The frequent emphasis in his novels on such phenomena as involuntary memory (*Coming Up for Air*), amnesia and slow recovery of memory (*A Clergyman's Daughter*), and dreams and nightmares (*Nineteen Eighty-Four*) suggests that Orwell was very much aware of the importance of extra-rational elements in human life and – equally – in literary creation.

His other important emphases are on the search for the right word, and on description. Orwell remembers himself as first selecting words for special purposes, but he tells us that later, in reading *Paradise Lost*, he all at once 'discovered the joy of mere words, i.e. the sounds and associations of words'. 'As for the need to describe things,' he adds in the same paragraph, 'I knew all about it already.' And he goes on to show how the double preoccupation with description and words determined the kind of books he wished to write in his youth.

I wanted to write enormous naturalistic novels with unhappy endings, full of detailed descriptions and arresting similes, and also full of purple passages in which words were used partly for the sake of their sound. And in fact my first completed novel, *Burmese Days*, which I wrote when I was thirty, but projected much earlier, is rather that kind of book.

Description – the urge to recount experiences, to picture scenes, to weave the odd observed facts of existence into the tapestry of prose – this is the original external purpose, to which is added very soon (at least as early as 'A Hanging' and doubtless before) the desire to discuss what has been described, so that argument follows experience. The eventual narrowing of discussion into moral-political polemics is merely a further development along the same lines. But all the time there is the concern for words, in their dual role as evocative sounds and as the means to exact description and argument.

This double movement of Orwellian prose can be seen most effectively in the kind of autobiographical-polemical reportage which he developed as his most characteristic form of writing. The structure of such works is determined by the peculiar Orwellian dialectic of presenting experience and then arguing from it. It is, essentially, a logical rather than an organic structure, governed by a rather simple system of balancing members.

In each case Orwell catches our attention by a fine descriptive set piece which serves as a kind of overture. We enter *Down and Out in Paris and London* to the sound of the morning squabbles in the Rue du Coq d'Or, we slide into the world of slums and unemployment in *The Road to Wigan Pier* through the sensationally seedy entrance hall of the Bookers' lodging-house, and the whole heroic tone of *Homage to Catalonia* is set by the high-keyed moment of Orwell's meeting with the Italian militiaman in Barcelona on the eve of his own joining up to fight for the Republican cause.

The alternation of narration and argument that follows can be observed in *Down and Out in Paris and London*. The first nine chapters tell how Orwell came to be destitute in Paris, and recount his attempts to fight off starvation up to the moment when he and his friend Boris get work in the Hotel X. This section has the progressive episodic flavour of a *picaresque*, but once the heroes have found work the pace slows, the atmosphere changes, and we settle down to another nine chapters which describe, with illustrative incidents embedded in the narration, the life of a great hotel as seen from below stairs. A further three chapters supplement this description with a scullion's-eye view of a fashionable Paris restaurant, and then the whole tale of Orwell's experience of Gallic destitution is rounded off with a chapter discussing the reasons for the survival of the occupation of dish-washer. Now, in the briefest of interludes, Orwell crosses the Channel, and the balancing second part of the book begins; it is about half the length of the first part and so avoids excessive symmetry. Some ten chapters, in which narratives of wandering from spike to spike are interspersed with descriptions of tramp habits, tramp ways of earning a living, tramp jargon and so on, are devoted to the world of London down-and-outs. The final three chapters offer Orwell's general reflections on tramps and what should be done to mitigate the social problem which they represent.

Basically the same form is followed in both *The Road to Wigan Pier* and *Homage to Catalonia*. *The Road to Wigan Pier* begins with the Bookers' house, goes on to tell of Orwell's impressions in the mines and his experience collecting information about life on the dole and slum housing, and ends with his arguments on what might be done to make conditions better. The second part (in this case the book is formally divided into two) begins with an autobiographical passage telling of Orwell's class-ridden childhood, his years in Burma and his first plunges into the underworld, as a prelude to a discussion on socialism from his own peculiar class point of view. In *Homage to Catalonia* there is again a sharp division about the middle of the book between the first part, narrating Orwell's experiences on the Aragon Front (with a central chapter of argument on the political nature of the war embedded in the narration), and the second part, which describes his return to Barcelona, the May fighting and the proscription of POUM. As in the first section there is a central chapter on the political implications of the situation and on the dishonesty of Communist propagandists and left-wing newspaper reporters, with remoter implications in terms of the falsification of history.

It is, in each case, a simple and unsophisticated form of construction. If it is not exactly linear, one might describe it as no more than undulant. It is true that a kind of development, through experience to understanding, takes place in each book, but it is interesting to observe that while Orwell is always anxious, like the good journalist he was, to provide an opening that will immediately involve the reader, he is so little concerned about his endings that more often than not he goes out with an anticlimax. The last chapter of *Down and Out*, with its vapid good intentions, is pointlessly bathetic, while *The Road to Wigan Pier* ends in a stale joke about the middle class – 'for, after all, we have nothing to lose but our aitches'. Only in *Homage to Catalonia* is there a lift in tension towards the end, when Orwell and his wife flee across the frontier from Barcelona to France, and then, with considerable artistry, there is the quiet release as the travellers cross to the dreaming land of England.

Such relaxed, undeliberate forms are appropriate to books of this nature, where the material of real life needs only the minimum of arrangement – a matter of what to leave out more than anything else – and where the sheer quality of the prose can be relied on to carry the subject-matter and the argument. This is why Orwell, with his zest for description and his passion for words that give the right feeling to a scene or a thought, is probably the best writer of reportage in a whole generation.

But fiction is quite another matter, and here Orwell has tended to succeed – where he has done so – in spite of great weaknesses in characterization and structure. Several of his critics, Tom Hopkinson and Edward M. Thomas among them, have argued that Orwell only took to novels because that happened to be the genre in which everyone was writing in the 1930s. His own accounts, however, suggest that he had been ambitious to succeed in fiction since childhood, and that his failure to meet his own expectations of what a novelist should be was a matter of great disappointment to him.

His difficulties began with characterization, for, though he could admirably sketch a person he had met in real life and observed from the outside (for example, Bozo the screever in *Down and Out in Paris and London*), he found it hard to create a fictional character, observed from within, who was not filled with Orwellian attitudes, even to the point of breaking at times into his creator's language and expressing his most characteristic thoughts. One hero alone, George Bowling in *Coming Up for Air*, develops enough vital autonomy to live in our minds as a credible character, though even he has his improbabilities – can one really imagine so genially vulgar a man being as well-read, articulate and sensitive to natural beauty as Orwell suggests? In their own agonized way, Orwell's major characters do learn about existence, and so there is always some kind of development centred round them, though usually their education consists of little more than becoming sadder and wiser as they realize that for all their efforts they are merely back where they started, with their comforting illusions removed by the surgery of experience.

Orwell's characters are, in fact, singularly passive for the creations of so active a man; all the important things in their lives happen to them, and whenever they themselves try to take action, which is usually in the form of rebellion against their passive role, it ends always in futility. What he is really saying is that in life most actions and most rebellions end in rather unheroic failure, but that, at the same time, it is better to act and to rebel than to do nothing at all; the little flame of dissent, like the little bit of coral in Winston's paperweight, is what really counts.

As with Dickens it is usually Orwell's minor characters, in whom there is no pretence of either growth or inner tension, who are the most effective in their obsessive intensities – characters like Mrs Creevy, proprietress of the evil Ringwood Academy; Ellis in *Burmese Days*, the fanatical hater of anyone with a coloured skin; and even, in a way, George Bowling, who is really a comic minor character magnified, seen from the inside, and provided with a history like the tail of a comet.

If Orwell finds it hard to create thoroughly convincing major characters, it is not merely because of their passivity, or because of the flavour of ineffectuality which lingers in one's mind when the book is read and they recede in one's mental vision. It is also because they are never really defined in their relationships with other people. Gordon Comstock in *Keep the Aspidistra Flying* has three major personal relationships, with his sister, with his friend Ravelston, and with his girl Rosemary. But in no case does the relationship come alive, and this is not merely because of Gordon's phenomenal self-centredness. It is rather because there is no real individuality about the other characters, and consequently nothing that can strike out against his egotism. The sister is a whining masochistic spinster, on whom Gordon preys constantly. We are told that he 'adores' Ravelston, but in fact he makes that insipid highbrow the butt of his most vicious attacks on the intellectual establishment and on the rich, whom he hates because of his own voluntary assumption of poverty. Neither the sister nor Ravelston reacts in any meaningful way; all they show is their ineffectual willingness to be exploited and insulted indefinitely. As for Rosemary, it is true that she plays the part of the seductive and eventually rapacious siren, but it is difficult, when one reads the juvenile dialogue that goes on between her and Gordon and when one sniffs the smell of hockey-field heartiness that hangs over her, to imagine how she succeeds. *Keep the Aspidistra Flying* is admittedly the worst example of Orwell's failure to involve his characters in credible relationships, and this is possibly because, in creating

Comstock, he concentrated so immoderately on the isolating emotion of self-pity.

In his other novels, it is where a touch of comedy or incongruity strikes a spark that his characters really come to life. Dorothy Hare's friendship with Mr Warburton, with its ever-to-be-repelled attempts at seduction and its slight flavour of vestry daring, is the best thing in *A Clergyman's Daughter*, and infinitely more credible than the lugubrious travesties of love affairs that go on between Gordon and Rosemary, and Winston and Julia. The only marriage in Orwell's novels that really arouses one's interest is that of George and Hilda Bowling, which, by the time we come upon it, has taken on the conventions of wedded life in one of Donald McGill's postcards, with the husband perpetually suffering for the suspicions aroused by his past adventures. In *Burmese Days* there is one very convincing and moving relationship – that between Flory and Dr Veraswami, with all its laughable misunderstandings and with the pathetic loyalty, all on one side, that rounds it off.

But *Burmese Days* contains another relationship – or perhaps rather a confrontation – which has an important bearing upon the partial nature of Orwell's success as a fiction writer. *Burmese Days* is the most conventional of Orwell's novels, and as a novel the most successful. In his other novels Orwell funnels the intensity of feeling through a single character because only one character is seen from within. But the true novel, as he in the end argues in his essay on Gissing, always contains 'at least two characters, probably more, who are described from the inside and on the same level of probability', and *Burmese Days* is the only one among his books that meets this requirement. Both Flory and Elizabeth Lackersteen are seen from the inside. It is true that no kind of intimacy is ever established between them, but that is part of the author's intent. What does take place is a confrontation in which they act upon and help to define each other, even though, by reason of Flory's inveterate romanticism and Elizabeth's abysmal selfishness, they are always at cross purposes and never even begin to understand each other. It is a relationship in the realistic tradition, and falls into the same class as that between Pierre Bezoukhov and Hélène, or Charles and Emma Bovary.

Orwell's failures in characterization are closely connected with the failures of general structure in his books. His concentration on the word as the vital unit of literature made him neglect the larger elements of literary planning, so that – except in *Burmese Days* – he never worked out an even approximately satisfactory form for a larger work of fiction. It is true that he was always searching, for the six works of fiction which he did write represented almost as many different types. *Burmese Days* can be accepted as a true novel in the tradition deriving from Flaubert. But it was followed by a regression, in *A Clergyman's Daughter*, to a loose picaresque with the elementary structure of a number of episodes strung on the thread of a journey, including at least one deliberately unrealistic passage (the Joycean scene among the derelicts in Trafalgar Square); several of the episodes owed their presence to the author's desire to describe his own experiences as a hop-picker, a down-and-out in London and a teacher in a small private school rather than to any evident needs of the plot. *Keep the Aspidistra Flying* is certainly not a novel in the traditional sense, and can probably be most kindly described as a burlesque, *Coming Up for Air* is a kind of prose dramatic monologue, held together mainly by the fascination of George Bowling's memories; it is a book almost without construction, with a vast middle section devoted to the past as Bowling's mind portrays it, and a disproportionately small final section describing episodically the trip back to Lower Binfield which is the main action of the book. *Animal Farm*, which Orwell described as a fairy tale, is really a fable, and it is also the only one of his books which is engineered with perfect tightness and economy, largely because it was built round an actual historical incident, the Russian Revolution and its betrayal. The problems of character are magnificently evaded by the stylization which becomes possible through the substitution of animals for human beings, and the simplified personalities that result are nearer to Jonsonian humours than to characters in the modern sense of the word.

Finally, *Nineteen Eighty-Four* is a Utopia, even if it is seen in negative, and, like other works of its kind, it has to find room for a great deal of detail of a kind that would be unnecessary in an ordinary novel. Here again, though perhaps not so successfully as in *Animal Farm*, Orwell takes a great deal more care over construction than he did in any of his pre-war books except *Burmese Days*. He solves one of the recurrent problems of Utopian writing, that of having to deal with the mass of unfamiliar inventions, appliances and arrangements in a society of the future, by assuming that the physical setting of London will not have changed, except to the extent of having become a great deal more decrepit; in other words, that Utopia may be something quite different from a steel-and-concrete paradise – may in fact be more than anything else a state of mind. He brings in a few inventions that are of use merely to the police so as to show the direction society has taken, and the space saved in this way he uses for long passages of theoretical material relating to the new society – particularly discussions on Newspeak, extracts from the spurious Goldstein book describing the history of Oceania and the Party, and dialogues between Winston Smith and O'Brien in the torture chambers. Here, of course, Orwell is adapting to fiction the pattern of his books of reportage; but while the arrangement helps the reader to understand the didactic message of the book, it tends to overwhelm the human drama that is – at least in fictional terms – the heart of the book. The main flaw of *Nineteen Eighty-Four* is in fact that it has two centres, a political and theoretical one and a human one; these centres come together when Winston is confronted by O'Brien in the Ministry of Love. For this is not only the point where Winston meets the power of the Party in all its inhumane force; it is also the point where the essentially human contact he thought he had established with O'Brien is betrayed. But instead of allowing the situation to speak in these terms, Orwell entirely spoils the effect by allowing O'Brien to argue and discourse at length, like an inverted image of himself, on the dialectics of power. Thus he fails at the crucial point to fuse the dual purposes of the book.

Orwell established his own manner of life, his own moral–political stance, his own way of using words, even his own form of reportage, but he never established, at least in the larger structural sense, a characteristic form for his fiction. Nor can it really be said that he spent the time in experimentation, since every one of the six different forms he took for his novels (to use the word 'novel' in its broadest sense) was a ready-made one picked from the general rack of serviceable forms developed over the centuries. It seems that just as Orwell was not interested in creating a system for his thought, so he was not interested in creating an overall structure within which to write. He was content to accept the structures other men had already developed, and even these he did not always use with great care. Sometimes one has the impression – it happens with a good book like *Coming Up for Air* as well as an indifferent book like *A Clergyman's Daughter* – that he got an idea and a vague shape in his mind and let the writing follow its course. Without very much exaggeration one might apply to him one of his own remarks about Dickens – 'a writer whose parts are greater than his wholes ... all fragments, all details – rotten architecture, but wonderful gargoyles'.

But though Orwell had little sense of fictional architecture and was a poor hand at characterization, the question as to whether he is a writer worth reading half a generation after his death hardly arises. He so obviously is, because what he liked doing he did superlatively well. His descriptions are magnificent; his polemical arguments, even when they occur in the wrong places, are always intensely readable; every one of his books contains episodes which most writers would give years of their lives to have written; his style in the narrower sense, his way with words, is inimitable.

Not since Swift, his great master, has there been a prose more lucid, flexible, exact and eloquent than Orwell's. But Orwell goes beyond Swift, for he can speak in the tone of humour as well as that of satire; he can sound the lyrical and the elegiac as well as the urbane and austere notes, and his style is capable of many variations. The tone in which he writes of Wigan, for example, is quite different from the tone in which he writes of Aragon, less heroic and rhetorical, as is appropriate to the different worlds he is presenting, and the style in which he argues is different from that in which he describes. In his fiction, even, there are several perceptibly different forms of the Orwellian style. Here are three samples drawn from books spaced out in terms of publication over the twelve years from 1933 to 1945.

In a moment the girl began to dance. But at first it was not a dance, it was a rhythmic nodding, posturing and twisting of the elbows, like the movements of one of those jointed wooden figures on an old-fashioned roundabout. The way her neck and elbows rotated was precisely like a jointed doll, and yet incredibly sinuous. Her hands, twisting like snakeheads with the fingers close together, could lie back until they were almost along her forearms. By degrees her movements quickened. She began to leap from side to side, flinging herself down in a kind of curtsy and springing up again with extraordinary agility, in spite of the long *longyi* that imprisoned her feet. Then she danced in a grotesque posture as though sitting down, knees bent, body leaned forward, with her arms extended and writhing, her head also moving to the beat of the drums. The music quickened to a climax. The girl rose upright and whirled round as swiftly as a top, the panniers of her *ingyi* flying out about her like the petals of a snowdrop. [*Burmese Days*]

The float dived straight down, I could still see it under the water, kind of dim red, and I felt the rod tighten in my hand. Christ, that feeling! The line jerking and straining and a fish on the other end of it! The others saw my rod bending, and the next moment they'd all flung their rods down and rushed round to me. I gave a terrific haul and the fish – a great huge silvery fish – came flying up through the air. The same moment all of us gave a yell of agony. The fish had slipped off the hook and fallen into shallow water where he couldn't turn over, and for perhaps a second he lay there on his side helpless. Joe flung himself down into the water, splashing us all over, and grabbed him in both hands. 'I got 'im!' he yelled. The next moment he'd flung the fish on to the grass and we were all kneeling round it. How we gloated! The poor dying brute flapped up and down and his scales glistened all the colours of the rainbow. It was a huge carp, seven inches long at least, and must have weighed a quarter of a pound. How we shouted to see him! [*Coming Up for Air*]

The windmill presented unexpected difficulties. There was a good quarry of limestone on the farm, and plenty of sand and cement had been found in one of the outhouses, so that all the materials for building were at hand. But the problem the animals could not at first solve was how to break up the stone into pieces of suitable size. There seemed no way of doing this except with picks and crowbars, which no animal could use, because no animal could stand on his hind legs. Only after weeks of vain effort did the right idea occur to somebody – namely, to utilize the force of gravity. Huge boulders, far too big to be used as they were, were lying all over the bed of the quarry. The animals lashed ropes round these, and then all together, cows, horses, sheep, any animal that could lay hold of the rope – even the pigs sometimes joined in at critical moments – they dragged them with desperate slowness up the slope to the top of the quarry, where they were toppled over the edge, to shatter in pieces below. Transporting the stone when it was once broken was comparatively simple. The horses carried it off in cartloads, the sheep dragged single blocks, even Muriel and Benjamin yoked themselves into an old governess-cart and did their share. By late summer a sufficient store of stone had accumulated, and then the building began, under the superintendence of the pigs. [*Animal Farm*]

The first is Orwell's earliest style, somewhat ornate, but by no means inappropriate to its rather exotic subject, a dance so stylized that it requires a stylized description. The sentence builds up in a series of phrases which suggest the dance's continuous movement. There are no less than four similes in this relatively short passage, none of them really redundant. The first, with its image of jointed figures on an old roundabout, sets the outlandish quality of the scene. The last gains its effect from the mild shock of thinking of snowdrops in the steamy heat of Burma. The choice in words is rather more pretentious and conventional in a literary way than Orwell would later have made, and there are a number of over-used phrases of the type he later condemned: 'incredibly sinuous', 'extraordinary agility', and so on.

The second passage shows an immense gain in vigour and immediacy. The language and the rhythms are, of course, far more colloquial, and the number of Latinized words is reduced to a minimum. The sentences are short, often exclamatory, so that the excitement builds up in a staccato rhythm quite different from the slow, fluent rhythm of the description of the Burmese dancer. The use of metaphor is not abandoned, but it is adapted to the manner of speech, so that all the similes are those which an ordinary man like Bowling with a country upbringing might have used, and which, in their proper context, retain a considerable freshness. There is a touch of exaggeration about the phraseology, but this reflects the personality and the humour of the speaker. It is the language of speech, using its rhythms, while the earlier language is the language of literature. One can imagine Bowling saying these words in one's ear; they project an image of the speaker as well as of the scene. One cannot imagine anyone making an oral description of the Burmese dance in language resembling that which Orwell used when he wrote *Burmese Days*.

The final extract shows the ultimate honing down of the language to a serviceable simplicity resembling that of Defoe. There is a quite deliberate formality, rather like that of an old-fashioned travel book, conveyed in the use of phrases like 'namely, to ultilize the force of gravity', 'a sufficient store of stone', 'under the superintendence of the pigs'; this is designed to establish the distance of the world of animals from that of humanity, and so paradoxically to enable us to look at humanity from the outside. But the functional quality is developed in the simplicity of the sentence-construction, in the economy of description, which tells one everything that is needed, but includes not a single unnecessary detail, and above all in the complete absence of metaphor (unless of course one might contend that the whole fable is a kind of extended metaphor). It is a model of direct, clear description, so transparent that even without the help of figures of speech we are able actually to visualize the animals at work on their human tasks.

This is the ultimate point of Orwellian simplification. But the language of *Animal Farm* is Orwell's highest literary achievement precisely because it is appropriate to that particular story.

It would not be appropriate to any other, and Orwell, even at the period when he wrote it, used variant styles for other purposes. More than any other writer of his time, perhaps more than any other writer of English, he learned to 'let the meaning choose the word', which meant to let every meaning choose its word and the tone of its word. The ultimate point in such a search comes when language and meaning are so close that one cannot drive the blade of a metaphorical knife between them. The style grows so near to the subject that one no longer thinks of it as a style. This Orwell succeeded in achieving more often than most other writers.

But the style, it is said rightly, is the man. And in that crystalline prose which Orwell developed so that reality could always show through its transparency, lies perhaps the greatest and certainly the most durable achievement of a good and angry man who sought for the truth because he knew that only in its air would freedom and justice survive.

A SELECTIVE BIBLIOGRAPHY

BOOKS*

The early works were published by Victor Gollancz, but the great majority of the books are now available in the *Uniform Edition* of Secker & Warburg. This includes:

Down and Out in Paris and London (1933)
Burmese Days (1934)
A Clergyman's Daughter (1935)
Keep the Aspidistra Flying (1936)
The Road to Wigan Pier (1937)
Homage to Catalonia (1938)
Coming Up for Air (1939)
The Lion and the Unicorn: Socialism and the English Genius (1941)
Animal Farm (1945)
Nineteen Eighty-Four (1949)
Collected Essays (1961), comprising the greater part of *Critical Essays* (1946), *Shooting an Elephant* (1950) and *England Your England* (1953)

Inside the Whale was published separately by Gollancz in 1940; it was then reprinted in *England Your England* and now forms part of *Collected Essays*.

James Burnham and the Managerial Revolution was published as a pamphlet by the Socialist Book Centre in 1946.

The English People (1947) was published by Collins.

Such, Such Were the Joys has only been published (1953) in New York, as part of a volume of essays which bears this title.

There are also two volumes of essays published by Penguin Books: *Selected Essays* (1957), reprinted in 1962 as *Inside the Whale and Other Essays*; and *Decline of the English Murder and*

* Dates of first publication are given.

Other Essays (1965). Many of the above titles are published in Penguin Books.

COLLECTED WRITINGS

The Collected Essays, Journalism and Letters of George Orwell, eds. Sonia Orwell and Ian Angus, 4 vols., (Secker & Warburg, 1968)

STUDIES OF ORWELL

Atkins, John, *George Orwell* (Calder, 1954)

Brander, Laurence, *George Orwell* (Longmans, 1954)

Hollis, Christopher, *A study of George Orwell* (Hollis & Carter, 1958)

Hopkinson, Tom, *George Orwell* (Longmans, 1953)

Rees, Richard, *George Orwell – Fugitive from the Camp of Victory* (Secker & Warburg, 1961)

Thomas, Edward M., *Orwell* (Oliver & Boyd, 1953)

Vorhees, Richard J., *The Paradox of George Orwell* (Purdue University, U.S.A., 1961)

INDEX

Adelphi, 65, 93, 103, 123, 240, 280

Air-Conditioned Nightmare, The, 192

A la recherche du temps perdu, 32

Anand, Mulk Raj, 13, 210–11

Anarchism; Anarchists, 16, 19–20, 28–9, 49–50, 112–13, 138–9, 185, 198, 219, 221, 223, 242–4

Animal Farm, 21, 26, 29, 33–4, 45, 67, 73, 81, 103–4, 118, 133, 139–40, 150, 152, 154–8, 165, 182, 195, 231, 246, 255, 262, 273, 276–8

Animal imagery, 67–70, 79–83, 154–7

Anna Karenina, 234, 239

Anti-Semitism, 203

Aragon, 136, 138, 180, 268, 275

Areopagitica, 255

'Art of Donald McGill, The', 12, 144, 207, 250, 253

'As I Please', 18

Atkins, John, 103, 280

Auden, W. H., 183, 198

Bakunin, Michael, 49

Balzac Honoré de, 160

Barcelona, 28, 127, 135–6, 138, 268

Barker, George, 20

Baudelaire, Charles, 160

Beggar My Neighbour, 212

'Benefit of Clergy', 238, 254, 257

Bennett, Arnold, 247

Bernanos, Georges, 185

Berneri, Marie Louise, 29

Bevan, Aneurin, 16, 20, 28

Bhagavad Gita, 220

Birth control, 122, 186, 205–6

Blake, William, 12

Blunden, Edmund, 13

'Boys' Weeklies', 248, 251–4

Brander, Laurence, 125, 159, 280

Brave New World, 166, 170, 192

Bread and Wine, 181

British Broadcasting Corporation, 13–16, 26, 31, 54, 153

British Pamphleteers, 280

Britten, Benjamin, 21

Brockway, Fenner, 22

Brooke, Rupert, 199

Burma, 27–8, 63–89, 105, 126, 128, 161, 179, 200, 213, 244, 265, 277

Burmese Days, 39, 51, 53, 64, 67, 73–87, 102, 116, 132, 155, 159, 162, 182, 200, 213, 231, 266, 270–73, 275, 277, 279

Burnham, James, 165, 173

Byron, Lord, 14, 57

Cabet, Étienne, 168

Campanella, Thomas, 168

Campbell, Roy, 116

Camus, Albert, 114, 171, 180, 182–3

Catalonia, 138

Cézanne, Paul, 56

Chamberlain, Neville, 204

Charterhouse of Parma, The, 235

Chase, James Hadley, 253

Chesterton, Gilbert Keith, 203

Churchill, Winston, S., 16, 203–4

Civil Liberties, 19–23, 41–3

Class, 24, 58–60, 70–72, 96–124, 127–33, 137–8, 163

Clergyman's Daughter, A, 38, 56, 62, 91, 102–16, 120, 144, 150, 231, 265, 272, 274, 279

Cobbett, William, 51

Collected Essays, 152, 240, 279

Comfort, Alex, 212

Coming Up for Air, 28, 34, 54, 56–7, 63, 102, 109, 122, 142–50, 152, 154, 165, 172, 188–90, 191–2, 195, 201, 206, 246, 252, 255–6, 265, 269, 272, 274–5, 279

Communism; Communists, 17, 19, 28, 42–3, 51, 53, 133–4, 136, 138–9, 155–6, 181, 198, 205, 220, 261, 268

Congreve, William, 250

Connolly, Cyril, 18, 21, 138, 143, 153, 160, 208–9

Conrad, Joseph, 239, 244, 247

Conservatism, 113, 122, 184–208, 219

Critical Essays, 279

Criticism, 150–53, 229–62

Dali, Salvador, 238, 254, 257

Darkness at Noon, 161, 180, 258–9

Deeping, Warwick 233

Defoe, Daniel, 104, 185, 277

Degas, E., 56

Deutscher, Isaac, 49

Dickens, Charles, 25, 30, 51, 151,

153, 164, 188–9, 217, 229, 236–8, 241, 245–6, 248, 270

Don Quixote, 239

Dostoyevsky, Fyodor, 160, 168

Douglas, Keith, 199

Down and Out in Paris and London, 25–6, 32, 59, 65, 73, 88–103, 119–20, 125, 133, 145, 200, 266–9, 279

Dreiser, Theodore, 171

Dryden, John, 7

Dunn, Avril, 24, 31, 64, 159

Education, 110–12, 158–62, 186, 216–18

Eliot, T. S., 20, 184, 198, 234, 236, 247, 280

Ellis, Havelock, 247

Empson, William, 13

Encounter, 280

Enemies of Promise, 153, 158

England, 135, 141, 190–92, 196–202

England Your England, 279

English People, The, 196, 201, 205, 210–11, 218–19, 224, 279

Existentialism, 114, 182

Family, 206–8

Fascism, 42–3, 127, 138, 197, 205, 218

Fielden, Lionel, 212

Flaubert, Gustave, 171, 272

Fontamara, 180–81

Foot, Michael, 28

Forster, E. M., 18, 20–21

Freedom, 29, 280

Freedom Defence Committee, 19–23, 42–3, 45, 153

'Freedom of the Park', 21

Freud, Sigmund, 114, 183

Fyvel, T. R., 88

Galsworthy, John, 247
Gandhi, Mohandas, 14, 199, 211–13, 258
Gangrel, 232
Gauguin, Paul, 56
Gem, The, 236, 252
Gide, André, 171, 184, 232
Gissing, George, 229, 238–40, 247–8, 254, 271, 280
Golden Asse, The, 239
Goldwater, Barry, 49
Gollancz, Victor, 103, 124, 126
Greene, Graham, 115
Grenfell, Julian, 199
Guild socialism, 31
Gulliver's Travels, 243–4

'Hanging, A', 64–8
Hardy, Thomas, 234, 247
Harrisson, Tom, 124
Hazlitt, William, 51
Heppenstall, Rayner, 56, 103, 123
Hitler, Adolf, 51–3, 54, 173, 247
Hoggart, Richard, 251
Hollis, Christopher, 49, 64, 68, 73, 114, 159, 280
Homage to Catalonia, 17, 26, 102–3, 118, 125, 133–4, 139–41, 149, 152–3, 180, 200, 221, 231, 267–8, 279
Hopkinson, Tom, 125, 269, 280
Horace, 189, 234
Horizon, 27, 33
Hornung, E. W., 253
'How the Poor Die', 29, 91, 95
Huxley, Aldous, 166, 170, 192, 198

Imperialism, 63–87, 88, 186, 209–16

Independent Labour Party, 16, 134, 136
India, 13–14, 142, 210–16
'Inside the Whale', 17, 143, 174, 187, 201, 248, 254–7, 279
Isherwood, Christopher, 183
'Isles of Greece, The', 14

James Burnham and the Managerial Revolution, 279
John, Augustus, 21
Joyce, James, 56, 255
Jura, 35–7, 37–41, 43, 73

Kafka, Franz, 160, 183
Keats, John, 56
Keep the Aspidistra Flying, 17, 24, 35, 37–8, 50, 91, 102, 104, 112–13, 117–24, 131, 144, 150, 154, 159–60, 206, 265, 270, 272, 279
Keyes, Sidney, 199
King Lear, 242
King Solomon's Mines, 239
Kipling, Rudyard, 211, 214–16, 234, 235, 240, 247–8
Koestler, Arthur, 139, 161, 179–81, 184, 229, 254, 257–9

Labour Party, 16, 21, 29, 37, 41, 43, 49, 128, 205, 211, 219
Language, 181–2, 184–5, 203, 262
Laski, H. J., 21, 124
Lawrence, D. H., 72, 118, 206, 247
'Lear, Tolstoy and the Fool', 233, 241–2
Lee, Jennie, 29
Left Book Club, 124–7
Left Review, 198
Lehmann, John, 67, 142, 239

284 *Index*

Letters from India, 210
'Letters to an Indian', 210
Lewis, Alun, 199
Lewis, Cecil Day, 198
Lewis, Wyndham, 198
Lion and the Unicorn, The,
    196–8, 201–2, 204, 281
London, Jack, 280
London Magazine, 23, 239, 280
'Looking Back on the Spanish
    Civil War', 140, 174, 217
Lyrical Ballads, 57

Macdonald, Dwight, 37
Machiavellians, The, 165
Madame Bovary, 239
Magnet, The, 236, 252
Malraux, André, 114, 179–81
Managerial Revolution, The,
    165
Marrakesh, 142
Marx, Karl, 30, 183, 260
Marxism, 49, 114, 127–8, 136,
    139, 172–3, 185
Mass Observation, 124
Menon, Narayana, 247–8
Miller, Henry, 17, 142–4, 184,
    192, 201, 236, 254–6
Modest, Proposal, A, 243
Moore, Henry, 21
Moralism, 171
More, Sir Thomas, 168
Morris, John, 26
Morris, William, 72, 186, 188,
    260
Mosley, Sir Oswald, 42
Muggeridge, Malcolm, 85, 214

Napoleon of Notting Hill, The,
    203
National Council for Civil
    Liberties, 20

Nationalism, 201–3
Nausée, La, 113
Nazism, 51, 199, 205, 249–50
Nehru, Jawaharlal, 14
New English Weekly, 24, 52,
    103
New Writing, 26, 67, 142
New Yorker, 160
News from Nowhere, 72, 186
Nineteen Eighty-Four, 16, 19, 24,
    28–9, 35–6, 43–5, 49, 53–5,
    60–62, 69, 76–8, 90, 104, 109,
    140, 143–4, 149, 152, 155, 158,
    160–75, 182–3, 191, 206–8, 223,
    231, 240, 243, 255, 259, 265,
    273, 279
No Orchids for Miss Blandish,
    253
'Notes on Nationalism', 201–2
Now, 28–9, 91
Noyes, Alfred, 234

Observer, the, 24, 39, 44, 216–17,
    240, 280
Owen, Wilfred, 199

Pacifism; Pacifists, 13, 50,
    198–200, 203
Panchatantra, 155
Paradise Lost, 266
Paris, 27, 94–9, 135, 197
Partido Obrero de Unificación
    Marxista (POUM), 133, 136,
    139, 268
Partisan Review, 13, 15–16, 28,
    50, 196, 212
Passage to India, A, 73
Patriotism, 15, 186, 188, 196–206
Péguy, Charles, 28, 185
Père Goriot, 125
Picture of Dorian Gray, The, 39,
    93–4, 145–6

Pitter, Ruth, 92
Plato, 168
Poetry London, 280
Poetry Quarterly, 240, 280
Polemic, 165
Politics, 37–8
'Politics and the English
    Language,' 182, 184–5, 255,
    262
'Politics vs. Literature', 223, 241,
    243–4
Popular literature, 248–54
Population, 186, 205–8
Potts, Paul, 20
Pound, Ezra, 248, 251
'Prevention of Literature, The',
    255
Priestley, J. B., 65
Progress, 141, 148, 186–95, 242
Proudhon, Pierre-Joseph, 28, 30
Proust, Marcel, 32, 148, 160

'Raffles and Miss Blandish', 238
Read, Herbert, 13–14, 18–22, 29,
    172, 185, 198, 229
Rebel, The, 183
Rees, Richard, 31 65, 189
'Reflections on Gandhi,' 12, 213
Religion, 105–15
Renunciation, 87–102
Reynolds, Reginald, 280
Road to Wigan Pier, The, 25, 32,
    49, 58, 64, 70, 77, 89–92, 94,
    101, 109, 110, 120 124–34, 141–2
    145, 159, 172–3, 188, 194–5,
    206, 217, 218–19, 224, 242–3,
    263, 266–8, 279
Romanticism, 57
Rossetti, Dante Gabriel, 56
Russell, Bertrand, 21

Sartre, Jean-Paul, 114, 181, 184

Sassoon, Siegfried, 199
Saturday Book, The, 254
Satyricon, 235
Savage, D. S., 212
'Second Thoughts on James
    Burnham', 165
Selected Essays, 279
Serge, Victor, 179
Shakespeare, William, 233–5,
    241–2
Shaw, George Bernard, 247
Shelley, Percy Bysshe, 57
'Shooting an Elephant', 64, 68–
    70, 213
Silone, Ignazio, 139, 179–82
Sitwell, Osbert, 21, 247
Slater, Humphrey, 165
Socialism, 15, 19, 28–31, 37, 49–
    50, 55, 68, 90–91, 113, 124–32,
    137–8, 149, 172, 181, 185–6,
    193–4, 204–6, 213, 217–25
*Soul of Man under Socialism,
    The*, 39
Spanish Civil War, 17, 28, 53, 73,
    125–6, 130, 133–42, 149, 156,
    165, 179, 187, 195, 198, 204
Spanish Testament, 180
Spender, Stephen, 15, 18, 20, 198,
    221
*Story of My Experiment with
    Truth, The*, 213
Stowe, Harriet Beecher, 235
Strachey, John, 125
Style, 133–4, 150–51, 153–4, 184,
    230–33, 262–79
Such, Such Were the Joys, 32,
    75, 158–63, 206, 209, 250, 279
Swift, Jonathan, 134, 151, 160,
    171, 223, 241, 242–6, 274
Symons, Julian 15, 19, 22–3, 29,
    45, 105, 229

Teruel, 136, 139

Thackeray, William Makepeace,
  229, 247

Thomas, Dylan, 20, 198

Tibet, 202

Tippett, Michael, 21

Tolstoy, Leo, 134, 184, 218, 221,
  233–4, 237–8, 241–6

Tribune, 16, 18, 21, 24, 27, 28,
  34, 41–3, 55, 97, 134, 153, 166,
  185, 199, 210, 218, 240, 280

Trotskyism, 16, 198, 203, 204

Turgenev, Ivan, 78

Twain, Mark, 247,

Twentieth Century Verse, 198

Uncle Tom's Cabin, 180

Utopias and Utopianism, 53, 61
  165, 167–70, 193–4, 223, 273

Virgil, 234

Wain, John, 41, 150–51

War and Peace, 234

War Commentary, 20, 29

Warner, Rex, 183

Way of All Flesh, The, 105

Way of the World, The, 235

We, 28, 166–70

Wells, H. G., 168, 187, 188,
  193–5, 229, 247–8

West, Anthony, 160, 162

Whitman, Walt, 12

'Why I write,' 230–32, 263–4

Wilde, Oscar, 12, 39–40, 92–4,
  247

Wodehouse P. G., 247–52

Woolf, Virginia, 198

Wordsworth, William, 57

Working class, 24, 58–60, 70–
  72, 96–8, 127–32

World Review, 184, 280

'Writers and Leviathan', 219–
  21, 236, 255, 261

Yeats, W. B., 72, 187, 234, 238,
  247–8, 264

Zamyatin, Evgeny, 28, 166–70

Zilliacus, K., 42

Zionism, 203

MORE ABOUT PENGUINS

Penguinews, which appears every month, contains details of all the new books issued by Penguins as they are published. From time to time it is supplemented by *Penguins in Print*, which is a complete list of all books published by Penguins which are in print. (There are well over three thousand of these.)

A specimen copy of *Penguinews* will be sent to you free on request, and you can become a subscriber for the price of the postage. For a year's issues (including the complete lists) please send 4s. if you live in the United Kingdom, or 8s. if you live elsewhere. Just write to Dept EP, Penguin Books Ltd, Harmondsworth, Middlesex, enclosing a cheque or postal order, and your name will be added to the mailing list.

Some other books published by Penguins are described on the following page.

Note: *Penguinews* and *Penguins in Print* are not available in the U.S.A. or Canada

THE COLLECTED ESSAYS, JOURNALISM, AND LETTERS OF GEORGE ORWELL

Edited by Sonia Orwell and Ian Angus

This collection of essays, reviews, articles, and letters which Orwell wrote between the ages of seventeen and forty-six, when he died, is arranged in chronological order and gives a wonderfully intimate impression of one of the most honest and individual writers of this century – a man who forged a unique literary manner from the process of thinking aloud, who was immune to shallow fashions in opinion or vocabulary, and who elevated political writing into an art.

Volume 1: An Age Like This – 1920–40

This first volume covers the years when George Orwell began to explore the life of the poor and struggled to establish himself as a novelist and factual reporter. Disillusioned with Communism in Spain, rejected for service in the war against Hitler, already ill, he faced hostilities in a mood of frustration.

Volume 2: My Country Right or Left – 1940–3

The second volume principally covers the two years when George Orwell worked as a Talks Assistant, and later Producer, in the Indian section of the B.B.C. At the same time he was writing for *Horizon*, *Tribune*, the *New Statesman*, and other periodicals. His war-time diaries are included here.

Volume 3: As I Please – 1943–5

For some eighteen months during the war Orwell worked as literary editor of *Tribune*, where he found a new freedom, which was expressed in the title and style of a regular feature he contributed – 'As I Please'. During the period covered he completed *Animal Farm*, the book most likely to immortalize his name: at least three leading publishers refused it.

Volume 4: In Front of Your Nose – 1945–50

This last volume contains the letters, reviews, and other pieces which Orwell wrote during the last five years of his life. The success of *Animal Farm* had eventually relieved him of financial worry, but during the drafting and writing of *Nineteen Eighty-Four* he was increasingly handicapped by the illness of which he died early in 1950.

Not for sale in the U.S.A.